CW00822799

A Contrast in Islands:

The Narrow Gauge Railways of Corsica and Sardinia

by

W. J. K. DAVIES

PLATEWAY PRESS

ISBN 1 871980 50 X

First published 2002

ISBN 1 871980 50 X

PLATEWAY PRESS
Taverner House, Harling Road, East Harling, Norfolk NR16 2QR

Printed in England by POSTPRINT
Taverner House, Harling Road, East Harling, Norfolk NR16 2QR

FRONT COVER ILLUSTRATION:
Sunset on the narrow gauge: A Sardinian 4XX class 2-6-2T winds down after a hard day's work.
(Derek Phillips)

BACK COVER ILLUSTRATION:
The modern scene in Corsica. l'Ile Rousse station with a CFD 2XXX series car; PW stock in the loop.
(Author)

TITLE PAGE:
Journey's beginning: SFS No. 3 takes a passenger train for Palau out of the north bays at Sassari, while a railcar for Alghero waits on the mixed gauge in platform 1.
(Author)

Contents

Maps and plans in text

Railway routes

Detailed layouts

Locomotive and stock drawings

Appendix 5: a drawing list is at the front of the Appendix.

Prologue

A Contrast in Islands

Why, one might well ask, try to contrast two islands which, even if they are neighbours, belong to two different nations with different railway systems? And why try to write a book as a contrast at all? Well, the second question is, perhaps, the easiest to answer. Even railway historians sometimes get fed up with the conventional round of history; route descriptions; locomotives and stock details...They are still needed but once the basics have been catalogued it makes a change to try and investigate what is different if otherwise similar places are under different influences and, after all, there are many basic similarities... The islands of Corsica and Sardinia, though one is nominally French and the other Italian, are near neighbours, sharing much the same climate and rugged geography; Corsica was under the dominion of one of the Italian states until 1768, both had similar communication problems to overcome... so, dear reader, bear with the idea – and if you spot that we know more about the systems of one island than the other, yes that is true. The problem, as the writer found with Portugal, is that very few enthusiasts visiting Sardinia in the mid-20th century bothered to record such mundane items as architecture and the minutiae of towed rolling stock and even the railways tend to regard such information as purely parochial – although items are beginning to surface here and there.

So what do we know about the background to the stories? In truth, they have a common beginning. Both Corsica (la Corse) and Sardinia (Sardegna) have a common geological heritage. They sit, Corsica above Sardinia, in the Tyrrhenian sea to the west of mainland Italy and south of mainland France. Both are essentially wild and barren, with population even now concentrated in a small number of substantial settlements and separated by vast, mountainous tracts of nowhere interspersed mainly with tiny hamlets clinging to dusty crags and, until quite recently, linked by roads that were little more than stony tracks; both were inhabited as far back as the neolithic period – the remnants of their former owners are still visible everywhere in Sardinia in the mysterious stone buildings known as Nuraghi. Up to the mid 18th Century, both were ruled by one of the Italian duchies – Sardinia by the kingdom of Piedmont and Corsica, after a lot of coming and going, by the Genoese... who sold it to the French in 1768. This was not entirely to the liking of the Corsicans who caused such trouble that it was not until the 1790s that Corsica, very reluctantly, accepted French rule, just in time to claim credit for one of its most famous sons – Napoleon Buonaparte. Both islands have a tradition of banditry and continuing urges for independence from what many of their inhabitants would see as occupying powers. Sardinia, indeed, is even more disparate in some ways since all its four provinces have different dialects and the inhabitants of the north-west are more nearly Catalan than Italian.

That having been said it is interesting to see, how, in this common heritage, the transport systems developed – and how important was the one big difference, the fact that Sardinia, as the second largest island in the Mediterranean, is over twice the area of Corsica which, itself, is still the fourth largest island even so.

Acknowledgements

These need really to be divided into individuals and organisations. As to individuals, in England, Harry Luff, Lance King, Fred Pugh, Trevor Rowe and Keith Taylorson, who visited the islands in the 1950s and 1970s have been an invaluable source of information and photographs; the late PM Kalla Bishop established most of the basic history of Sardinian railways as far back as 1969 and Wilfrid Simms' little guides of more recent years have also proved very useful. I must add Derek Phillips of "Steam and Safaris" (no connection) whose well-planned trips enabled a latecomer to study the whole surviving Sardinian system in comfort and who has provided the splendid cover picture. On the continent, the contributions of Jean Arrivetz, José Banaudo and Bernard Rozé have been invaluable. Thanks are also due to Sulzer Marketing & Technology Ltd, successors to SLM, who kindly provided drawings and photographs of the SFSS 2-6-0Ts.

As to organisations, as usual I thank FACS (Federation des Amis des Chemins de Fer Secondaires) and APPEVA for their constant notes and articles on Corsica. For Sardinia the Italian Railways Society has searched its library which includes most of PM Kalla Bishop's correspondence and Marco Boi of the Museo Ferrovie at Monserrato has kindly dug up old photographs, drawings and a precious stock inventory. The SNCF management in Corsica have also been very helpful. There is still much to discover about Sardinia in particular and any observations or information will be gratefully received by the publishers or myself.

W. J. K. Davies

Wheathampstead, 2001

PART 1

A General History

CORSICA and SARDINIA in their surroundings

CHAPTER 1

Genesis and development of island railways to the mid-1920s

Differing initial approaches in Corsica and Sardinia

As with may other areas of continental Europe in the mid 19th century, the islands of Corsica and Sardinia were largely undeveloped and consisted, effectively, of great tracts of uninhabited landscape punctuated by small isolated settlements with very poor communications – the position is well reflected by the oft-reported citation that warships used regularly to fire their heavy guns for target practice against the west coast of Sardinia because they knew that no one was likely to be harmed! Just as elsewhere, however, there was a strong desire to improve the lot of rural populations and the new-fangled railways seemed to offer a possible solution.

It is interesting to see how differently the problem of rail communication was approached in the two islands. In Corsica, possibly because of a comparatively late start (1877) and the French predilection for use of the narrow gauge in mountainous territory, metre gauge was adopted at the beginning and used thereafter. In Sardinia, the early date of starting (1863) and, no doubt, the distances to be covered, determined that initial efforts would be on the standard gauge. To be fair, the first railway operating in that island was actually narrow gauge, being a mineral line of 800mm nominal gauge to rail centres and 760mm (actual) gauge from the mines of San Leone in the south west to Santa Luzia and a port at Maddalena. It was relatively substantial, being some 15km long and drew some attention from French theorists of the period as an example of narrow gauge working. At the same time its poor track, crude wagons running on plain bearings, and primitive Schneider-Le Creusot 0-4-0Ts were not a good advertisement for the genre. It was, as they say, without issue and indeed, if the late PM Kalla-Bishop is to be believed, had regressed to mule haulage in later years – there are indications that the locomotives did no good to the track even when new.

The early 1860s, however, were too early for serious consideration of long narrow gauge lines and Sardinia was in any case large enough to need at least a north-south railway spine to link the major towns of three out of the four provinces. In 1862 a concession was granted by the State of Piedmont, which then owned the island, to the Compagnia Reale delle Ferrovie Sarde (Royal Sardinian Railways) who started construction in 1863 but stopped it five years later before any section had been completed - the usual reason, lack of money, was to blame they said. Indeed lack of money was a common complaint of Italian railway entrepreneurs at the time and in August 1870 a law had to be passed providing for substantial subsidies once serious construction was underway. In Sardinia this led to a 26km section being opened from Cagliari on the south coast, northward through Decimomannu to Villasor in May 1871, and thence, in stages, to a provincial capital, Oristano, about half-way up the west coast, (January 1872) and on through the inland town of Chilivani by December 1878. Here it was joined by a separate branch coming down from Porto Torres on the northern coast through the second town of Sardinia, Sassari; this had been operating as a detached branch since 1874.

Meanwhile, the semi-industrial south west corner of the island was demanding railway access and a branch was pushed westward from Decimomannu to the rising industrial centre of Iglesias in May 1872. Here it did not quite connect with the independent Monteponi Railway, the first 16km-long section of which had actually been opened in May 1871 from zinc and lead mines at Monteponi to the west coast at Portoscuso. The gap was filled fairly quickly by the Sardinian Secondary Railways (see below) who were conceded a route between Iglesias and Monteponi. Initially, the Monteponi was a mule-hauled mineral line and disproportionately important for us in that it appears to have determined the Italian "standardised" narrow gauge of 950mm. This is said to have come about because of the, then current, European fashion for measuring gauge from the centres of rails – a scheme which converted the irritating British standard gauge of 4ft 8½ inches to a convenient 1,500mm rather than the, equally irritating, 1,435mm it later became. The snag, as perceptive readers no doubt realise, was that as rails became heavier – and therefore wider – the actual gauge between rail edges decreased... hence a reluctant but necessary change of plan! The Monteponi had originally been metre gauge to rail centres with a true gauge of 960mm but when it decided to extend some 3km to a better transhipment port at Porto Vesme, reached in March 1879, and to introduce steam traction it naturally used heavier rails: hence the final "real" gauge of 950mm which, since the Monteponi was one of the first true narrow gauge lines in Italy, was eventually adopted as the national standard. Perhaps fortunately its other "innovation" – side buffers and chain link couplings – was not widely perpetuated. The Company was so pleased with its railway and its new motive power that a passenger service was introduced throughout in May 1881 and lasted until 1918. From October 1898 it was also linked to the standard gauge at Monteponi as noted below.

Completion of the standard gauge network in Sardinia

That, however, is a digression. From its 1878 railhead at Fraigas the main standard gauge line was pushed eastward to the north east coast at what is now Olbia by March 1881 and then on to a deep water port at Golfo Aranci in July 1883. By now, however, narrow gauge had been developed to a point where its superiority for mountain work was becoming clear and the standard gauge had only three further extensions – a short branch to Cagliari harbour in 1893 and two branches to serve the industries in the south west: from Iglesias to Monteponi in 1898 and from a point near Iglesias (Villanassargia) down to the coal mines at Carbonia as late as 1956. Of these the Monteponi bit was actually built by the, otherwise narrow gauge, Strade Ferrate Secondarie della Sardegna (SFSS) and remained standard gauge until it was converted to 950mm gauge and handed over to a local company in 1926; it is not to be confused with the Monteponi railway itself. The Carbonia branch was intended to relieve transhipment problems but continued in use as a general carrier even after the mines closed. It will be noted that, by mainland standards, even the standard gauge lines are considered as secondary branchlines and worked as such; they are all single track (except for a recent doubling to Decimomannu) and worked by CTC under secondary railway rules.

Start of the public narrow gauge system in Sardinia

All this was fine but, in the early 1880s, still left much of the island without reliable communication for the roads were unspeakable (and barely negotiable) besides being infested with bandits. In particular the remaining provincial capital of Nuoro and important centres like Tempio Pausania in the north, Sorgono up in the centre and Arbatax on the east coast felt entirely neglected. Fortunately the 1880s and 1890s were a period of opening up country districts throughout Europe and the use of narrow gauge was becoming very much the vogue, especially in mountainous areas. It was cheaper than standard gauge, indeed it was often the only feasible solution and, at the time, appeared a huge advance however slow and tortuous its routes. Both France and the new Italian State certainly thought so and were prepared to promote and largely finance such railways. In Corsica, as we shall see later, this resulted in a homogeneous system that became the railway network. In Sardinia the state planned, and offered out a series of separated lines that were really extended feeders to the existing standard gauge network.

The initial concession for building and operating the major systems was taken up by the Societa Italiana per le Strade Ferrate Secondarie della Sardegna (Sardinian Secondary Rail Roads or SFSS). 40% of construction cost was to be met by the provincial authorities, the remainder being found by the company but reimbursed by the state through a 90-year subsidy. Lines were to be 950mm gauge and steam-worked with stock provided by the company; ruling grade varied between 1 in 36 and 1 in 40 although this included long stretches of 1 in 33 in the central mountains.

Four separate systems were constructed and opened between 1888 and 1893, a very creditable feat given the nature of the countryside traversed! They were:

- Monti, on the standard gauge line between Chilivani and Olbia, north to Luras and then west to Tempio Pausania where the depot was; length 40km. This was opened throughout on 15 February 1889.
- Cagliari – Mandas – Isili – Sorgono, running north from Cagliari up the southern plain to the central hills; this opened to Isili on 15 February 1889 and then in stages on through the mountains to Sorgono by 3 November 1889. From Mandas, where an intermediate depot was established, a most difficult and

Early days on the Sardinian Secondary (SFSS): a posed shot at a special occasion; SLM 2-6-0T with original spark-arresting chimney for wood-burning. (MUSEO FERROVIE, CAGLIARI)

Maintaining equipment on the SFSS: an SLM 2-6-0T receiving attention at Cagliari old station. (MUSEO FERROVIE, CAGLIARI)

spectacular line was built east and north through the mountains via Nurri, Villanovatulo and Ussassai to Gairo and then on to Lanusei and down to the coast at Arbatax. Construction was started from both ends, the final section between Villanovatulo and Ussassai being linked up on 20 April 1894; a short branch southward from Gairo to the little town of Jerzu had already opened the previous November. The system was extensive enough to have major depots at Cagliari, Mandas, Seui, Sorgono and Arbatax with lesser servicing points elsewhere. Its total length was about 337km.

- Bosa, about half-way up the island on the west coast, up a steep escarpment and through the hills to Macomer on the standard gauge line south of Chilivani and then on across the central plateau via Tirso to Nuoro. It was opened from Bosa to Tirso on 26 December 1888 and on in two stages to Nuoro by 6 February 1889. It was soon joined by a link between Chilivani and Tirso, completed on 1 April 1893, through very difficult country. The major depot was at Macomer with a subsidiary shed at Ozieri on the Chilivani branch. Total length was about 198km.
- Sassari southwest to Alghero, a port and resort down on the west coast (depots at Alghero and Sassari Santa Maria). This was a comparatively straightforward route, 35km long and opened throughout on 1 April 1889.

This company also built the 6km standard gauge link between Iglesias and Monteponi in the south-west of the island.

Development of suburban and urban tramways at Cagliari

This book does not specifically cover urban tramways but at this point one should, perhaps, include mention of the SA Tranvie della Sardegna who opened a steam-worked suburban tramway from Cagliari town via Monserrato to Quartu S.Elena (10km) on 32 September 1893 with a branch along the coast to Poetto (7km) on 14 July 1913. It operated with a succession of standard Krauss tram locomotives towing railway-type trailers and according to GA Baddeley was originally operated by the SA Tranvie del Campidano e Poetto. It was electrified in 1925 (Poetto) and 1930 (Quartu S.Elena), in effect being assimilated into the town tramways latterly operated by Azienda Communale Transporti di Cagliari. Known details are in Appendix 6. It is of interest in that parts of these routes were traversed by the SFSS and its successor when they needed access to the quayside tracks.

Glimpses of Cagliari suburban trams: an original motor car with bow collectors and trailer on the electrified Quartu S. Elena route, at Monserrato old station... (H LUFF)

...and an ex-steam trailer in use on the electric lines. (H LUFF)

Later additions to Sardinian narrow gauge up to 1925

There was then a considerable pause, indeed until the second decade of the 20th Century when two more 950mm gauge lines were offered. The concession for these was taken up by a new and ambitious company, the Ferrovie Complementari della Sardegna SA (Sardinian Complementary Railways or FCS). Between 1913 and 1915 the FCS built a total of some 91km, consisting of a long line springing from the SFSS Sorgono route a little north of Isili at Sarcidano and running southwest to Villacidro via Villamar, whence a branch ran northwest to Ales; at Sanluri standard gauge station, some six kilometres from Sanluri town itself, the Villacidro line linked to and crossed the standard gauge. At its eastern end, it had running powers into Isili which, as a major town, was a rather more sensible terminus than Sarcidano. The FCS appears to have been ambitious from the start, firmly intending to take over the much larger but rather tired SFSS which it did on 1 January 1921. The SFSS negotiated to retain the annual subsidy – which was in effect the guarantee on its original capital; although this was no doubt ravaged by inflation at least the company wasn't actually losing money any longer. The exact terms of takeover are not clear but since stock was not renumbered it may well have been on a management (fermière) basis rather than total assimilation. In any case the FCS soon negotiated a reasonable operating subsidy for the combined system, to run from 1925, and promptly spent some of it on new rolling stock – three handsome 2-6-2T and at least one batch of vestibuled bogie coaches.

The situation in Corsica

So much for the first wave of Sardinian railway mania. The approach in Corsica over the same period was very different. Certainly the Corsicans – in the mid-1870s only a century or so out of Italian control after all – had eyed the early attempts to provide internal communications in Sardinia and, seemingly, decided that anything the Sardinians could do they could do better. Fortunately by that time the use of narrow gauge in mountainous territory was becoming accepted so standard gauge was no longer "in the frame". Corsica was, therefore, to be served by metre gauge - the national "standard" for narrow gauge – from the start. Furthermore the French State decided that it was no use expecting private enterprise to take the risks and decided to take construction of a basic network under its direct control. In 1877 the national Ponts et

Sardinian train in service: an SLM 2-6-0T with SFSS luggage van and an FCS coach – so probably post-1921.
(MUSEO FERROVIE, CAGLIARI)

Chaussées (Bridges and Highways) department was charged with surveying and building a network of lines to join up the main population centres in the island – Bastia in the north east, Ponte-Leccia and Corte in the centre, Ajaccio about two-thirds of the way down the west coast, Calvi in the north-west and a string of isolated settlements down the east coast ending at Bonifacio in the south east corner. As a start, work concentrated on the Bastia – Ajaccio link which was undoubtedly the most difficult, cutting as it did right across the very rugged central massif. Initially the two extremities, from Ajaccio inland to Ucciani and Mezzana and from Bastia to Corte were surveyed and declared of Public Utility in June 1878. Work on their construction and on a survey of the missing link was started immediately, this (Mezzana – Corte via Vivario) being declared of Public Utility in December 1879. Meanwhile three other routes had been included in the national Plan Freycinet agreed in July 1879: these were a line down the west coast from Ajaccio to the port of Propriano; a branch from Ponte Leccia northward to the sea coast at Calvi; the east coast line down to Bonifacio from a putative junction with the central route at Casamozza. Given the early state-of the art, a prestigious committee of (largely main-line) railwaymen was set up to advise the government on infrastructure and material needs.

By 1882 work on the original sections was advanced enough to make the government look around for someone to operate the system – and to build any further sections since this was no longer considered to be a state function. Their urge to pass the problem on was no doubt increased by a long wrangle over the route of the Calvi branch once it got near the coast; inhabitants of a string of inland settlements felt that the line should run along the hills via them, with a branch to the burgeoning port of l'Ile-Rousse; the Ile-Roussiens were firmly of the opinion that the main line should serve their town and then reach Calvi via the coastal plain. Since this was both shorter and apparently cheaper to build, the proponents of l'Ile-Rousse option had their way and the line was declared of public utility in August 1882. At the beginning of that month, agreement was also reached on the much less contentious line from Casamozza to Bonifacio which was duly authorised on 5th August.

Unusually, since the whole thing was a State initiative, the normal concessionary process did not apply (this was, indeed, the first serious experiment with a reseau of Intérét Général on the narrow gauge). Hence the State looked round for a known operator to whom it could entrust, or affirm, the development of the system on a management basis. The choice fell on the Cie des Chemins de Fer Départementaux (CFD)

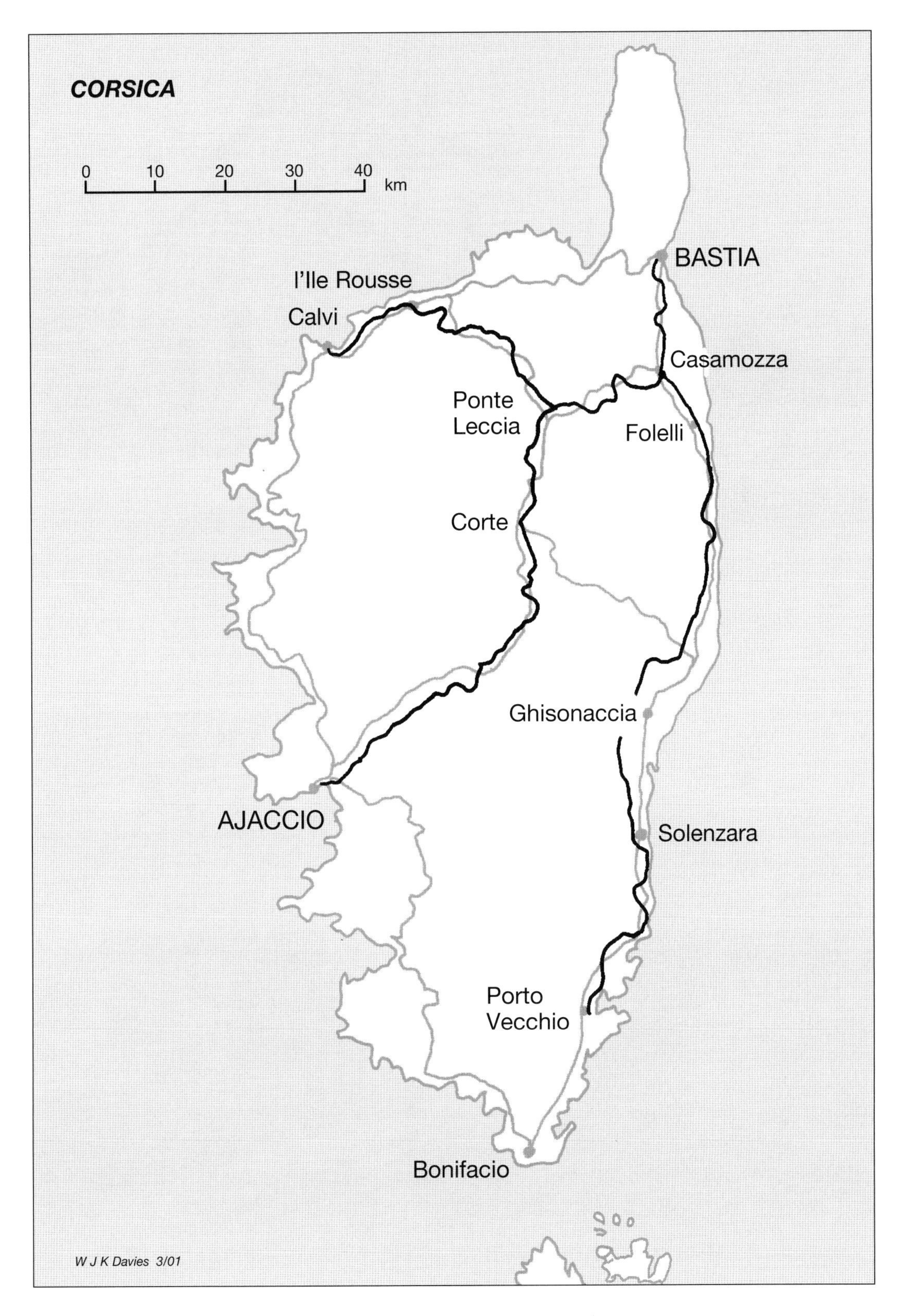
CORSICA
0
10
20
30
40
km
BASTIA
l'Ile Rousse
Calvi
Casamozza
Ponte
Leccia
Folelli
Corte
Ghisonaccia
AJACCIO
Solenzara
Porto
Vecchio
Bonifacio
W J K Davies 3/01

Early days in Corsica: Calvi station with an 0-6-2T and original stock. (FACS/JOSÉ BANAUDO COLLECTION)

Corsican trains in service 1: Vizzavona station with 0-6-2T No. 34 and a mixed bag of original 4-w and bogie stock. (FACS)

which was by now well established in operating extensive systems of Intérêt Local throughout mainland France. In February 1883 the CFD was therefore entrusted with an initial term of 15 years during which it would, on behalf of the state, build the lines to Calvi and down the east coast as far as a point known as Fium'Orbo, provide all movable equipment and then operate the complete system, including the Bastia – Ajaccio link as and when that was completed. "All movable equipment" appears to have meant just that – station furniture, tools, machines and appliances, locomotives and rolling stock. When the 15 years was up, the agreement could be extended on a rolling three year basis so long as both parties agreed.

The CFD quite naturally provided its "standard" patterns of locomotives and stock, or derivations of them, basing its main workshops at Bastia and operating the Bastia – Corte section plus the east coast line as far as Tallone from the beginning of February 1888; a further section from Tallone to Ghisonaccia followed in June and at the beginning of December the detached line from Ajaccio was opened to traffic, initially as far as Bocognano but extended to Vizzavona the following July. This forced the CFD to set up a separate base at Ajaccio, complete with maintenance facilities. Meanwhile the first section of the Calvi branch, to Palasca, was opened in January 1889 although the remainder, to l'Ile-Rousse and Calvi, took until November 1890 to complete because of the difficult terrain. The central link took even longer, Vizzavona – Vivario being opened in October 1892 and the last stretch to Corte not until December 1894...since the whole included some 23 tunnels, 11 viaducts and a huge sweeping "boucle" or return loop at Vivario, this was not entirely surprising. The east coast line took longer still, the Ghisonaccia – Bonifacio section not being authorised until 1911 and then stalled by the outbreak of the 1914-18 war.Indeed the only further extensions during the period were two short branches to the harbours at Bastia (authorised 1896) and Ajaccio (1902).

And what of the line down the west coast from Ajaccio, you may ask? Well, it remained in the list of projects for many years and, indeed formed part of a grand plan for a west coast route from Calvi through Ajaccio and on round to Bonifacio which really never stood a chance; somehow even the original branch never got declared of public utility and in practice nothing was done before increasing road competition and the Second World War put an end to the plans. Meanwhile, in the years surrounding the first world war the plans continued to be put forward in both islands and the 1920s seemed to be an era when progress would be continued.

Corsican trains in service 2: Venaco station with a Mallet-hauled train, showing the typical relationship of a mountain town and its station! (José Banaudo collection)

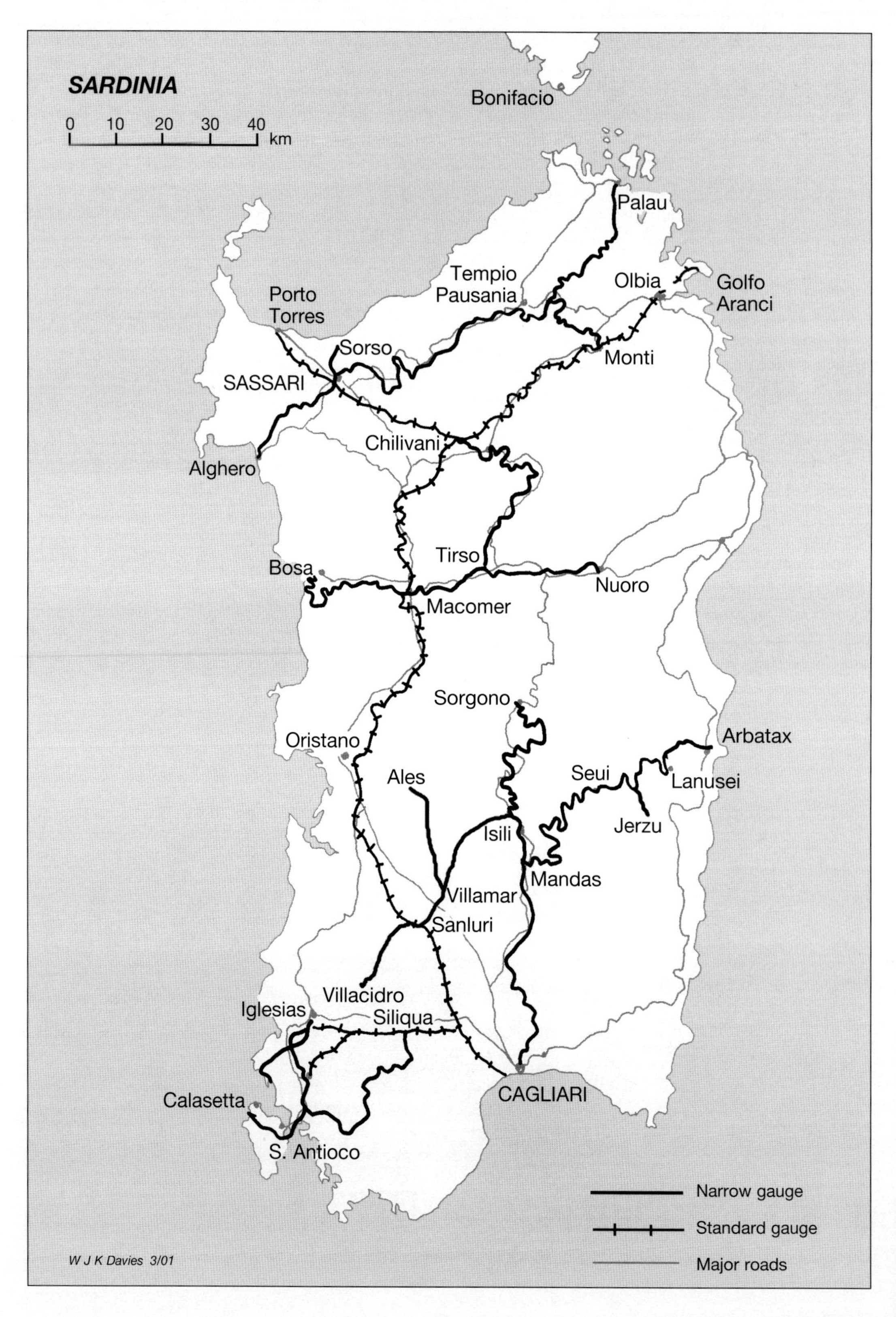
SARDINIA
0 10 20 30 40 km
Bonifacio
Palau
Tempio
Pausania
Olbia
Golfo
Aranci
Porto
Torres
Sorso
SASSARI
Monti
Chilivani
Alghero
Tirso
Bosa
Nuoro
Macomer
Sorgono
Arbatax
Oristano
Ales
Seui
Lanusei
Jerzu
Isili
Mandas
Villamar
Sanluri
Villacidro
Iglesias
Siliqua
Calasetta
CAGLIARI
S. Antioco
Narrow gauge
Standard gauge
Major roads
W J K Davies 3/01

CHAPTER 2

1925-1945: The final flings

Schemes and dreams continue – in both islands

Despite the First World War and its immediate aftermath, the planning authorities had by no means finished with either island. In the mid-1920s, even on the mainland of Europe, local railway systems were still being built despite increasing competition from road transport. Sardinia and Corsica were no exception although the respective scales of development were very different.

In Corsica attention was concentrated on completing the east coast line and no particular urgency was shown. A further section from Ghisonaccia down to Solenzara was opened in September 1930 and this was carried on to Porto Vecchio almost exactly five years later; only the final stretch to Bonifacio was still in the planning stage when war broke out in 1939 and ended expansion. As already recorded, this also finally put paid to the Ajaccio – Propriano line and the rather vaguer idea of the coastal circuit.

In Sardinia, however, there were two further substantial bursts of railway building, both narrow gauge, in the late 1920s and early 1930s. The two routes of the SA Ferrovie Meridionali Sarde (Sardinian Southern Railways or FMS) came first, down in the south west and there was at least some justification for them. During the first world war brown coal deposits south of Iglesias had been opened up and, in spite of the poor quality, demand was sufficient to develop them properly during the 1920s and 1930s. Much of the terrain was broken enough to make narrow gauge a sensible choice for local transport since most product would be used locally or exported by sea and the FMS was the result. By 23 May 1926, when it opened throughout, it had converted to metre gauge the existing standard gauge link between Iglesias and Monteponi and built south from Monteponi roughly paralleling the Monteponi Railway to a developing mining area known as Bacu Abis. It then diverted south east to a proposed new mining town of Carbonia (eventually built in the 1930s) and finally scrambled across a low saddle to descend to the coastal plain and

A CFD train at Calvi in 1938 shows little change except that the locomotive is a 2-6-0T; stock includes original bogie coaches with semi-saloon portion. (K TAYLORSON COLLECTION)

transhipment ports at Sant' Antioco and Calasetta on the presqu'ile of Sant' Antioco – a total of 55 km. Just before crossing the causeway it also threw off a long (59 km), and somewhat rambling line which eventually curved north east and ended up at Siliqua on the standard gauge branch from Decimomannu to Iglesias. Originally it was equipped as a typical rural railway but not for long. It was all very much dependant on the coal traffic and the Government, particularly in the depression years of the early 1930s, was quite willing to throw subsidies at the area and provide extra help to keep the coal traffic alive and expand operations - even though of poor quality it was home-produced coal and would save valuable foreign currency. Hence the FMS became basically a heavily loaded mineral railway, acquiring extra motive power in the shape of some large and handsome 6-coupled Mallets from ex-Military lines in the Dolomites and later a succession of rack-equipped tank engines surplus to requirements from the FS lines in Sicily; it even had a fleet of bogie container wagons for the coal traffic to ensure easy transhipment, while four Fiat light railcars ran most of the passenger services from 1935-on.

The other new system had, one would have thought, rather less justification, except as an unemployment relief measure and was in the far north. A new company, the Societa Anonima Ferrovie Settentrionali Sarde (FSS), was formed in 1927 to build lines across the north of the island. Between 1930 and 1932, it built two lines from Sassari; the shorter one, out to Sorso, probably did have potential for suburban and commuter traffic although the official excuse was that it might be extended to the north coast as a link to Corsica. This was also apparently one reason for the other line, 150km of very difficult construction roughly paralleling the standard gauge in a north-easterly direction, though some 20km to the north. This meant that it had to battle some extremely rugged country, including a complete spiral at Bortigiadas, before it even reached Tempio Pausania and an end on-junction with the FCS (ex-SFSS) branch from Monti. Thence it had running powers over the SFSS for 11km to Luras before struggling off on its own again to end up on the north east coast at Palau opposite the wild and charming Maddalena archipelago. Palau was certainly a minor port with possible connections to southern Corsica but hardly a good reason for a line that was likely to be massively deficitary from the start; indeed there were only two trains daily throughout from the time of opening on 18 January 1932. Nevertheless, there it was, a solidly engineered system laid with fairly heavy rail and well equipped with a set of powerful 2-6-0T, matching bogie coaches and four-wheeled goods stock - even fitted with the vacuum brake from new which was most unusual in Sardinia! The other lines were largely making do with handbrakes and the locomotive reverser. In 1933, the company was taken over by a Genoa-based concern, the SF Pugliesi SA, who quickly formed a local subsidiary, the Strade Ferrate Sarde SA (Sardinian Railroads Co or SFS), by which name it was known thereafter.

To work all these lines, the three companies, in the early 1930s, had the following basic locomotives and stock:

Company	*Locomotives (all types)*	*Coaches (bogie/4w)*	*Goods stock Total*
FCS*			
- Cagliari divn:	38	53 (37+16)	352
- Macomer divn:	20	41 (14+27)	162
- Tempio line:	4	12 (2+10)	27
- Alghero line:	4	25 (9+16)	19
SFS original	14	31 (28+3**)	133
FMS original	8	15 (10+5)	80***

* *of which, the original FCS provided 7, 12 and 39 items respectively*
** *3, 4w coaches ex SFSS according to PM Kalla Bishop*
*** *later supplemented by 250 coal container wagons*

Services pre-war in both islands

It is significant that, even in the pre-war era with poor road communications, the level of service required on the rural lines of both islands was not high. In a typical year (1933/4) at what might be thought of as the peak of development, the following frequencies applied:

In Sardinia there is a newcomer: though taken in 1958, this could have been anytime after opening of the Ferrovie Meridionale Sarde, with Breda 2-6-0T No. 105 on a typical mixed train at Calasetta... (H LUFF)

Corsica

Bastia – Corte – Ajaccio:	2 through trains each way daily, plus one short working from Corte to each end and return; one thrice-weekly "express" boat train each way.
Bastia – Calvi:	2 trains each way daily
Bastia – Solenzara:	2 trains each way daily

Sardinia

Sassari – Sorso:	5 trains each way daily
Sassari – Alghero:	2 each way daily; one extra in summer
Sassari – Tempio:	3 each way daily
Tempio – Palau:	2 each way daily
Tempio – Monti:	2 return workings daily, operated from Tempio
Bosa – Macomer:	2 each way daily
Macomer – Nuoro:	3 each way daily
Chilivani – Tirso:	1 through each way daily plus 1 short return working between Ozieri & Chilivani; 1 return working Bono – Chilivani, weekdays only.
Cagliari – Mandas – Arbatax:	1 through daily working, plus 1 daily return working Isili – Mandas – Cagliari and 1 return working Seui – Cagliari (weekdays only); 1 daily return working Seui – Arbatax.
Gairo – Jerzu:	2 return journeys weekdays only, operated from Jerzu; 1 return ditto, sundays only.
Mandas – Sorgono:	2 daily each way (one being weekdays only)
Isili – Villacidro:	1 daily, 1 weekdays only each way.
Villamar – Ales:	1 daily each way; 1 weekdays only. Timings differed.
Siliqua – Calasetta:	2 daily each way
Iglesias – Palmas Suergiu:	2 daily return journeys each way.

NB: Where return journeys are not shown, departures from each end were at similar times. Most of these workings would have been mixed trains, shunting at stations as required.

...and the same applies to this FCS mixed train at Gairo composed of SFSS stock: a 3XX class 2-8-0T heads two vans, an early luggage van and a Bauchiero composite. (H Luff)

Probably in the 1940s: an FCS short goods train with a 4XX class 2-6-2T crosses a fairly run-down viaduct; interesting in showing the state of infrastructure. (Museo Ferrovie, Cagliari)

Welcome to modernisation in Sardinia: an enthusiastic throng greets the introduction of the new OM railbuses at Bosa Citta in 1934... (MUSEO FERROVIE, CAGLIARI)

...and an equally excited crowd admires them at Macomer FCS station; note the original stocksheds behind. (MUSEO FERROVIE, CAGLIARI)

It will be noted that only Sassari-Sorso, even then clearly an almost suburban line, had a reasonable daily train service and that even the "new" SFS and FMS in Sardinia, and the Solezara extension in Corsica had only two trains a day, a morning and late afternoon working sufficing in each case. The pattern of short workings is also interesting, showing the relative importance of Corte (Corsica), Seui and Tempio Pausania as operating centres with substantial facilities on long branches.

Even given this low level of traffic, all systems in both islands recognised even in the 1930s that costs had to be reduced and journey times cut if they were to survive – although roads in both islands were still totally inadequate they were improving between major centres and threatening the short distance commuter traffic that was the only faint hope of profit. Both, therefore, acquired what were for the 1930s fast and efficient railcars: the FCS, after flirting with some bus-like four-wheelers, pitched on an excellent Fiat semi-streamlined bogie diesel car for its central system and the FMS quickly followed suit; in Sardinia only the SFS held out but then it, after all, had only just been built! Corsica adopted a parallel strategy by first dabbling with a couple of petrol-electric vehicles but then getting serious with two very modern looking series of bogie cars by Billard of Tours. Both types revolutionised passenger services on their respective systems and, for the period, were very advanced.

The Second World War and its effects

By 1939, therefore, the narrow gauge systems in both islands were substantially in their final form, the standard gauge in Sardinia having settled down under State Railways (FS) control since 1920 and been equipped as a secondary cross-country line to tie the whole thing together. So what effect did the war have?

In Corsica, railcars have arrived also: Billard A150D 112 and purpose-built trailer at a wayside station; although taken post-war, this was typical of prewar railcars in Corsica... (BERNARD ROZE)

...but steam still holds sway for much work; a fives Lille 0-6-2T shunts at Bastia in 1938. (K TAYLORSON COLLECTION)

In Sardinia it appears to have had comparatively little effect. Italy did not enter the war on the Axis side until June 1940 and effectively withdrew from it in 1943 after being invaded by the Allies and agreeing an armistice. Sardinia, naturally, was Italian-controlled and the retreating German land forces had plenty to do without trying to take and hold it so it was largely bypassed. There was a certain amount of strafing and the Cagliari installations were damaged by bombing but the major effect on Sardinian railways appears to have been the ever increasing difficulty of obtaining supplies from outside the island – a quite serious consequence being a need to burn the local brown coal which did the locomotive boilers and fireboxes no good at all. The standard gauge was able to recover quite quickly since FS resources were available by the existing train ferry service but the independent concerns had no such recourse. Details are sparse but the narrow gauge lines were certainly in a very run down condition by 1945 and both the FCS and SFS were taken over in 1947 by an entrepreneurial concern called La Ferrotranviaria SA, based in Rome. It is worth noting that, to economise on road transport, the Monteponi railway ran a passenger service between Bacu Abis and Portovesme from 1944 to 1949; this is said to have been provided by the FMS using their railcars and utilised an existing link between the two lines.

The war affected Corsica considerably more. So far as Corsica in general was concerned, it was officially in the unoccupied zone of France – ie under Vichy government control – and initially continued as before except that the Corsican office of CFD was thrown more or less on its own resources. Nonetheless a new 5-year management contract was agreed with CFD in 1941. The operating problems were exacerbated in November 1942 when the German forces abolished the, so-called, unoccupied zone and the German army occupied the island. This alas had serious consequences the following year when, following their invasions of Sicily and Italy, allied forces also liberated Corsica in November; the retreating Germans not only blew up many of the engineering works along the east coast line but also destroyed a vital bridge on the central line between Casamozza and Ponte Nuovo and damaged much of the stock. The east coast was effectively interdicted to seaborne traffic; hence, although the railway was considered vital for keeping the island supplied, all traffic had to come through Ajaccio. To assist, a prefabricated military bridge was brought over from Algeria to fill the central line gap and two heavy 0-10-0T (originally ex the CFD du Côte d'Or) were temporarily allocated to the system together with at least four Algerian Mallets. Regrettably, nothing was done about the east coast line which had always provided a large slice of the receipts and in 1945 the CFD company therefore surrendered its contract. The State once more accepted responsibility and, after a short interregnum, charged the Ponts et Chaussées organisation with operating the system and bringing it back to health.

CHAPTER 3

After the war was over

1945 to 1965: Change and decay

As noted at the end of the last chapter, 1945 saw the railway systems of both islands in some disarray and distinctly short of money. What was interesting was the contrasting way in which their overlords reacted. In Sardinia, the initial reaction was "more of the same". That is, the FS sorted out its standard gauge branches, exchanged the oldest and most worn equipment for successive batches of new and more powerful railcars and, in 1962, introduced D342 class diesel hydraulic locomotives to supplement the existing 740 class 2-8-0s. The narrow gauge was left to the private sector, the FMS continuing to be supported by its subsidised coal traffic, while La Ferrotranviaria SA of Rome took over the FCS and SFS in 1947, although retaining the existing company names and structures. It did, however, rationalise matters somewhat by transferring operation of the FCS northern lines to the SFS, which thus acquired responsibility for Sassari – Alghero and Monti – Tempio Pausania together with the associated equipment, although the Alghero line appears to have remained physically separated from the rest.

Patterns of post war services

Services at this time were only just settling down after the strains imposed by the war and, as road competition returned, they were cut back to some extent. Soon after the war, the following applied and can be compared with those of pre-war. In general all services were 1st and 3rd class:

CFC Corsica (1947)

Bastia – Ajaccio:	1 steam mixed each way daily, 1 thrice weekly boat train.
Corte – Ajaccio:	one mixed return working daily
Corte – Bastia:	1 return railcar, weekdays only
Calvi branch:	1 through return railcar weekdays only, 1 twice-weekly mixed to Ponte Leccia and return
Bastia – Folelli:	2 return railcars daily.

Sardinia (1952)

FCS Cagliari division (all trains weekdays only)

Cagliari – Arbatax:	1 through mixed train, each way
	1 return mixed train, Isili – Cagliari
	1 return mixed, Seui – Lanusei.
Sorgono – Mandas	1 through mixed train, each way
Gairo – Jerzu	2 return mixed trains

FCS Macomer division (daily unless shown)

Bosa – Macomer	2 return all-stations railcars
	1 mixed train, weekdays only
Macomer – Nuoro	2 railcars, 2 mixed trains each way
Tirso – Chilivani	1 through mixed, each way, weekdays only
	1 return passenger, weekdays only Bono – Chilivani
	2 return mixed daily Ozieri – Chilivani

FCS original lines

Isili – Villacidro	1 return mixed weekdays only
Ales – Villamar	1 return mixed weekdays only

SFS

Sassari – Palau	1 through mixed train each way, weekdays
	1 return mixed, Tempio – Sassari, weekdays
	1 return mixed Palau Marina – Tempio weekdays
Sassari – Sorso	4 mixed trains each way, daily
Sassari – Alghero	3 mixed trains each way, daily
Tempio – Monti	1 return mixed, weekdays only

FMS

This concern had more complex timetables reflecting the importance of the line to its mining communities.

Between Iglesias and San Giovanni there were five trains one way and six the other daily, the unbalanced one being an express railcar from San Giovanni at the early hour of 4.00am, but on Sundays an early morning working to and from Iglesias was cut out and on high days and holidays a late evening working was put on from Iglesias. Railcars ran roughly half the services.

Between Siliqua, San Giovanni and Calasetta, there were three daily railcar services each way, one being cut out on holidays, plus a rather complex mixed which ran through from Calasetta to Siliqua on weekdays only but had a daily return working except that on sundays it ran only between San Giovanni and Calasetta. There was also a daily railcar return working from Calasetta to San Giovanni in the morning and a daily mixed in the morning returning late afternoon. Lastly there was one daily afternoon railcar return working between Calasetta and S. Antioco and there were two unbalanced workings from Calasetta to San Giovanni, an early morning mixed on weekdays only and an early evening railcar daily.

"return" indicates and out-and-back working.
"each way" indicates parallel departures from each end.

In Sardinia, steam was retained for many mixed services. Here an FCS 2-6-0T heads a mixed train at Macomer as late as 1969... (D Trevor Rowe)

...but from 1958, diesel-electrics took an increasing role. Here a DE 6XX series locomotive heads a mixed train out of Macomer in 1969; one of the Reggiane 3/1/luggage coaches in original condition at the rear. (D TREVOR ROWE)

Modernisation and its results

In terms of post-war modernisation, Sardinia came off best. After considerable argument, the Italian State, by a law of 1952, provided substantial subsidies of up to 75 per cent during the 1950s for capital works on proper rehabilitation and upgrading of track and rolling stock. So far as stock was concerned this meant that all companies were enabled to order modern diesel equipment which arrived in 1958-59. The FMS got least, a series of six bogie diesel-electric railcars with four trailers; the FCS lines acquired a similar set of twenty cars with matching trailers and fourteen 700hp diesel-electric locomotives while the SFS got five almost identical locomotives and eleven less powerful railcars with some trailers. These latter cars were diesel mechanical, rather than diesel electric, the official explanation being that the comparatively gentler curves and gradients of the SFS did not warrant the complications of electric drive.

So far as the infrastructure was concerned, modernisation had two tiers. Attention was concentrated on those lines thought to offer most potential. Thus Cagliari - Mandas - Isili, Macomer - Nuoro and Sassari - Alghero were relaid with 18m long rail weighing 27kg/m in place of the original SFSS lengths of 9m and 21kg/m, opportunity being taken to provide some minor realignments especially on the approaches to Nuoro. At Nuoro the line was also truncated by about 700m for urban development, a new terminus being built. On the first two sections, many stations and depots were also reconstructed in what can only be termed a blockhouse style of architecture using brick and concrete. The other surviving lines, excluding the FMS, were resleepered and reballasted, with some rail being replaced by better material, largely from those lines which were closed and, it is said, a total of 23.4km of minor deviations to smooth out the worst curves.

One says "surviving lines" because the sting in the tail, so far as the railway system was concerned, was that subsidy was calculated on a complex formula based on traffic, population in the area served and length of line; under a certain figure, the line had to be closed and replaced by bus services. In practice this meant that the original FCS routes from Sarcidano and the ex SFSS branch from Gairo to Jerzu closed in the summer of 1956 together with the SFS-operated section from Monti to Luras; there was little complaint about the FCS routes which had long been reduced to a single daily train but opposition around Monti was so ferocious that the track was left in place for some years in case it had to be re-opened.

In 1958 the FCS also got modern railcars: here a brand-new ADe 04 awaits ceremonial acceptance. (H LUFF)

All sections of the system also benefited by general building refurbishment, renewal of some tunnels and masonry structures, replacement of many time-expired metal bridges, rectification of superelevation and curvature to accommodate higher speeds, and improvement of station facilities. Notably, operation of points at important stations was changed from flagmen to groundframes sited at the main building, most disc warning signals were replaced by dual-aspect colour lights and important road crossings were automated with flashing light indicators for both road and rail and, in many cases, lifting barriers. Passenger coaches were also upgraded and modernised to some extent for those trains (usually mixed) which were still locomotive hauled.

Thus by the late 1950s the surviving lines were in good shape and had the advantage that the railways were also running most of the supplementary bus services. Certainly, over the next few years, the modernisation appeared to be succeeding. In the first "new" year, Sassari – Alghero, for example, carried 270,271 passengers as against 87,733 the previous year and over the six years from 1957 to 1963 passengers on the Macomer division, on an annual basis, rose from 176,728 to 697,411 and on the Cagliari lines from 133,012 to 1,228,452; this was undoubtedly helped by introduction of a network of bus feeder services to strategic points and more frequent and faster railcar services. Freight also benefited to some extent and transporter bogies were introduced at Macomer and around the Sassari area.

As examples of passenger service improvements, in the late 1960s, even the Sorgono branch had four daily through workings (two by bus, two by railcar) with extra buses as far as Laconi; Alghero had no less than nine daily railcars plus a mixed train; and the Sassari – Palau line had two daily through railcars and a diesel-hauled mixed besides various short workings and parallel buses. Even the bustitution service for Monti - Tempio gave three daily workings each way while the ex FCS lines had a positive glut compared with their previous one-train daily: no less than three through bus services over the former main line, with additional short workings to meet local needs, and a similar set between Villamar and Ales. Only the Arbatax route seems to have suffered, the only through working being a daily freight which conveyed passengers when required.

As for the Sardinian Southern lines, they were caught both ways. None of their traffic was really profitable, even the coal mining industry existing only by virtue of a substantial subsidy, but so long as that lasted the railway was safe also. When mining declined, the company was not able to sustain the consequent losses and in 1952 went into receivership. Its operations were taken over by the State in 1955 – more specifically by a Government Office in Rome which was set up to administer all such failing concerns if they could not be closed. Non-coal goods traffic was minimal and while there may well have been some national relief when EU pressure forced closure of the heavily subsidised mining in 1959-60, the FMS was hit hard. A small import traffic in coal remained for several years using standard gauge wagons on transporters transhipping at Carbonia and the company tried to retain traffic, even putting on a through bus service between Cagliari, Iglesias, Carbonia and Calasetta, but closure could not long be delayed. Meanwhile all the surviving lines soldiered on; the new equipment speeded up passenger services but otherwise there was little apparent change, steam locomotives being retained in most places for goods and shunting work except on the SFS routes. The Arbatax mixed still took over twelve hours in practice to stagger through to Cagliari but then it was really what the Germans rather pedantically class as a "goods train with passenger accommodation" and there was always the sea route for through passengers!

The Corsican experience

Meanwhile, over in Corsica, a similar situation had been handled entirely differently. Initially, following the CFD withdrawal, a "Service de Controle" was set up to ensure uninterrupted operation. The Ponts et Chaussées organisation took over officially from February 1948, operating the system "en regie" (ie under direct administration) on behalf of the state. In some ways the situation was worse than that pertaining in Sardinia as the service standards mentioned above indicate. The railway did already have the advantage of a substantial railcar fleet built only just before the war so the authorities were able to get away with ordering just eight powerful ABH-type bogie railcars from Renault to operate express services between Bastia and Ajaccio, together with two of a batch of ten diesel-electric locomotives being built for various minor railways. Goods traffic was small enough that, even so, steam traction was abandoned in 1954. On the other

In Corsica, there was limited modernisation: two new diesel-electric locomotives took over the goods workings.
(Bernard Roze)

Renault ABH railcars took over the express services between Bastia and Ajaccio, here seen at Corte.
(BERNARD ROZE)

hand money in general was tight and the operating deficit continued to rise, which made rehabilitation of the infrastructure quite difficult. The remaining stub of the east coast line, from Casamozza down to Folelli-Orezza was closed entirely from the beginning of July 1953 and an attempt was made to close the Calvi branch in 1955; as at Monti in Sardinia, the public objections were vigorous and prolonged, so much so that the branch was reprieved. A similar attempt to shut the whole system in 1959 met with total obstruction from both populace and the départemental authorities but, though the system was reprieved, lack of money for maintenance and deficits getting almost out of control meant that it decayed rapidly. By 1964 the situation was so serious that something drastic had to be done. A thorough study by a State Commission decided that the railway had to be saved because it was still almost the only reliable trans-island communication link, particularly in winter. The problem was how should this be done?

1965 – 1985: A patchy revival in Corsica

What was done in Corsica appeared at first to have great potential. After discussions with various reluctant private operators – including the CFD – the State decided to turn operation over to the Societé Auxiliaire pour les Chemins de Fer Secondaires (SACFS). This small company had, in the late 1950s, taken over the Castres system of the ailing CFD du Tarn and transformed it into an efficient railway with an accompanying drop in deficit. The CFDT was closed in 1962, a road-minded Council having decided it was still not viable, but the experiment was seen as at least partially successful. From 29 May 1965, the Corsican system was therefore conceded to the SACFS for a term of 14 years 7 months (ie until the end of 1979) with an annual subvention. Stipulations included partial renewal of the permanent way, the restoration of the harbour branches and the construction of spurs to serve the airports at Bastia and Ajaccio. The SACFS would have use of existing equipment, together with one new diesel locomotive at the State's expense, and agreed to bring in material of its own which had been acquired second or third hand from a variety of closing systems in mainland France. (see list in Appendix 1). In line with its experience on the Tarn, the new operator proposed to institute fast passenger services on the main line (with a surcharge), to provide separate messageries services and to provide a frequent shuttle in season along the coast between Calvi and l'Ile Rousse – to be known as the Ligne de Balagne. More controversially, from the staff point of view at least, it reduced most intermediate stations to unmanned halts and rationalised operation.

Corsica got shabby under the SACFS and the CFD locomotives came out in red and yellow stripes – here at Bastia. (D TREVOR ROWE)

A period of rejuvenation of a sort followed but, alas, not for long. The rather miscellaneous gaggle of small Billard cars and six-coupled diesel tractors imported by the SACFS was not really up to the job, even though some were rebodied and overhauled before coming to the island. The airport branches were never built and only the harbour line at Ajaccio was recommissioned – it is said this got little use since locals had become accustomed to using the main station and did not change their habits. It is not clear whether the financial situation was largely irremediable or whether the company's management was not really capable of coping with such an extensive system; in any case the deficit, after an initial blip, continued to increase and the company, stuck with an agreed subsidy, got seriously into debt. It was forced into receivership and, from 7 January 1972, the railway was placed under an administration. The sole real legacy of the SACFS reign was the institution of the seasonal shuttle service along the north coast between Calvi and l'Ile Rousse, marketed as the "Ligne de Balagne".

The administrating company was another of the major French operators, the Societé Générale des Chemins de Fer et de Transports Automobiles (CFTA) heir since 1966 of an amalgamation between the Societé Générale des Chemins de Fer Economiques (SE) and the Cie des Chemins de Fer Secondaires et de Transports Automobiles (CFSTA). This concern, once a great rival of the CFD, was confirmed in post from 1st February 1972 and immediately set about studying how it could improve the situation. Its proposals, agreed by the State in 1974, envisaged the following:

- complete renewal of the permanent way and reconstruction of the stations at Ajaccio, Calvi and Bastia.
- transfer of the workshops to new buildings at Casamozza
- acquisition of five new railcars and rebodying of some trailers
- implementation of a suburban service between Bastia and Casamozza down the developing eastern coast.

This programme was at least partly implemented – indeed the Bastia suburban service as far as Bigulia had been started at the beginning of January 1973. The new workshops were built, Bastia becoming a running shed and first-line maintenance depot while Bastia station itself was completely reworked as part

Most of the SACFS stock ended up on a huge dump at Borgo, south of Bastia; this selection included a Billard draisine, tractor 3 and a selection of Billard A80Ds... (JOSÉ BANAUDO)

...but under the CFTA and SNCF things have improved. Modern Soulé cars cross at Vivario. Note the bullhead track still in place within station limits. (JOSÉ BANAUDO)

of an urban development programme, the harbour branch being removed entirely. The best of the old railcars – the Renault ABH – were modernised and five new bogie cars (2001-05) bought from the CFD Montmirail Works. Timetables were markedly improved and the track renewal programme started. As a result CFTA was confirmed as operator for a period of five years from January 1977 with annual extensions thereafter. The programme of track renewal with 39kg/m rail was started in 1974 and completed by 1984, allowing all vehicles to run throughout the system. To complement it, a 3.5km realignment took place south of Bastia, cutting out three level crossings of the main road, and Bigulia station was rebuilt to act as a terminus for the suburban operation; at the other end, a realignment of about 1km was undertaken at Ajaccio, to allow urban development.

In practice, however, the CFTA got only one extension, the regional authorities considering that, as a state-owned property, the railway should logically be operated by the state owned SNCF which was seen as having greater expertise and resources (no doubt it also took into consideration the strongly expressed opinions of the staff who preferred the enhanced conditions of service offered by SNCF). Services settled down to their present pattern, comprising three or four trains daily between Bastia and Ajaccio, with the inevitable short workings to and from Corte, a twice daily through service between Calvi and Bastia, and the Bastia suburban shuttles together with the seasonal shuttles between Calvi and l'Ile Rousse.

Under recent laws, responsibility for local communications has been handed over to the Regions Autonomes, of which the relevant one is the Collectivité Territoriale de la Corse which combines the two Corsican Départements, and from 1983 onward the system has been managed by the SNCF's Marseilles Division under a succession of five-year contracts. This is essentially a management scheme, the equipment, infrastructure and staff being owned and employed by the Region with a small cadre of SNCF managers in control. The Region has provided finance for upgrading the current fleet with new railcars and for continued improvements to stock and track. There is even talk of rebuilding all or part of the former east coast line using EU funds as has happened in the neighbouring island of Sardinia.

Parallel changes in Sardinia

If the Corsican system was still largely unchanged at the end of this period, the same could not be said of its Sardinian neighbours. True the FS had stabilised its standard gauge operations with more modern diesels and retirement of the steam fleet. On the narrow gauge, however, there had been sweeping changes. Down in the south, the remaining coal traffic went over to road transport, and the FMS started dying. The least used sections (Iglesias - Monteponi and part of the Siliqua branch as far as Narcao) closed in 1969 and 1968 respectively – because of a collapsed tunnel on the Iglesias branch and flooding for a new dam north of Narcao on the Siliqua branch – and the rest followed in stages by 1975. The six newer railcars were sent to the FCS but the rest – barring a 2-6-0T and a Fiat railcar which were "preserved" in the open to rot away – was scrapped.

Nor was the FCS exempt from change. True, a new depot and workshop complex was built at Monserrato on the northern outskirts of Cagliari in the late 1960s, and a start was made on constructing a 7km link across town to a site near the FS station. On the other hand the Cagliari terminus was cut back to a gloomy site at Piazza Repubblica "as a temporary measure owing to conflict with road transport" and to release a valuable site for development. In 1969, too, the branch from Tirso to Chilivani was closed to all traffic; as with Monti – Luras, the local reaction was so strong that the track was left in place for some time and the replacement bus service is still prominently marked as such.

All this, alas, was insufficient and the FCS/SFS operation went the way of most Italian secondary narrow gauge railways – it had to be taken over by the State Office set up to control such affairs when they became insolvent but were considered indispensable. Initially La Tranviaria went into receivership in 1971 and the Government Office put the existing lines under administration while retaining the old company frameworks. In 1989, however, they did the logical thing, all surviving lines coming under the control of an administrative commission, the Gestione Governativa Ferrovie Della Sardegna, otherwise known as the FdS. Massive injection of European Union funds for deprived regions followed which at once bolstered and threatened the railway system. Threats came because the funding included drastic and rapid improvement

Other things changed in Sardinia too. This is the old, and impressive, Cagliari terminus at Viale Bonaria which closed in 1968 or thereabouts... (MUSEU FERROVIE, CAGLIARI)

of the island's road system which gradually led to diminution of services on the outlying sections – in particular Bosa – Tresnurages – Macomer (Bosa – Tresnurages substituted by road services from 15 June 1981 and the railway service eventually discontinued completely by 1997). Nulvi – Tempio – Palau; Isili – Sorgono; Mandas – Arbatax also lost their year-round scheduled services in 1997 together with the final cessation of freight workings. Seasonal workings remained in force between about May and October over certain sections – for example the Sorgono branch had an out and return daily from Mandas, and the Arbatax line had two trains each way.

Funding bolstered the system in that the other lines (and even parts of the failing ones) were massively improved with new or refurbished stations, general track and signalling upgrading and drastic realignments over considerable distances. Even at time of writing these are still continuing and have greatly altered the Cagliari – Mandas, Macomer – Nuoro, Sassari – Sorso and Sassari – Alghero branches which are considered to have potential as commuter lines. The two latter may eventually be incorporated into a rapid light transit system which is projected for the Sassari region. This is being built to the 950mm gauge to allow future linkups with the FdS and the first part of Line 1, 2.4km of single track with one intermediate loop, from the FS station to Emiciclo Garibaldi, is under construction in 2001. Four modern articulated sets have been ordered from Ansaldo-Breda and future plans envisage an "intermodal interchange" at the FS station, together with several other routes. One is projected to use a short portion of the FdS Tempio line, another to run parallel with the Sorso branch on the same formation into the north-west suburbs before curving away. In the longer term, electrification of the FdS lines to Sorso and Alghero is the subject of feasibility studies, together with the possibility of a branch of the latter to Alghero airport and, even, a return through Alghero town to the harbour area. On the other hand a grandiose plan for electrifying both standard and narrow gauge lines in the Cagliari area foundered, although the standard gauge catenary had been erected (it is still there) and some standard gauge locomotives delivered; the FS, it is said, simply refused to operate the new system as uneconomical, while the narrow gauge link was never completed.

...and the Cagliari trams, reduced to the Station – Poetto link, closed also. A Tallero car in the harbour area, Cagliari.
(José Banaudo)

In Sardinia, the daily commuter workings may be dullish and modernised – an unrebuilt DM railcar of series ADm 5X on the modern Alghero branch. (AUTHOR)

The daily special workings board at Mandas for a typical weekday in May 2001 shows that there is still a fair amount of activity even on the officially mothballed lines. (AUTHOR)

The equipment picture has changed less. With declining traffic the FCS saw the writing on the wall and decided not to modernise further, keeping the best of its steam power serviceable into the 1970s for shunting and occasional traffic peaks. As a result, the existing power, supplemented by the ex-FMS railcars, proved sufficient to cope with traffic. The only additions have been, in 1995, a series of eight modern diesel-electric railcars and five matching control trailers from Ferrosud; legend has it that these were designed to be convertible to straight electrics if the electrification project had materialised. As a substitute for new stock, the existing railcar fleet is being progressively upgraded with new fibreglass-clad monocoque bodies on the reconditioned running gear of existing vehicles, while some of the more modern bogie coaches and some diesel locomotives have been refurbished.

Simultaneously, an EU-backed initiative was started to safeguard those lines not chosen for wholesale renewal. Under the generic title of "Trenino Verde" (little green train) this involved the provision of seasonal tourist services over those lines (which are, of course, the really scenic ones), together with a drive to offer charter trains for groups. These are popular with both locals (for example school trips or social club outings) and railway enthusiasts and, in 2001, appeared to be replacing most of the former scheduled seasonal services - ie most, while running in the same paths, are now "on request" or "on demand" and thus have a guaranteed passenger load if they run. The infrastructure is kept in good repair, which presumably provides continuing work, and there may well be little financial difference between a once daily scheduled

Besides railcars these often include locomotive-hauled workings. Here is a typical tourist train (Trenino Verde) of LDE 502 and an SFS refurbished coach on the northern line. (AUTHOR)

While steam charters are by no means unknown, SLM 2-6-0T 43 GOITO is seen with restored "heritage" stock on the western end of the Arbatax line. (AUTHOR)

train running almost empty and a succession of seasonal workings that are at least well-used. The "verde" label ties in with a general attempt to promote "green" tourism, including such activities as organised mountain-biking trips.

In connection with the tourist, or historic train, operations, a small museum has been opened at Monserrato and several ex SFSS and SFS bogie coaches have been restored together with a nominal fleet of six steam locomotives. At the time of writing, economies are threatening the continuation of this policy and both the northern and southern lines are marred by a widespread outbreak of graffiti on normal service stock.

The position is somewhat complicated by recent political changes. From 16 June 1997 FS officially took over responsibility for the FdS although little appeared to change on the surface save partial and erratic application of UIC numbers to selected stock. On the other hand regular passenger services on the outlying sections were definitively suspended, leaving only the seasonal ones mentioned above. From 1st January 2000, the situation changed again, control of all railways, including the standard gauge, being transferred to an Island administration. Goods traffic has effectively effectively been discontinued over the whole narrow gauge system but the passenger services seem fairly safe, although little money is left for further improvement - as usual with EU projects, capital expenditure is comparatively easy to obtain but continuing maintenance must come from revenue or local taxes.

CHAPTER 4

Railway geography and routes in Corsica

A metre-by-metre chronicling of the very considerable route kilometrage in both islands would take too much space and be excessively boring: to envision the very spectacular scenery and the impressive engineering works it is really necessary to visit and to ride the trains, or perhaps to view one of the videos listed in the bibliography. There is still sufficient kilometrage in traffic to get a very good idea of the whole and if one wants a vicarious impression of the atmosphere, D. H. Lawrence in his "Sea and Sardinia" describes very graphically a voyage on the Sorgono line in its heyday. This chapter and the next are intended only to give an overall impression and to allow some comparison to be made between what are at once very similar and very different landscapes. For details, Appendix 2 gives an annotated list of stopping places with their main features and Chapter 11 typical layouts and comparisons of the more important stations.

Corsica and its railway routes

Each of the three surviving sections of Corsican line is different from the others. The Bastia – Ponte-Leccia stretch is coastal plain followed by a steep gorgelike river valley; The Calvi branch, for much of its length, is arid rolling country covered with maquis and most of the rest is sandy pinewoods and coastal bathing places; The main line south to Ajaccio cuts across the grain of the high country east of the mountainous north-south spine before burrowing through it to descend to Ajaccio half way down the west coast – a much "closer" country than most of the Sardinian mountains though requiring equally massive engineering works. The now defunct east coast line ran mainly on the plain, coming close to the coast in several places and only taking to serious engineering works when the terrain got rocky and rugged – indeed it only had one serious tunnel, although there were sufficient bridges and viaducts to doom it once they were destroyed in the Second World War.

All the best light railways tangled with the streets: In a shady side street on the Bastia harbour branch, tractor 2, ex the VFD, is frustrated by a carelessly parked van. (D TREVOR ROWE)

Bastia – Casamozza – Ponte Leccia

The system has its headquarters in the thriving port of Bastia up on the north east coast and the capital of Upper Corsica (Haute Corse). The railway originally had a sprawling station, with a typical French station building and goods shed on the east side and the extensive running sheds and works to the west, while a long spur led off down to the harbour. In the 1980s, however, this was drastically altered by an "urbanisation programme" which cut off the harbour branch and destroyed most of the east side buildings in favour of city spread. They were replaced by a modern station, administrative HQ and goods shed immediately alongside the works yard and facing east instead of west, while the yard itself was truncated; thus the whole site appears to have pivoted westward and the line now curves sharply to enter the impressive tunnel of la Torreta (1,422m) under a steep hill. At the same time the "Works" has been reduced to the status of a running shed.

The line down the eastern plain as far as Casamozza is now unashamedly suburban, its only real points of interest being a girder bridge at Bevinco and the newish deviation which has done away with several level crossings of the main road that parallels it most of the way. The five stations are little more than commuter halts, with Bigulia as the normal terminus, but Casamozza itself (21km) was rebuilt after the war in a very austere style and now houses the main repair works - two standard modern industrial buildings and some sidings on the eastern side; any obsolete derelict equipment tends to get dumped here.

Casamozza was also junction for the former east coast line but only the partly destroyed trackbed and buildings of that survive. The current route crosses the River Golo and turns south west to climb up its increasingly rugged valley, crossing from one bank to the other occasionally. Barchetta (29.6km) and Ponte-Nuovo (39.1km) are the only serious stops but there is also scenery, five tunnels and a collection of quite impressive bridges before the junction of Ponte Leccia (46.7km) is reached - and this is only the beginning of the serious work. This was always an important stop, with a two-road sub-shed, locomotive servicing facilities and a buffet, and the Calvi branch trails in from the north east to a cross-platform interchange.

A typical goods train, with 405 in charge, leaving Mizille viaduct on the way from Bastia to Ponte Leccia.

(José Banaudo)

A very French atmosphere at Ponte Leccia itself, as tractor 114 ambles around in the way of all minor railway operations. (JOSÉ BANAUDO)

The Calvi branch

The branch from Ponte-Leccia northwest to the seaside resorts of l'Ile Rousse and Calvi always seems to me to be unfairly neglected. Apart from the quite common challenge of seeing off the odd weighty cow – or, not, as the case may be; the bovine attrition rate is fairly spectacular since they like lying down in the coolth of tunnels and a random couple of journeys in summer once claimed one dead, one retired hurt and one very near miss - the branch has its own kind of charm. Certainly it has little of the forested hills and towering gorges of the main line but it starts with a crossing of the River Asco and a steady 1 in 50 climb up the Navaccia tributary through Pietralba (km 52.7 from Bastia) and Novella (65.3km) to its summit before starting a long rambling descent across the barren and dusty central highlands. It must have been a heartbreaking line for the traffic department. The occasional stations, now mostly derelict and crumbling, seem to have no hinterland at all and as the chestnut forests give way to scrub and rolling vistas the line has to follow the contours up and down re-entrants, cutting through them in no less than nine short curving tunnels as soon as the land allows. Palasca (km 75.1) is vaguely near its station but Belgodere (82.8km) is a good 150 metres uphill and just before it the line has pierced a final ridge via the Croce tunnel before dropping steadily across the wide plain of the Balagne to Le Regino (88.1km and only 60m up). A final scramble across a low intervening ridge and it reaches the sea at last, at the now flourishing resort of l'Ile Rousse (98.1km). l'Ile Rousse is a pleasant town and ferry terminal with a nice seafront along which the train mingles with the holidaymakers and the bicyclists (who may, of course be one and the same). l'Ile Rousse station is just along a sandy track to the north and is one of the few properly manned in season because it is terminus for the shuttles of the Ligne de Balagne. From it the line wanders behind dunes and scrubby woodlands, pausing now and then to pick up or drop casual passengers from the bathing places. There are only two real stations, (Algajola, 106.3km and Calenzana-Lumio, 115.5km) which are needed as

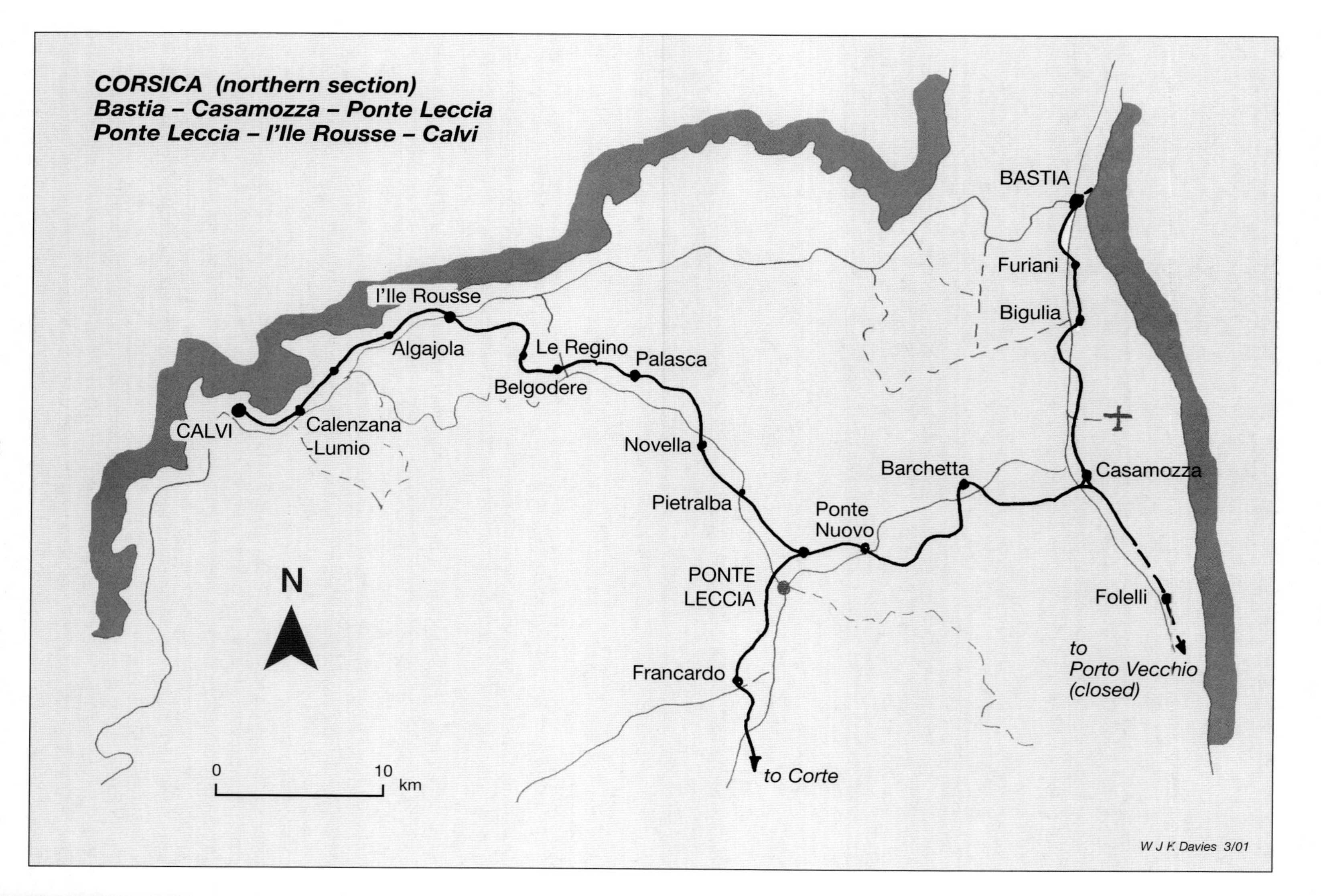
CORSICA (northern section)
Bastia – Casamozza – Ponte Leccia
Ponte Leccia – l'Ile Rousse – Calvi
BASTIA
Furiani
Bigulia
Casamozza
Folelli
to
Porto Vecchio
(closed)
Barchetta
Ponte
Nuovo
PONTE
LECCIA
Francardo
to Corte
Pietralba
Novella
Palasca
Le Regino
Belgodere
l'Ile Rousse
Algajola
Calenzana
-Lumio
CALVI
N
0
10
km
W J K Davies 3/01

Typical inland scenery on the Calvi branch, as BB 404 hauls a permanent way train between Novella and Ponte Leccia.

(JOSÉ BANAUDO)

Where the Calvi branch meets the sea, with l'Ile Rousse in the background. 114 on a short goods train of a van and a car transporter – with no vacuum brakes it was restricted to four wagons and the extra safety chains at chassis corners are visible... (José Banaudo)

...and west of l'Ile Rousse, the Balagne shuttle of an ABH car and control trailer 113 carries on – but which way? (JOSÉ BANAUDO)

passing places in high season but there are plenty of request halts before the outskirts of Calvi and a run in to the refurbished station on its western edge. Calvi (120.0km) is a delightful town, especially in the low season when it is not swamped by people and, if it were not for the infrequent services to anywhere but l'Ile Rousse, would be the ideal place to stay. Even so, a few days lounging on the beach or walking in the nearby hills cannot be bad and the frequent shuttles in season give an excellent excuse for being there.

Ponte Leccia – Corte – Ajaccio

The really difficult country was between Ponte Leccia and the west coast. In order to serve the major settlements of Corte (once the island's capital) and Vizzavona, the railway cannot take the most direct route but must climb from and descend into no less than three horrendous river gorges, painfully scaling the flanks of one before burrowing through the watershed to reach the next. At first it continues up the Golo valley but after Francardo (54.6km) it swings away up a tributary. Short tunnels and bridges give a taste of what is to come before the route passes Omessa (61.0km), crosses a watershed at St Quillico tunnel (363m) and drops down a gorge to the Tavigliano river and up it to the old town of Corte (Km.73.8; altitude 396m). Corte itself, high on its hill with the fortifications above, is worth a visit and is actively promoting tourism; there are short workings to here from Bastia and more could probably be done to encourage traffic. As it is, the railway is now entering the most spectacular part of its course – it is no wonder that the central section took so long to complete. No less than eleven short tunnels and two major viaducts (Maures and Morte) have to be traversed before arriving at Venaco (85.9km) although there is only one intermediate stop, at Poggio-Riventosa (82.1km). Another two tunnels, one of them the watershed crossing of San Pietro (604m) and five viaducts or major bridges (plus a couple of sheltered "arcades" to stave off snow and avalanches) are needed on the remorseless scramble across to the River Vergato and to Vecchio (89.8km, 475m) – and if that was hard the next 17km or so on to Vizzavona are an almost constant 30mm/m (1 in 33) As an aside, the CFD seemed quite at home with this sort of grade – the long climb from Le Cheylard to Saint-Agrève on the Vivarais was very similar in its intensity and the crews used flippantly to call it "la

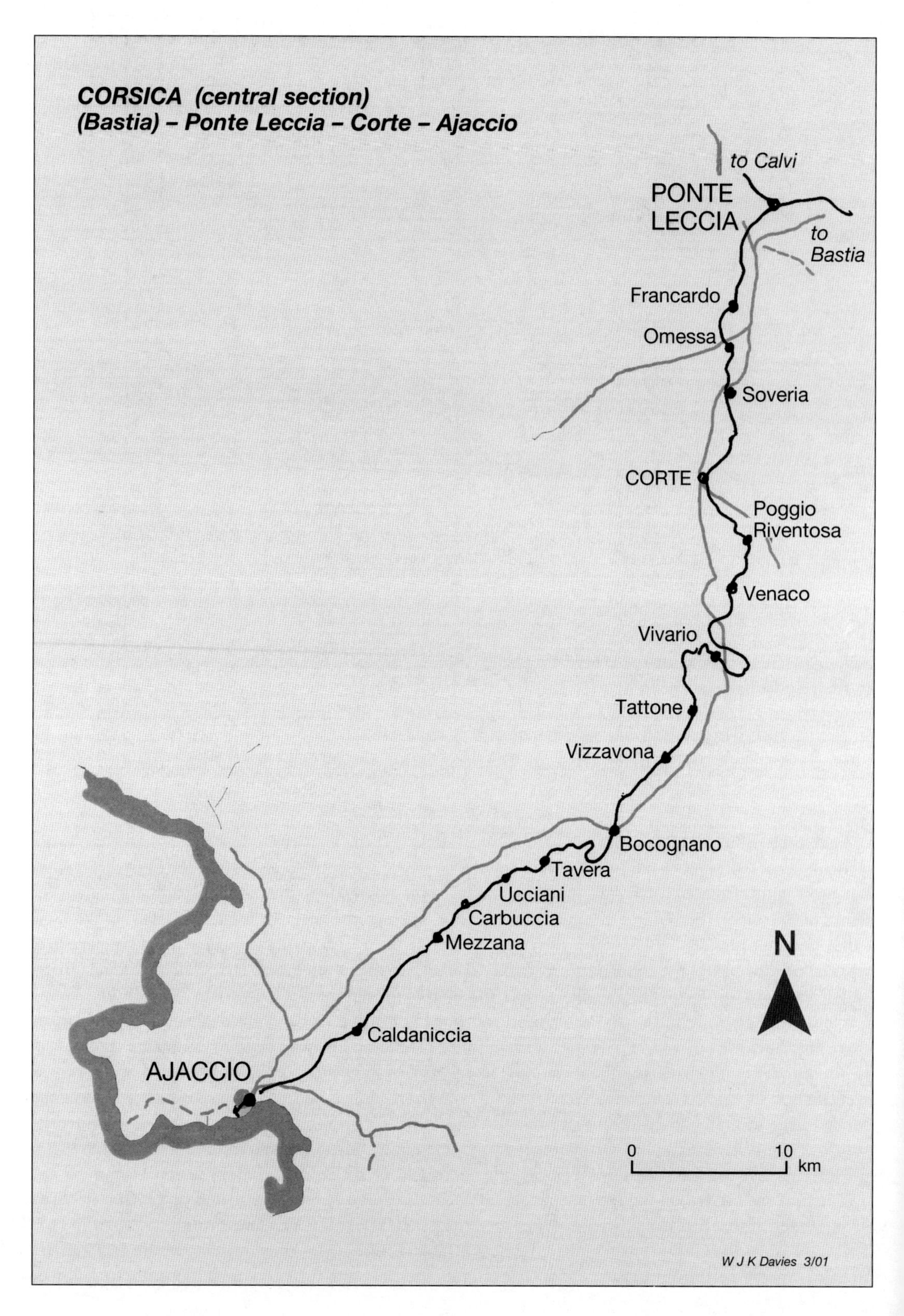
CORSICA (central section)
(Bastia) – Ponte Leccia – Corte – Ajaccio
to Calvi
PONTE LECCIA
to Bastia
Francardo
Omessa
Soveria
CORTE
Poggio Riventosa
Venaco
Vivario
Tattone
Vizzavona
Bocognano
Tavera
Ucciani
Carbuccia
Mezzana
N
Caldaniccia
AJACCIO
0
10
km
W J K Davies 3/01

A typical townscape in central Corsica: a Renault ABH and rebuilt Billard trailer leaving Vivario in the central highlands. (D TREVOR ROWE)

petite colline" – and the Sardinian Arbatax and Palau lines have stretches with very similar sustained gradients. In Corsica, the climb starts with the spectacular metal Vecchio viaduct across a tributary of the Vergato which it then climbs painfully along to the, justly famous, boucle (horseshoe) of Vivario. Even with a 1 in 33 ruling grade, the line is forced well out of its direct course right up, across and back along the rocky valley to curve once more round its flank for another 180 degrees and enter Tattone (alt. 802m; km 102.8). The last four kilometres into Vizzavona itself (106.7km, 906m) are just as hard and immediately afterward the line plunges into its longest tunnel, under the Vizzavona col (3916m long). In traversing this the line drops straight as an arrow, losing some 78m in the process (it is claimed that with the right weather

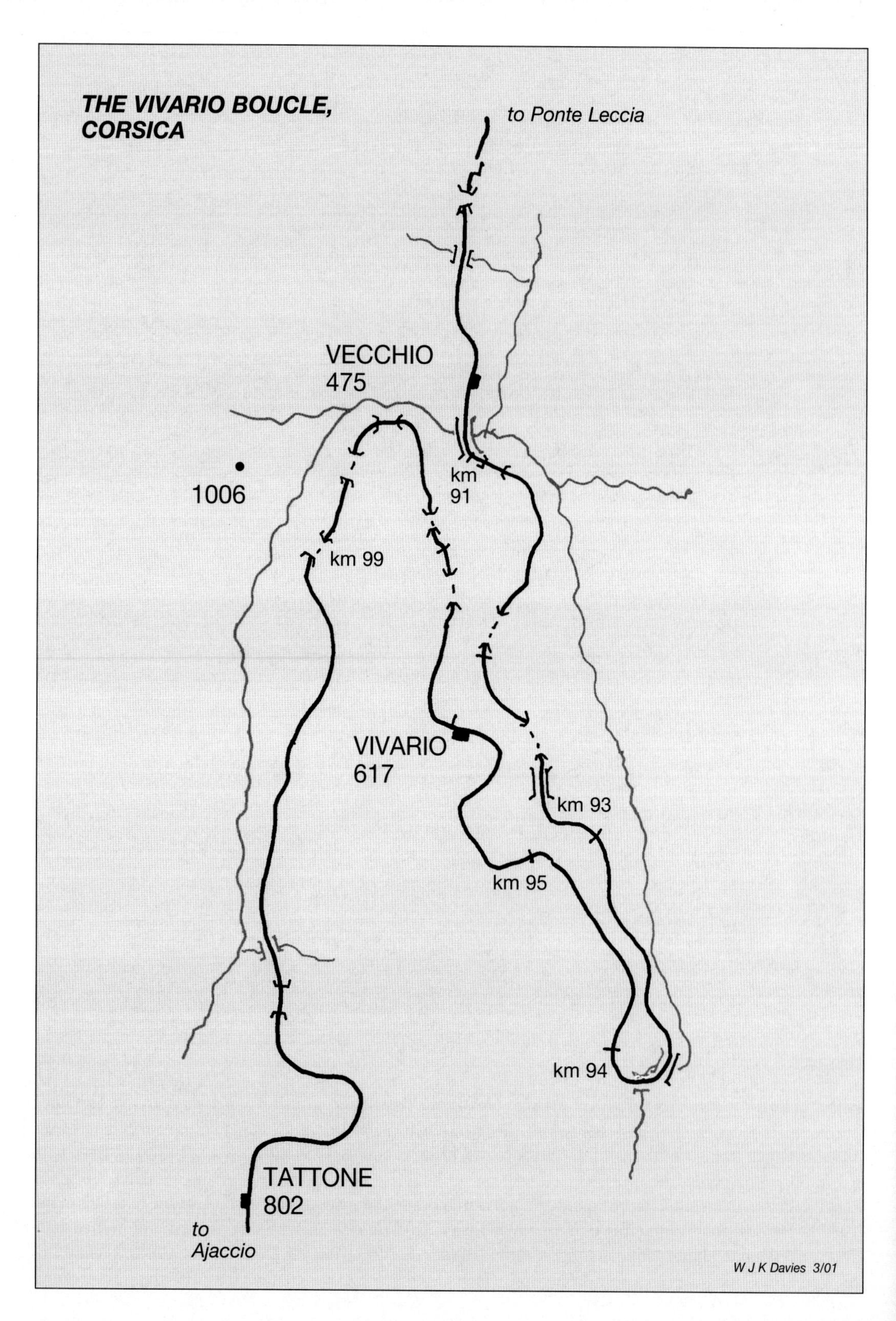
THE VIVARIO BOUCLE, CORSICA
to Ponte Leccia
VECCHIO
475
1006
km
91
km 99
VIVARIO
617
km 93
km 95
km 94
TATTONE
802
to
Ajaccio
W J K Davies 3/01

conditions you can see right through although the writer has never tested it!). This is THE major watershed between east and west and the line then drops steadily at between 1 in 40 and 1 in 50 right down to Mezzana (144.9km). This is not to say that the countryside becomes much easier - the traject includes a view of a spectacular waterfall and a crossing of the equally spectacular Granato stone viaduct beside numerous short tunnels and bridges and a cluster of halts of various kinds but it is the last fling. From Mezzana the line makes its way down to the coast along which it runs into Ajaccio proper and Ajaccio station on the seafront. There was for many years a harbour branch and for some years in the 1970s passenger services carried on into the harbour area to a featureless halt which the SACFS hopefully named Ajaccio Centre but no one much used it and the extension has now been abandoned. Certainly this section can compare well with anything in Sardinia and, with its forests and craggy gorges even surpasses it in many peoples' eyes.

On the main line again, a Soulé set crosses a typical viaduct by Venaco. (JOSÉ BANAUDO)

Nearing Ajaccio, a Billard A150D6 and trailer by the famous "bride's veil" waterfall... (D TREVOR ROWE)

...and, finally, the public face of a local railway. The street frontage of Ajaccio station with hardly anything to tell you "here are trains". (AUTHOR)

Casamozza – Folelli – Ghisonaccia – Solenzara – Porto Vecchio (closed)

The former long line down the east coast has now been closed, in large part, for nearly 60 years and is consequently not recorded in detail: parts of it, in particular near the southern end, have even been subsumed into, or obliterated by, road improvements and even photographs are rare. The following notes are only a skeleton description.

The first part to open, and the last to close, was over a continuation of the coastal plain through Arena-Vescovata (24.2km from Bastia) and on to Folelli, parallelling the main road with only a halt (St Pancrace at c.29km) in between. Folelli, or more properly Folelli-Orezza (31.9km) for most of its life, remained in use up to 1953 and was a typical "Ponts et Chaussées" station, as indeed were all structures down to Ghisonaccia; the CFD took over construction thereafter.

The railway on to Ghisonaccia ran along the coast, crossing the main road several times to maintain its height. Apart from several halts there were three proper stations - Prunete-Cervione (46.8km) right on the coast (Cervione being about three kilometres inland); Tallone (67.6km) where the line swung inland for a while; and Aleria (73.2km), some distance from its name town on the main road to Corte. Ghisonaccia (85.3km) was terminus for over forty years, the remainder being opened by the CFD between 1930 and 1935. This latter is the section where mountains meet sea and where the road has replaced it in some places. There was a station a few km south of Ghisonaccia serving the scattered hamlets of Prunelli and Pietropola, a station at Ponte do Travo where a viaduct led over the Travo river, and two halts, before Solenzara (109.9km), once more a temporary terminus for some five years. The last stretch came back to the coast and the road, through a string of halts and a proper station at Ste Lucie (134.4km) before again swinging inland and returning to Porto Vecchio (150.9km) at the head of its little bay. The interesting thing is a comment from a French enthusiast who has managed to follow the line – that they seem to have managed to build a road over the difficult part of its course while claiming that destruction of engineering works was sufficient to ensure closure of the railway. Detailed statistics will be found in Appendix 2.

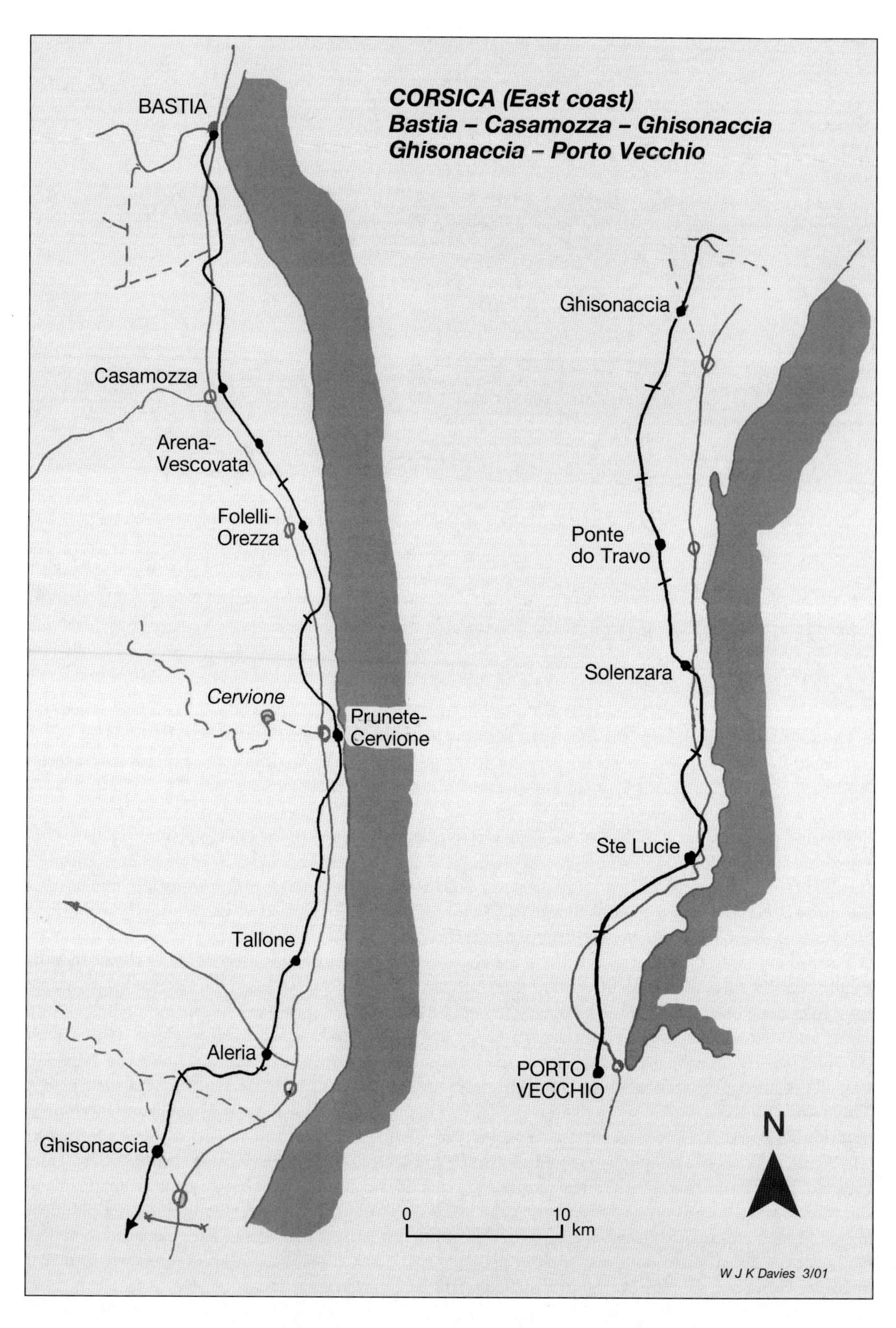
CORSICA (East coast)
Bastia – Casamozza – Ghisonaccia
Ghisonaccia – Porto Vecchio
BASTIA
Casamozza
Arena-
Vescovata
Folelli-
Orezza
Cervione
Prunete-
Cervione
Tallone
Aleria
Ghisonaccia
Ghisonaccia
Ponte
do Travo
Solenzara
Ste Lucie
PORTO
VECCHIO
N
0
10
km
W J K Davies 3/01

CHAPTER 5

Railway geography and routes in Sardinia

Because Sardinia is so much larger than Corsica its railways are geographically more diverse. The existing narrow gauge ones divide into three distinct systems: the southern group with its headquarters at Cagliari Monserrato and extending north through Mandas to Sorgono and east from Mandas to the east coast at Arbatax; the central system, which basically runs from the west coast at Bosa to a standard gauge junction at Macomer (headquarters) and thence east to Nuoro which is a provincial capital; the northern system, centred on its standard gauge junction of Sassari and with three lines running west to Alghero; north-east to Sorso; and eastward to the coast again at Palau. The closed systems, other than those branches depending from the above, were different again but a car is needed to examine what remains except where they deviate enough to require hiking. All of the existing systems encounter difficult country somewhere; the major visual difference from Corsica is the noticeable lack of trees en masse - the Greeks and Romans used up most of them and their successors, with a constant demand for firewood, ensured that the place remains largely deforested although regeneration is taking place and many hillsides are covered with scrub and young growth. In general, too, the mountains are more open, with sweeping vistas as one climbs higher, and the railways are less inclined to hug deep river gorges. The final difference is of recent origin. Massive injections of European Union (EU) funding have been used on the most used railways to undertake some drastic realignments which have radically altered the character of some sections; instead of winding sinuously around the contours, they now cut almost arrow straight across the landscape, using cut and fill to avoid any really heavy gradients with new viaducts where necessary. The lines between Cagliari and Mandas, Macomer and Nuoro, Sassari and Sorso and Alghero are particularly affected. In all cases, therefore, distances given are indicative only, based on pre-1990s timetables which appear generally accurate within 1km. Detailed original distances, where known, are in Appendix 2. Note that descriptions in this chapter, in general, are oriented as most visitors will find them (eg Sassari - Alghero, although the line was originally run from Alghero).

1. Southern (Cagliari) system

Cagliari – Mandas – (Isili): distances prior to realignment except where noted

The SFSS used to start at a major terminal in Cagliari town, down on a wedgeshaped site fairly near the waterfront between Viale Bonaria and Viale Armando Diaz, where it had running sheds and main workshops and from which a goods extension reached the harbour front to run, latterly along the municipal tram tracks, to a freight link with the FS harbour lines. The station itself ran west to east, fronting Viale Bonaria and there is still an "alley of the old station" (Stazione Vecchio) joining the two roads. Thence the line swung north through the town, with far too many level crossings for comfort in the typical car-ridden environment of an Italian city. Under the 1970s plan to divert passenger services to near the FS station, this terminal site was sold off for development and a "temporary" station established on the old route at Piazza Repubblica where the line turned away from the streets. This, variously described as "like a garage" or "a concrete chasm" consists simply of two platforms and a utilitarian facade closed off by metal grilles and is now the permanent terminus – which is a pity. The old station was quite impressive with its imposing two-storey passenger building and offices flanking four dead-end tracks whose two platforms, under a vaulted overall roof, looked out across an ornamental fence to the city beyond. Even in later years when the roof was stripped to bare girders, the associated goods shed, workshops and running sheds made for a lot of interest. Now, from its dreary beginning, the so-called "Cagliari metropolitan" section climbs out of the town among the back gardens and general urban mess to serve a string of passenger halts before emerging about 5km out at the suburb of Monserrato. Here a modern concrete station with a passing loop replaces the former station of Monserrato-Pirri, the never completed trackbed of the 1970s diversion trailing off westward from its south end. Monserrato also hosts the main works and running sheds of the FdS, together

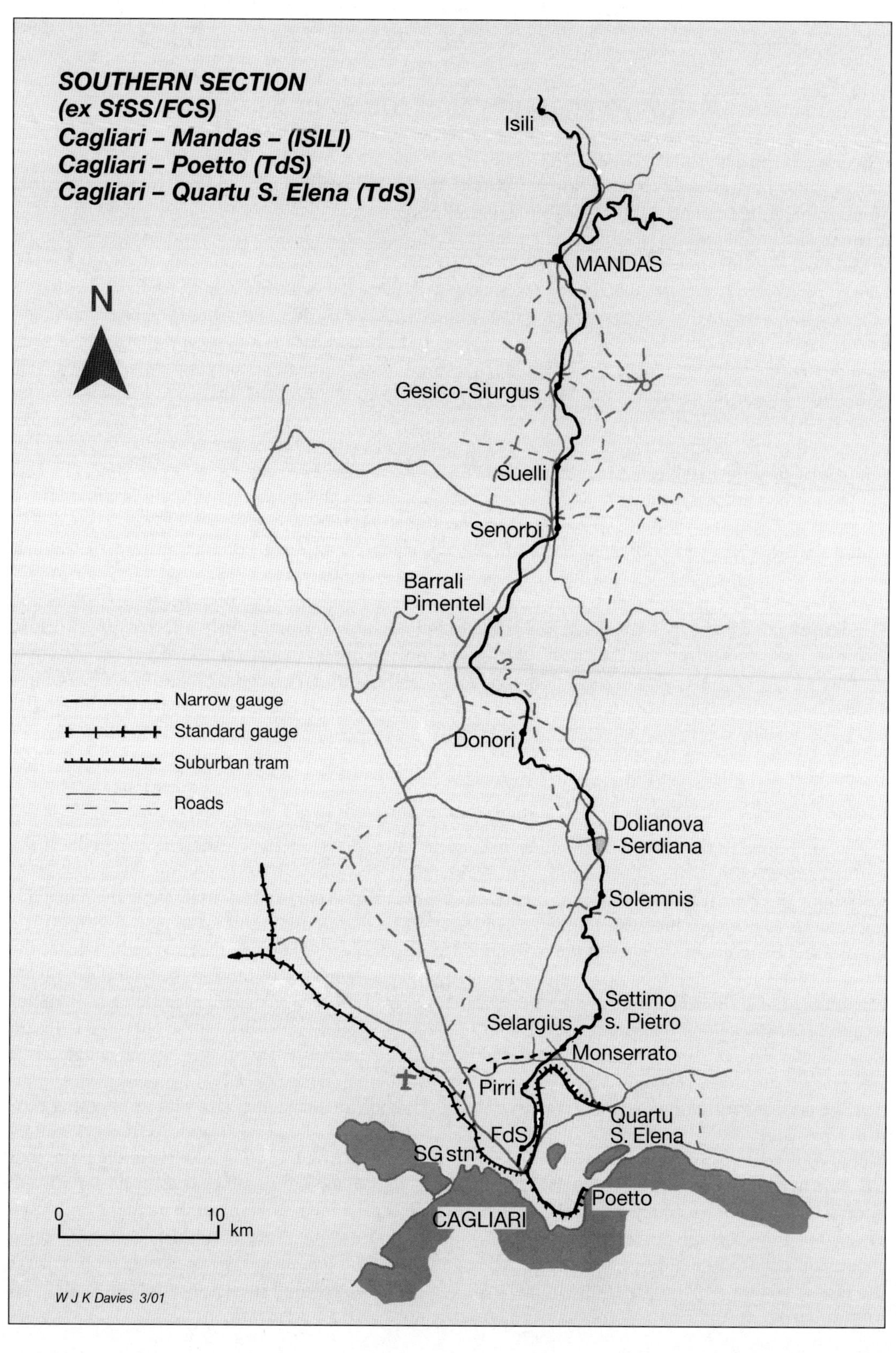
SOUTHERN SECTION
(ex SfSS/FCS)
Cagliari – Mandas – (ISILI)
Cagliari – Poetto (TdS)
Cagliari – Quartu S. Elena (TdS)
N
Isili
MANDAS
Gesico-Siurgus
Suelli
Senorbi
Barrali
Pimentel
Donori
Dolianova
-Serdiana
Solemnis
Settimo
s. Pietro
Selargius
Monserrato
Pirri
Quartu
S. Elena
FdS
SG stn
Poetto
CAGLIARI
Narrow gauge
Standard gauge
Suburban tram
Roads
0
10
km
W J K Davies 3/01

Where it all started from: a bird's eye view of the old FCS station at Viale Bonaria, looking to the dead end...
(F PUGH)

with a small but new railway museum set up with EU funds. The line north to Mandas appears to have been to some extent modernised in the 1950s with new or rebuilt station buildings and in the late 1990s has been drastically shortened and realigned in many places. Indeed the first realignment comes between Monserrato and the first real station, Settimo-S. Pietro (12km) as the line heads off across the central plain with its intensive agriculture. The setting of this line is not very scenic, being bland rolling countryside with the "new" line cutting straight through it, evidence of its former winding course appearing successively on each side with much of the track still in place, at least in 2001. Solemnis (21km) is a standard station which has lost its siding, Dolianova-Serdiana (24km) has two loops with platforms and a turntable and serves as outer terminus for some suburban workings. The line continues climbing past remnants of old meanders to Donori (35km), a standard station with an extra stock siding and then reverts to the original formation as far as Barrali (44km), another standard layout, before being realigned once more - a fairly drastic realignment, this one, cutting off great loops each side of the main road and saving two difficult road crossings. Senorbi (51km, now 43km) is a little more elaborate with extra sidings and a turntable plus an additional halt for schoolchildren at the north end of town. Suelli (55km) is standard and then the line is into rolling, hilly country on its original formation as far as Gesico-Siurgus (62km, now noted as 53km) which for some reason has retained its original building, refurbished by kind permission of the EU; since neither Gesico (to the west) nor Siurgius (to the east) are particularly close it was presumably not thought worthwhile to rebuild it. Mandas (nominally 68km since cutting back the Cagliari terminus) is the logical terminus and has a big 1950s station, an extensive yard and a three-road locomotive shed with servicing facilities. On the evidence of the occasional revised kilometrage display, the real distance must now be about 60km.

...and where the scenery starts: Mandas station, looking north to the branch junctions. (AUTHOR)

(Mandas) – Isili – Sorgono (original distances from Mandas)

Both the Sorgono branch and the line to Arbatax plunge right into the Gennargentu, the craggy mountainous heart of Sardinia which provides some of the most difficult terrain in western Europe. The Sorgono branch continues north from Mandas, passing the standard station of Serri (5km) in 1950s style before arriving at Isili (13km). Isili is the terminus for several workings from Cagliari, was effectively terminus for the original FCS, and its station reflects this. It is a watering point and currently a centre for local bus services and was as far as the modernisation of the 1950s reached. Continuing, there is a newish concrete platform halt on the outskirts of Isili town and the line starts climbing eastward past a reservoir which has clearly modified the road and railway routes. Currently the line crosses this at its eastern end, to swing 180 degrees round into Sarcidano (18km), with its loop, former goods siding and a long stock siding ending in a turntable. The space available is considerable and it was presumably more extensive before 1958 when the FCS had a junction here; its former route is just traceable dropping down toward the west.

The SFSS line now climbs fairly steadily northward through broken, mountainous country most of the way to Sorgono. The next station is Nurallo, (23km) a standard SFSS wayside affair on a ledge, then comes Sulau halt, just a long loop with a lengthman's cottage to break up the section in the middle of a stiff gradient as views open out to the left before Laconi (38km). This was a normal wayside station but the loading dock has been flattened and paved as a passenger area since it is terminus for some tourist workings although the town is some 2km away down a steep hillside. Funtanamela (44km) is currently a halt with loop and crossing keeper's cottage; Ortuabis (48km and 774m up) with its loop and spur is derelict and is near the summit. There follows a twisting up-and-down section along the hillside, with a couple of nameless concrete platforms before the next real settlement of Meana Sardo (60km) with its standard station, again about 3km from its name town. Castiau must have been a halt once, Belvi-Aritzo (76km) is standard SFSS but Desulo-Tonara (81km) has a real goods shed and a headshunt as well despite being no less than 7km from Tonara and nearer eight from Desulo. Then there is a steady drop with the odd tunnel and past Illare halt (90km?) with its small two-storey building and siding to an open loading bank. Sorgono (97km), the terminus, is just below the town, has a big refurbished station building with attached goods shed, an extra loop with siding for goods and a locomotive yard with a two-road shed (now reduced to one road and used mainly for buses); the main line ends in a turntable and just to confuse the issue the building

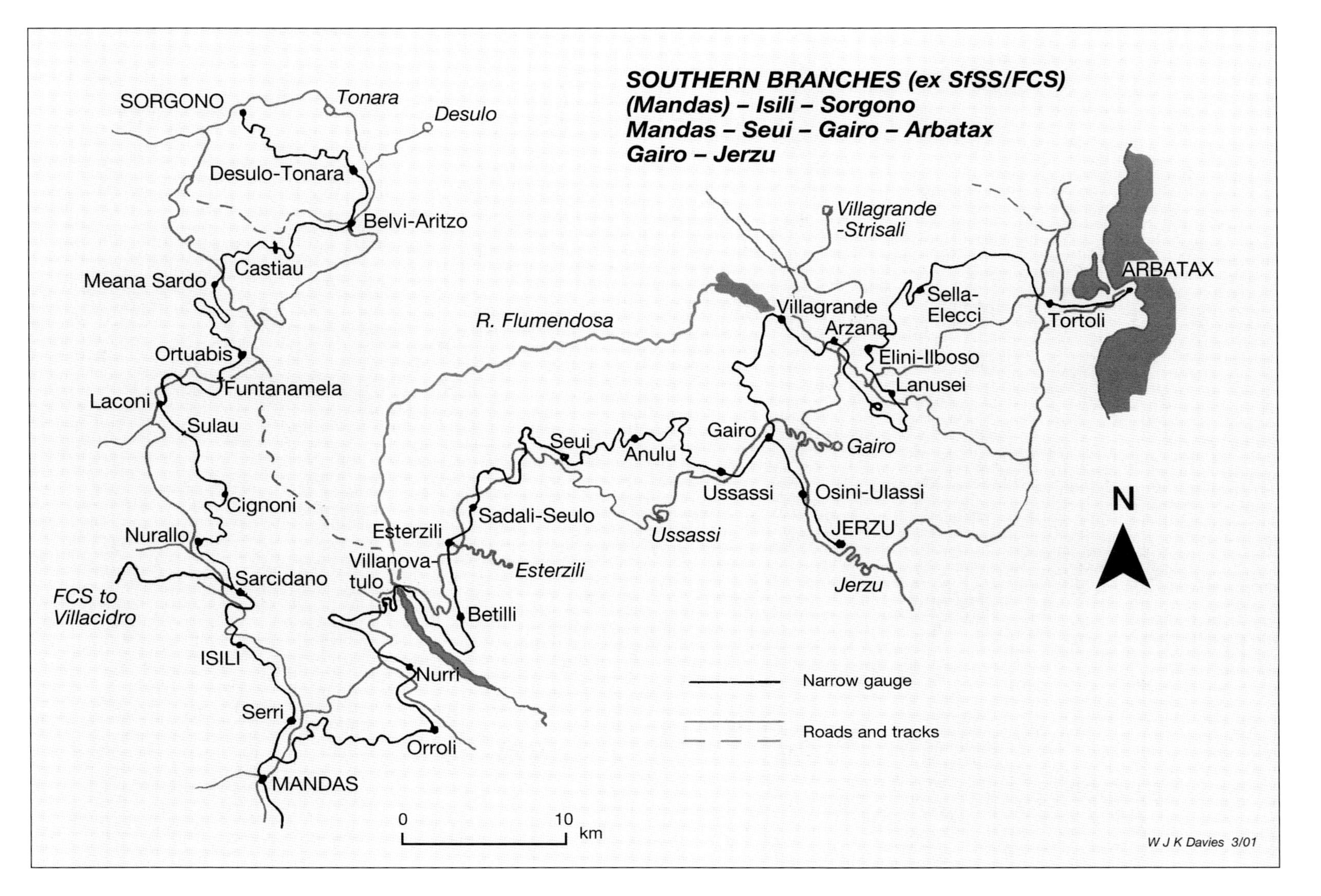

SOUTHERN BRANCHES (ex SfSS/FCS)
(Mandas) – Isili – Sorgono
Mandas – Seui – Gairo – Arbatax
Gairo – Jerzu
SORGONO
Tonara
Desulo
Desulo-Tonara
Belvi-Aritzo
Castiau
Meana Sardo
Ortuabis
Funtanamela
Laconi
Sulau
Cignoni
Nurallo
Sarcidano
FCS to Villacidro
ISILI
Serri
MANDAS
Orroli
Nurri
Villanova-tulo
Esterzili
Esterzili
Betilli
Sadali-Seulo
Seui
Anulu
Ussassi
Ussassi
Gairo
Gairo
Osini-Ulassi
JERZU
Jerzu
R. Flumendosa
Villagrande -Strisali
Villagrande
Arzana
Elini-Ilboso
Lanusei
Sella-Elecci
Tortoli
ARBATAX
N
Narrow gauge
Roads and tracks
0
10
km
W J K Davies 3/01

The trip to Sorgono is much greener and more wooded, while Laconi has tidied itself up for tourists... (AUTHOR)

...and even the odd scheduled railcar tends to stop at wayside springs for everyone to fill their water bottles. (AUTHOR)

proclaims it as 95.310km from Piazza Repubblica. The town (688m above sea level) is pleasant, has one or two good restaurants in season and tends to trade on its DH Lawrence connections.

Mandas – Arbatax (distances from Cagliari, apparently from Piazza Repubblica)

Mandas, as noted above, is a major servicing point and the Arbatax line starts at a facing junction a short way to the north; it is interesting that, so isolated was the country, lengthmen's cottages appear to have been provided every kilometre or so. At first it parallels the Sorgono line for quite a distance before swinging away east to cross the neighbouring road. The first twenty kilometres or so twist and turn all over the place but in total gain little height. Orroli (89km, 520m), a standard affair for the branch with 2-storey station house, open loading dock, loop and siding, and close to its village, is the first real station since stops are well spread out in this desolate countryside. Thence the line climbs hard through convoluted country past Nurri (94km, 557m), a similar station but with a turntable spur, and then drops to Villanovatulo (104km, 346m), a standard station perched on the hillside almost 3km away from and about 210m lower than its village and once a watering point. Soon the route brests a summit and descends in sweeping curves to the northern point of the artificial lake that has replaced the Flumendosa river in this stretch. Here a 1961-vintage road and rail bridge over the lake neck somewhat eases what must originally have been a very sharp set of curves in the narrow valley – the old route is still visible. There follows a phenomenal straight slog at about 1 in 30, straight up along the mountainside with the lake winding below, past a nameless modern halt platform and round the hill-end to Betilli halt (116km, 518m). This was originally a lengthman's cottage (now in private hands) and is clearly there to promote tourism – it neighbours a shelter, a water tower and a picnic area, has excellent views and a siding which breaks up the long section operationally. The harsh grade continues almost until the standard station of Esterzili (km 123km, 680m) and only eases off shortly after cottage No.80 (or at least the cottage for length 80!). Thence it runs through gorse and rocky outcrops to Sadali-Seulo, (128km, 763m) another 2-storey station with loop and siding quite near Sadali but with little current trace of Seulo. Then there is more of the same, climbing to a summit of approximately 900m, which occurs in a tunnel, and descending over difficult country to the major station of Seui (141km, 812m). Seui

On the Arbatax line the scenery soon gets craggy. A typical charter train in the wilderness. (AUTHOR)

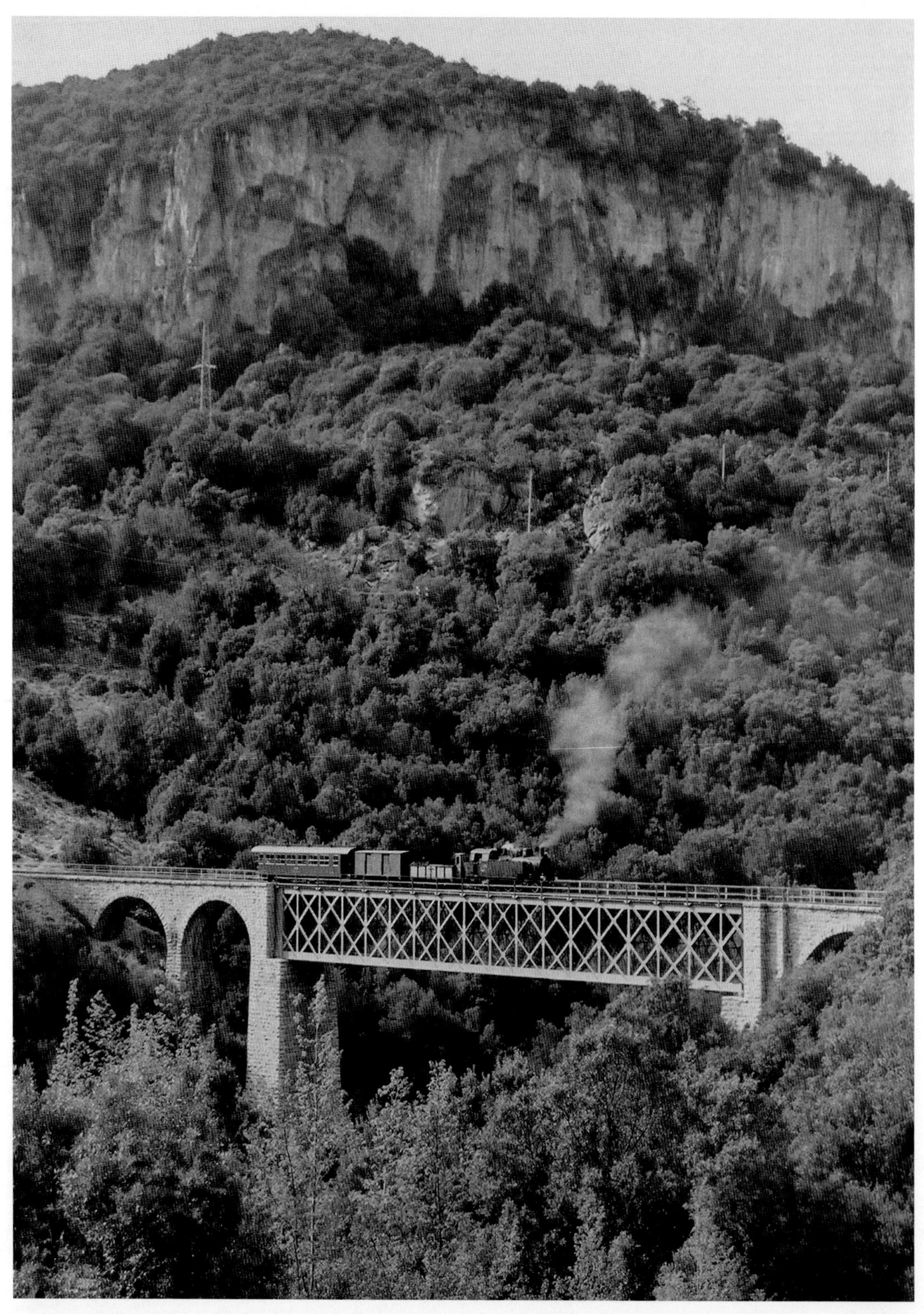

On the southern edge of the Gennargentu, the scenery gets very impressive. The same train on one of the typical girder bridges. (AUTHOR)

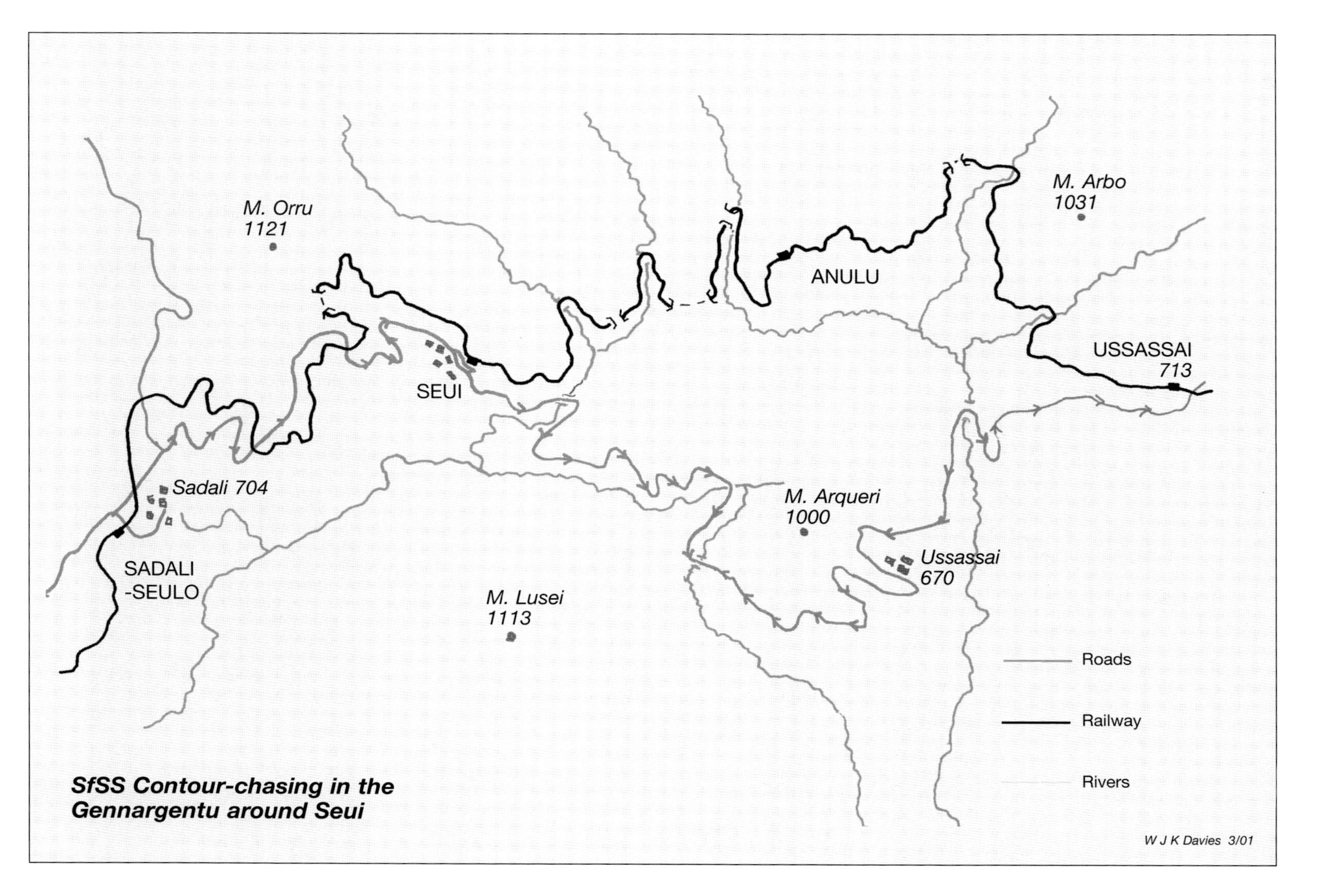

SfSS Contour-chasing in the Gennargentu around Seui

has two loops, a yard and a two-road shed with turntable and water and was a staging point in steam days besides being a start and finish point for short workings. Now it tends to be a lunch stop for the tourist trains since the town is immediately adjacent.

From Seui, the line has to desert the road entirely, tunnelling through a watershed, contour chasing up and down narrow reentrants. The Vivario boucle in Corsica is justly celebrated but the engineers on this line had to repeat the exercise in miniature many times over as they forced a path through this convoluted countryside and it becomes almost common to see the line retracing its path above or below on the other side of a rocky valley. As to habitation there is little or none. Anulu (152km; 765m altitude), a totally isolated place in the middle of this section a little before cottage 99, is just a siding with water but is used for passing out-of-course workings (as for example charters which have almost expired on the climbs so far!) and the next "real" station is Ussassai (163km; 713m) whose only distinctions are that its loop actually precedes the station site – and that it is a good 9km from Ussassai village.

This up and down scramble, with its remote settlements, is a foretaste of what is to come. Gairo station (167km; 784m) is much more elaborate, with traces of its former status as branch junction for Jerzu in its double loop and small locomotive shed (now a church, though apparently disused) with turntable and water. It is also over 200m vertically and a couple of kilometres horizontally as the crow flies from Gairo itself over a diabolical road which plunges down the valley side in a slew of hairpins and then struggles up the other side past the old town of Gairo, abandoned to landslip in the 1950s, to the present replacement – about 8km of travel in reality. The Jerzu branch course can still be seen high across the valley, passing its own apparently abandoned settlement on its ledge.

Here again, to avoid impossibly steep climbs, the main line swings wildly north up a rocky streambed, round a ridge to the end of another lake that is actually the source of the Flumendosa river. Here is Villagrande station, (179km; 811m) an otherwise standard affair which has been titivated, even if its village is 8km out of sight across a ridge – although Arzana (183km and 855m) a similar place but with a turntable and former shed has not although it is effectively the summit; perhaps the fact that its village is 5km away has something to do with it. On this section, the line now descends steadily, describing a complex set of spiral and horseshoe bends to get down to the major town of these parts, Lanusei (194.822km to be precise and 595m altitude). Lanusei, on a sharply curved ledge below the main town, has a standard layout plus a

and Lanusei reflects the typical relationship of a Sardinian hill town to its railway (a hill village would be too far away to have one!). (AUTHOR)

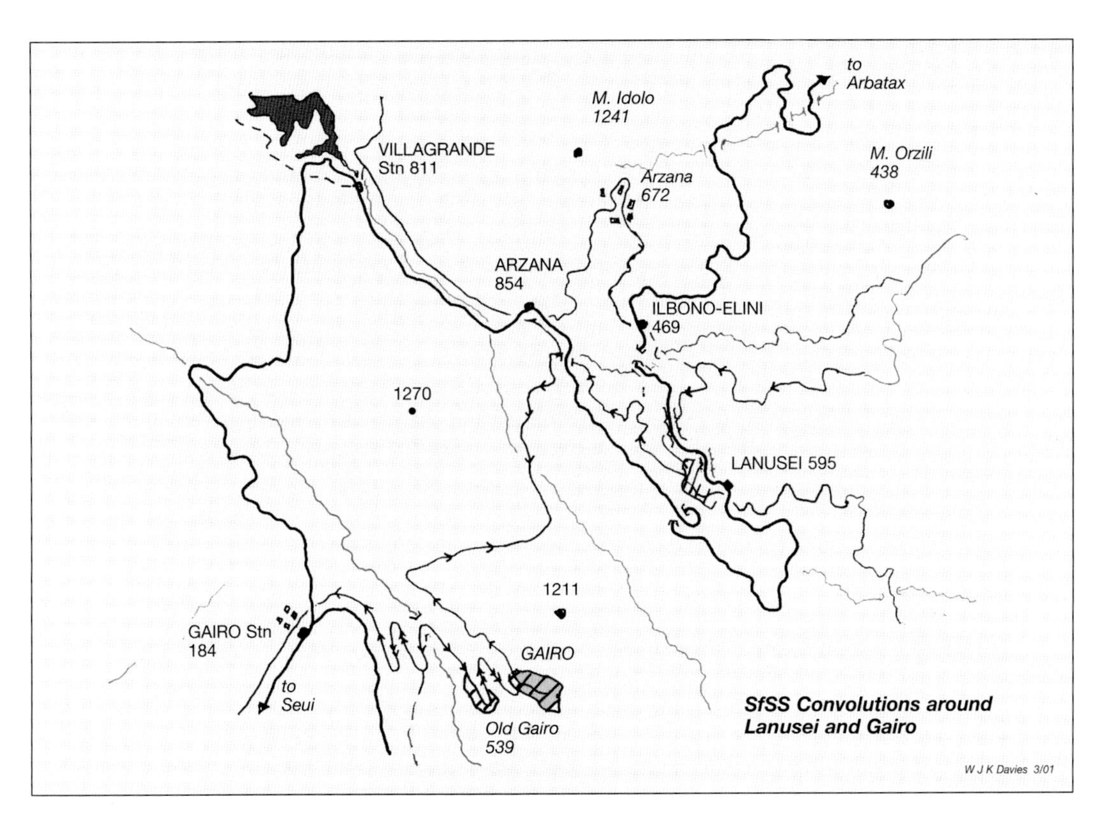

Diesel train at Arbatax old station with FCS coach. (F PUGH)

yard with separate goods shed and locomotive shed with turntable. From it the line curves round the town, with a very photogenic viaduct en route, and then descends gradually through hilly country to the sea. Elini (197km), formerly Elini-Ilbono, is a standard wayside station, but Sella Elecci halt (209km; 220m) has only a narrow loop preceding a ganger's cottage with attached water tower. Tortoli, (224km and only 12.6m above sea level) down on the coastal plain, has an extra loop and a goods shed and was originally Arbatax-Tortoli, Cartiera is but a halt and Arbatax itself is right down by the seashore. Arbatax is a busy port and ferry terminal besides being a reasonably pleasant town. The locomotive facilities, comprising offices, a long siding with turntable and a one-road shed, are a few hundred metres before the terminus which is now simply a double loop before a concrete platform but once had an odd little goods shed at right angles to the line, to ease transfer to the road above. The line formerly crossed a bridge over one of the harbour basins to run past the station building (228km) and onto the quayside but this portion is currently disused.

The Gairo - Jerzu branch ran roughly south east up a valley opposite Gairo, a straight gash along the valley side well above a road, with only the double-barrelled halt of Osini-Ulassi (6km) to break the journey before halting at Jerzu station (9km) for Jerzu village, vertically close but horizontally about 4km away downhill over a very twisty road.

The trouble with describing the Arbatax branch is that one cannot convey the reality. It is still one of the most impressive narrow gauge journeys in Europe but it has to be experienced.

2. Central system

Bosa – Macomer

The central system is arguably the least impressive of the three. It started on the west coast, from a terminal at Bosa (Citta) some way up the river Temo and ran briefly seaward alongside a main road, crossing it twice on its way to Bosa Marina (3km) which is now the (EU enhanced) terminus; the old Citta station is still in use as a bus depot and dumping ground for derelict stock and most of the intervening track is still in place – as is the old station at Bosa Marina although it has been replaced since 1997 by a new building and platform at the roadside, courtesy of the EU. The most spectacular part of the line, however,

On the central system, the really spectacular part is the climb from Bosa. Here FCS5 SULCIS takes a single coach up the cliffside section, with Bosa town spread out to the north. (AUTHOR)

is that from Bosa Marina along the cliffs and up the hillside in great sweeping curves past Modolo with its village and semi-derelict station, and past an isolated EU-inspired tourist halt on the hillside, to Tresnuraghes on the central plateau. The section is spectacular since the railway bends back and forth with wide views out to sea as it struggles up the steep hillsides. Tresnurages (20km from Bosa) currently bears the portmanteau name of Tresnurages-Magomadas-Cuglieri, presumably awarded when railhead for regular services was cut back to here in 1981 although Cuglieri in particular is so far off as to be virtually detached. Tresnurages to Macomer is a comparatively tame run across rolling upland via Tinnura (24km) and Sindia (35km), past a former industrial siding which was also the request stop for Bara lake (43km) to run into Macomer FdS alongside the line on to Nuoro.

Macomer (49km from Bosa Citta) is system headquarters with a large depot mixing modern and old buildings and is but a short street away from Macomer standard gauge station. Indeed a sharply curved spur runs down through 180 degrees to a bay platform in the SG station and gives access to the main line goods yard which includes a transporter bogie pit. The Nuoro line is unusual on the island in having used transporter bogies (rollbocke) to convey standard gauge wagons over its whole length and the facilities are still present, both here and at various stations along the line. The line to Bosa, however, although refurbished, has been closed to regular traffic since 1997 and is now used only for charters and the occasional tourist train.

Macomer – Nuoro

Nuoro, set on the edge of a large upland plain, and some 61km to the east of Macomer by rail, is one of the four provincial "capitals" and so still has a reasonable scheduled train service, although it is not a commuter line. For the same reason, the narrow gauge has been extensively realigned over both its western and its eastern section and equipped with some working colour light signalling and with automated crossings over the main highway which it roughly parallels for much of its course. From Macomer FdS (571m above sea level) the branch first parallels the Bosa line and then swings away to climb briefly round the town and then descend past Birori halt (6km) and on to the first real station of Bortigali (9km, 458m), a standard two-storey affair with loop and siding. Silanus (14km, 386m) is very similar but then realignment starts, cutting straight across a succession of shallow and wide meanders where, in 2001, the old track was still in place. Rolling agricultural countryside of the central plateau follows through Lei (17km) and Bolotana (21km, 285m), both "standard" two storey affairs with loop and siding and not that close to their villages, before more realignment takes the line into the major intermediate crossing place of Tirso (27km, 217m). This was junction for the, now closed, Chilivani line and the junction triangle is still in place at the west end. The buildings are standard 1950s pattern but the layout is elaborate, including a loop across the forecourt behind the buildings and a set of storage sidings normally containing derelict stock. It once had a small shed and servicing facilities; the station currently houses a small museum of signalling equipment.

Continuing along the plain, the route has again been extensively straightened, through Iscra (31km; 183m) which was originally a halt but now has a double loop and a transfer siding with rollbocke pit and standard gauge section. From here, massive deviation works, completed only in 1998, take the line up to Orotelli (41km; 343m) a standard intermediate station some 3km from its village and on to the similar Oniferi (44km; 379m), 7km from its name town but complete with new colour-light signalling and, unusually, the remains of a livestock loading pen. Hereabouts the line, now climbing gently over undulating foothills, meets one of the new dual carriageway roads which it parallels into Nuoro past the standard station of Prato Sardo (55km). There is evidence of earlier realignments here, probably dating from the 1950s modernisation and the final approach to Nuoro, across a steep-sided valley from the town perched on its hill, is the most impressive part of the journey. Nuoro station itself dates from the mid 1950s when it was relocated here on the west edge of town to make way for urban redevelopment. It has a modern station building, a big, three-road depot and two goods sheds, one of which is served by a standard gauge siding off a transfer pit. Official records give it as now 61km from Macomer and some 540m above sea level but, with all the realignment, kilometrages must now be historical only; old timetables suggest that some 2km in all has been saved.

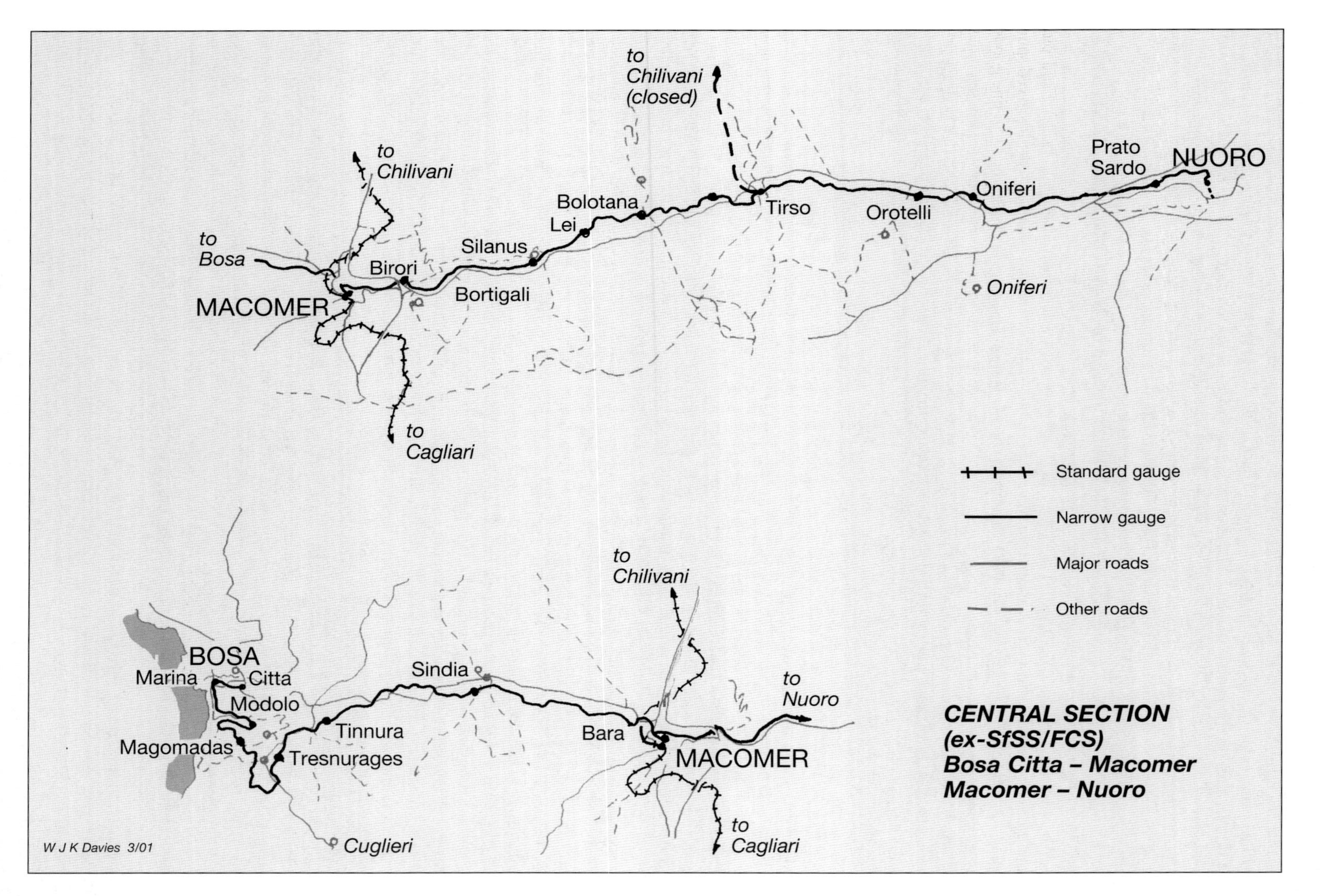

to Chilivani (closed)
to Chilivani
Prato Sardo
NUORO
Oniferi
Bolotana
Tirso
Orotelli
Lei
to Bosa
Silanus
Birori
Bortigali
Oniferi
MACOMER
to Cagliari
Standard gauge
Narrow gauge
Major roads
Other roads
to Chilivani
BOSA
Marina
Citta
Sindia
to Nuoro
Modolo
Tinnura
Bara
Magomadas
Tresnurages
MACOMER
CENTRAL SECTION
(ex-SfSS/FCS)
Bosa Citta – Macomer
Macomer – Nuoro
to Cagliari
W J K Davies 3/01
Cuglieri

3. Northern system

Sassari, as the island's second city, is a very important town with a very populous hinterland – there are serious plans for a light transit system and in 2001 tram track was being laid in the streets – and its narrow gauge railways are correspondingly well-used and heavily modernised.

Sassari – Alghero

This line, originally about 35km long, was initially built and operated by the SFSS and its FCS successor. It was intended to link Sassari with the old fishing port and minor resort of Alghero out on the west coast and was very much a rambling SFSS venture with its own headquarters at Alghero Porto and a sub-shed at Sassari Sta Maria, a few hundred metres south of Sassari main line station. Thence it first swung away and then crossed over the standard gauge to drop through a jumble of gorges and ravines past Molafa (6km) to the San Giorgio Area where it chased the contours down past Arcone to the coastal plain near Olmedo (23km; now 20km) and thence by devious means to Alghero town. There it ran along the seafront via a waterfront halt at San Giovanni to a harbour terminus (Alghero Porto; 35km). Under FdS control it has altered markedly. The central section has been drastically realigned in the last few years, a new and rather fortress-like station at San Giorgio (11km) replacing the old one which can still be seen away to the south on a former trackbed. The country in general has become much more populous, around Olmedo in particular, and there are halts although the only passing place between Olmedo and Alghero is Mamuntanas (28km, now 25km) which still has a loop. The Alghero terminus, which once ended in a walled enclosure at the harbour edge (35km) was cut back in 1988 to an area of new residential development at San Agostino on the northern outskirts – just why is not clear since the old trackbed down to the former terminus near the old town still exists, largely on reserved right of way, and would, one feels, be a source of tourist traffic if not of local commuters; Alghero and its surroundings are now a definite tourist destination in season and many flights use Alghero airport. San Agustino (33km, now 30km) is a modern passenger station with loop and bay platform and a quite extensive yard with a goods shed (disused), a turntable spur and a two-road stockshed. The line is now very much a modern commuter railway with automated road crossings and

In the north, the Alghero route used to be a sleepy seaside line terminating at Alghero Porto just by the harbour. (K TAYLORSON)

Now it is a modern commuter railway, with smart stations and a full set of automatic signalling. Olmedo is typical, though with partly refurbished buildings. (AUTHOR)

Sassari is a busy mainline station. Here a railcar train for Alghero departs from the north-end bays. (AUTHOR)

colour-light signalling much in evidence. Trains now start from the main line station in Sassari, using a mixed gauge through line on platform 1 and being serviced at Sassari (SFS) depot. The three-rail mixed gauge currently (since the early 1990s) serves platform 1 but linked originally via the far side of the island platform (line 3) and then via line 2. It was rerouted to avoid an unnecessary crossing of the standard gauge. Probably the only real features of continuing interest for the traditional railway enthusiast are the crumbling remains of Sassari Sta Maria and a group of sidings between Arcone and Olmedo which are used to house derelict stock. It appears that, for many years after the SFS "takeover", the line was not connected physically to the SFS routes or depot which explained the continued existence of Sta Maria and the facilities at San Agustino.

Sassari – Sorso

Now the shortest narrow gauge line on the island, this SFS-built line was always seen as a commuter and fresh-produce adjunct to Sassari itself and joins the rapidly growing settlements along its routes to the big metropolis. Trains always started from bay platforms at the north end of Sassari main line station and then ran past the SFS depot before pottering off down to a rich agricultural plain and across it to Sorso with its small locomotive shed (now disconnected). Now the first two kilometres or so are double-tracked to allow for a metro extension and a new suburban station replacing the original (Roda Quadda; 3km) has been built on Sassari outskirts together with several halts including Crabulazzi (6km). The usual sprawling loops have been realigned between Funtana Niedda (7km) and Sorso, including an elegant new concrete viaduct, and surviving road crossings have been automated. Sorso itself is simple for a terminus, just a loop and siding serving a goods shed and loading dock, together with a, now disconnected, single road locomotive shed. The line ends in a turntable and the station building and surrounds have recently been refurbished. An intensive service (for Sardinia) is operated with eight or nine trains daily at peak periods; the intermediate stopping places have been rationalised into passenger halts without surplus trackage. Like the Alghero line, it could probably be incorporated into a light transit system with little more than electrification.

The Sorso branch is fairly flat but is being heavily modernised. This viaduct appears to be built with double track in mind even if the charter train is elderly. (AUTHOR)

Sassari – Nulvi – Tempio Pausania – Luras – Palau

This, which was originally the longest single narrow gauge line in Sardinia if you take the Arbatax route as starting at Mandas, has had a complex history in spite of being built as late as 1930-32. It was originally two distinct portions, Sassari - Tempio Pausania and Luras - Palau, joined by an existing stretch of the, now closed, SFSS branch from Monti to Tempio, and for years trains worked east and west from Tempio. For a long time, however, it has been run as a single entity. Its western end, to the flourishing town of Nulvi, is considered to have considerable potential as a commuter line, has been partly realigned and has a reasonable daily service to Sassari FS where it shares the northern bays with the Sorso line. The eastern part, however, is effectively closed except for charters and a few seasonal scheduled tourist trains but has nevertheless received some improvements, particularly at Palau.

The line can only be described as a switchback. To reach Nulvi from Sassari (176m above sea level) it has to scramble up into the mountains, first clinging to a ledge above a deep valley as far as Achettas (11km), a halt with siding that is not mentioned in old maps or timetables and may be an upgraded lengthman's cottage. Then it climbs along a hillside with views to the south to the standard station of Osilo (17.8km; 438m) and across a rolling plateau to Fenosu halt (26.4km; 535m). About half a kilometre further is a curious structure, clearly once served by a loop siding, which appears to be a former ropeway terminus. In fact it is a ballast crusher, built to take advantage of the plethora of stone scattered about the surrounding countryside, and consists of a tall tower served by a chain and scoop elevator at the rear; thence the stone dropped through the crushing device to pour through chutes into wagons on the track alongside.

From here the line descends again, contour-chasing down and through a tunnel to reach Nulvi (34.7km; 463m) perched on its hillside above a wide plain. Nulvi has been cleaned up and "commuterified" but, considering its importance as a terminus, is not much modified operationally; it still has just a loop and siding with the usual building and goods shed and a lengthman's cottage at the nearby road crossing.

The line now drops down towards the plain - in the other direction Nulvi can be seen for kilometres across it – having to detour away from the road it has hugged since Fenosu and crossing various streams on stone viaducts before climbing again to Martis (45km; 235m) which was clearly once operationally more important than Nulvi; it has water columns and a turntable in addition to the standard features and old maps show the two settlements to have once been much of a muchness. Even this far east the road crossings have been automated and the line occasionally uses them as it loops across the rolling upland through the standard stations of Laerru (54km, 120m) and Perfugas (59.0km, down to 53m) and the little halt at Coghinas (63.4km and even lower at 42m) to Scala Ruia (67.6km and 66m). Scala Ruia, with a loop but no goods facilities just for a change, marks the start of a major climb. This culminates in the impressive Bortigiadas spiral, partly in tunnel, to reach Bortigiadas itself (81km, 334m), again a standard station with an extra headshunt, from which one can look down on the levels of track below. A succession of deep valleys, tunnels and ledges through increasingly rugged terrain follow until the line reaches first the little town of Aggius (87km, 478m) with its halt (2 storey building plus loop) and then the far more substantial settlement of Tempio Pausania (91km, 548m and the highest station on the line). For the tourist this is a pleasant spot to visit on a tour or on a daytrip from either Palau or Sassari; for the railway it is a major station with a two-road shed, steam servicing facilities, and evidence that each railway once had its own facilities.

The journey onward is much the same, rugged but fairly open country, past Nuchis (100km; 2 storey building and siding but no loop or goods shed) with the main difference as far as Luras (102km) being the rather more gimcrack architecture of the old SFSS. Luras is a standard station with water; Calangianus (103km; 443m), the first station after Luras, is just a small 2-storey halt, the town's real station having been on the Monti branch. It marks the beginning of a long descent toward the eastern coast but there are five more intermediate stations before that coast is reached at the tourist resort of Arzachena (136km; 87m) with its standard station. For the record St Linaldo (111km; 258m) is similar to Calangianus, S.Antonio di Gallura (120km; 221m) is standard, Oddastru (128km; 112m) is a halt with siding, Capichera (not in old records) is probably an ex-ganger's cottage, Caldosa (132km; 66m) is a standard halt. Rio Piatto, once a halt at km 115, appears to have disappeared entirely, perhaps under the newish lake which seems to have caused

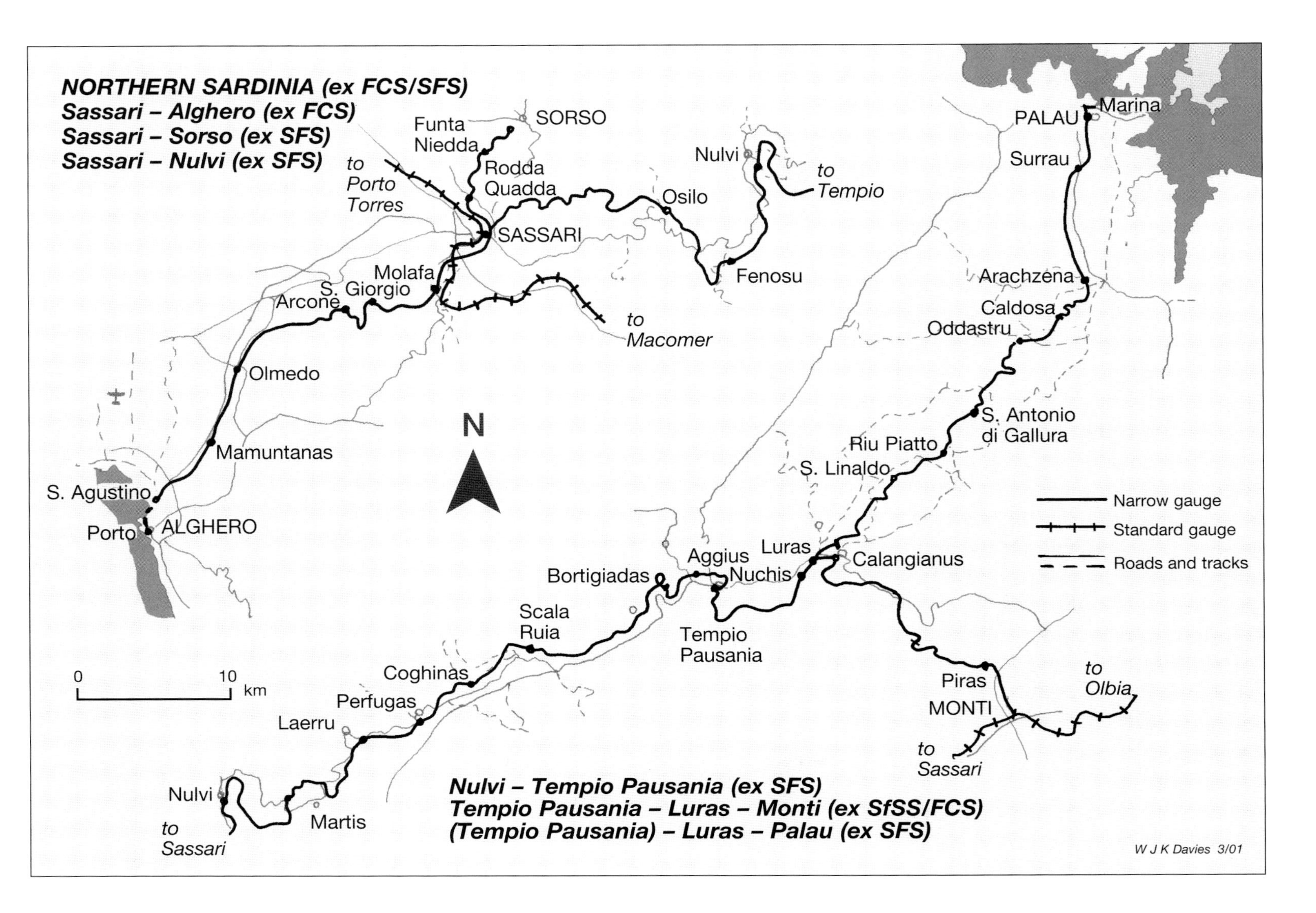
NORTHERN SARDINIA (ex FCS/SFS)
Sassari – Alghero (ex FCS)
Sassari – Sorso (ex SFS)
Sassari – Nulvi (ex SFS)
Funta Niedda
SORSO
Rodda Quadda
to Porto Torres
SASSARI
Nulvi
to Tempio
Osilo
Fenosu
Molafa
S. Giorgio
Arcone
to Macomer
Olmedo
Mamuntanas
S. Agustino
Porto
ALGHERO
N
PALAU
Marina
Surrau
Arachzena
Caldosa
Oddastru
S. Antonio di Gallura
Riu Piatto
S. Linaldo
Luras
Calangianus
Aggius
Nuchis
Bortigiadas
Tempio Pausania
Scala Ruia
Coghinas
Perfugas
Laerru
Martis
Nulvi
to Sassari
Piras
MONTI
to Olbia
to Sassari
Narrow gauge
Standard gauge
Roads and tracks
0
10
km
Nulvi – Tempio Pausania (ex SFS)
Tempio Pausania – Luras – Monti (ex SfSS/FCS)
(Tempio Pausania) – Luras – Palau (ex SFS)
W J K Davies 3/01

Once away from the coast the Palau line has its moments. You can look down from the top of the spiral at Bortigiadas and see the specials trundling past below. (AUTHOR)

a small diversion of the railway's course… A feature of the old SFS, now being steadily covered under bland EU paintwork but still visible on this section, was the elaborate brick and paint decoration of the buildings in local style.

The tourist development – mainly apartments, holiday cottages and the much more luxurious accommodations of the exclusive Costa Smeralda – is frenetic once the coast is reached and seems at times to be covering all the bare hillsides, although more elegantly than on, say, the Costa Brava. The railway almost ignores it, carrying on past the lengthman's cottage which constitutes Surrau halt (144km; 44m) to Palau town, (149km, 17m) a dusty station by a dusty road, with large station buildings, a double loop and a (now disused) locomotive shed with turntable spur. It then uses a reversal to drop the final 15 metres or so to the refurbished quayside station that is Palau Marina (150km, 2m) – a simple dead end with a trailing siding to a former goods shed. With its ferries to and from the renowned Maddalena Archipelago and its general air of prosperity, Palau should be good news for the railway but its future is actually very much in the balance at the time of writing.

4. Closed lines

Tirso – Chivivani

The defunct Tirso - Chilivani route is of particular note since it remained in situ for years after closure and an advertised replacement bus service still follows its rugged course for anyone who wishes to do so. For most of its route it contour-chased along the mountains, closely paralleled by the only practicable road

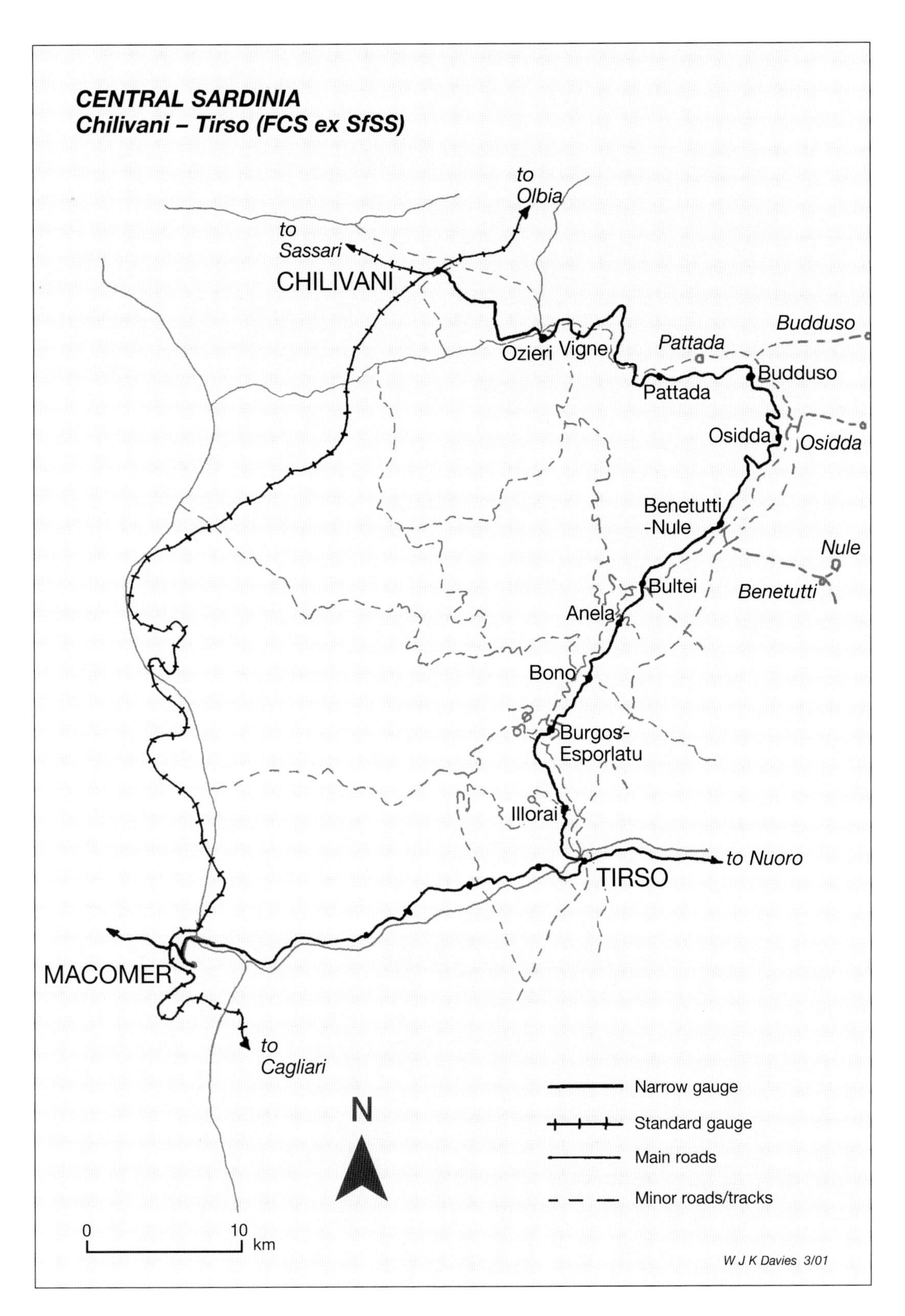

CENTRAL SARDINIA
Chilivani – Tirso (FCS ex SfSS)
to Olbia
to Sassari
CHILIVANI
Ozieri
Vigne
Pattada
Budduso
Pattada
Budduso
Osidda
Osidda
Benetutti -Nule
Nule
Bultei
Benetutti
Anela
Bono
Burgos-Esporlatu
Illorai
TIRSO
to Nuoro
MACOMER
to Cagliari
N
Narrow gauge
Standard gauge
Main roads
Minor roads/tracks
0
10
km
W J K Davies 3/01

and serving tiny settlements. Illorai was a good three kilometres away but otherwise, for the first 40 or so kilometres these were close to the line. True, the twin villages of Burgos and Esporlatu, confronting each other across a valley, were both about two km away to the west of their joint station (10km; 357m) but Bottida (12km; 358m); the township of Bono (17km: 447m); Anela (22km; 396m) and Bultei (25km; 409m) were close to their respective settlements as the line struggled generally upward. This was not the case later. Benetutti was 16km away from the station of Benetutti-Nule and Nule even further. Osidda was about 8km to the east of its station (42km; 581m) up a hairpinned track, Budduso, at 49km from Tirso and 628m up, was nearer 13km from its station and the inhabitants of Pattada, although they might have hurled a stone down to the line below, had a 4km trudge down to either Budduso or their own station (km 55; 674m). Thence it was a twisting drop down to Ozieri (70km; 412m) which acted as main depot for the line and had a two-road engine shed. Then it was another drop to Chilivani (79km; 225m) and a junction with the standard gauge in the valley. One can see why traffic was low but also why the few inhabitants complained about the withdrawal of their communication links.

Monti – Tempio Pausania

This originally isolated SFSS/FCS branch must have been a natural candidate for closure, whatever the locals said. Its raison d'etre was simply to give the important settlement of Tempio Pausania a link to the outside world and, once the SFS put in its connection with the provincial capital Sassari, the importance of the branch declined sharply. For the first few kilometres from Monti it roughly paralleled a road but then it struck out westward across barren hills past the miniscule hamlet of Piras (7km) with only a totally isolated request stop before it regained road contact and dropped down to Calangianus (27km, where it had its own station) and a (later) junction with the SFS at Luras station (29km) – itself about a kilometre from its name village. The final stretch into Tempio (40km) was again away from the road with only the hamlet of Nuchis (31km) to serve.

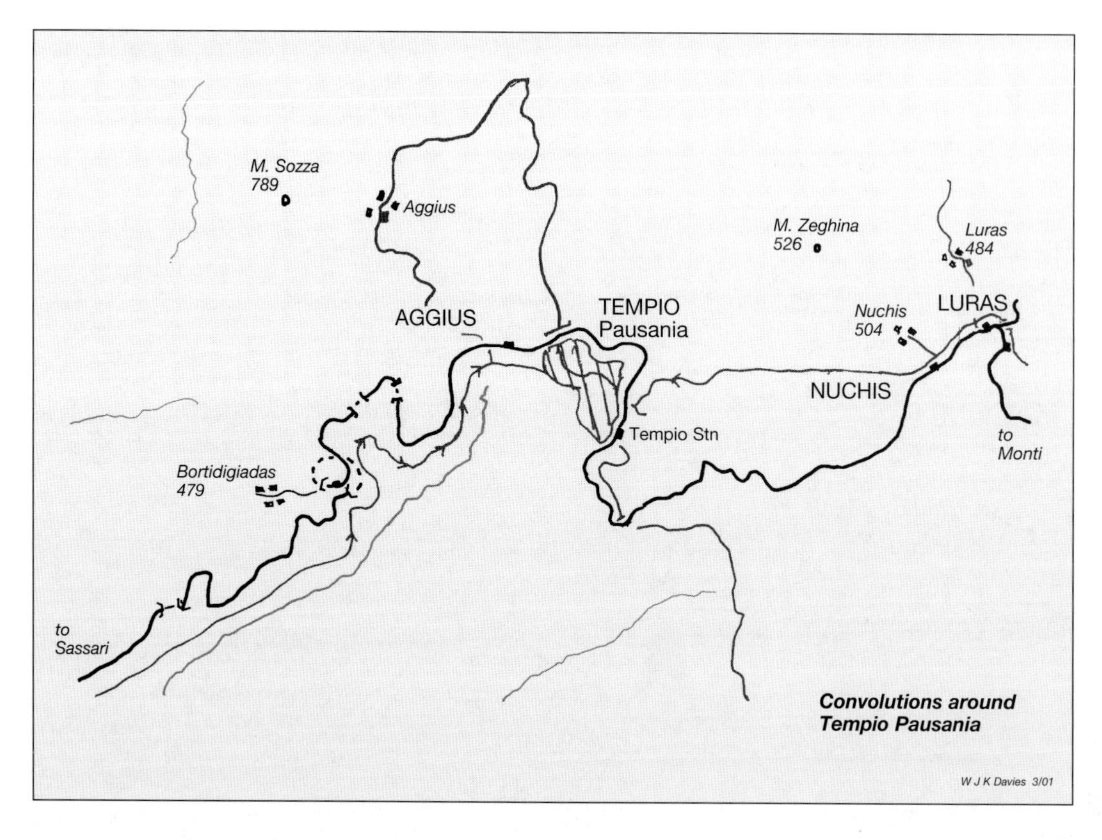

Convolutions around Tempio Pausania

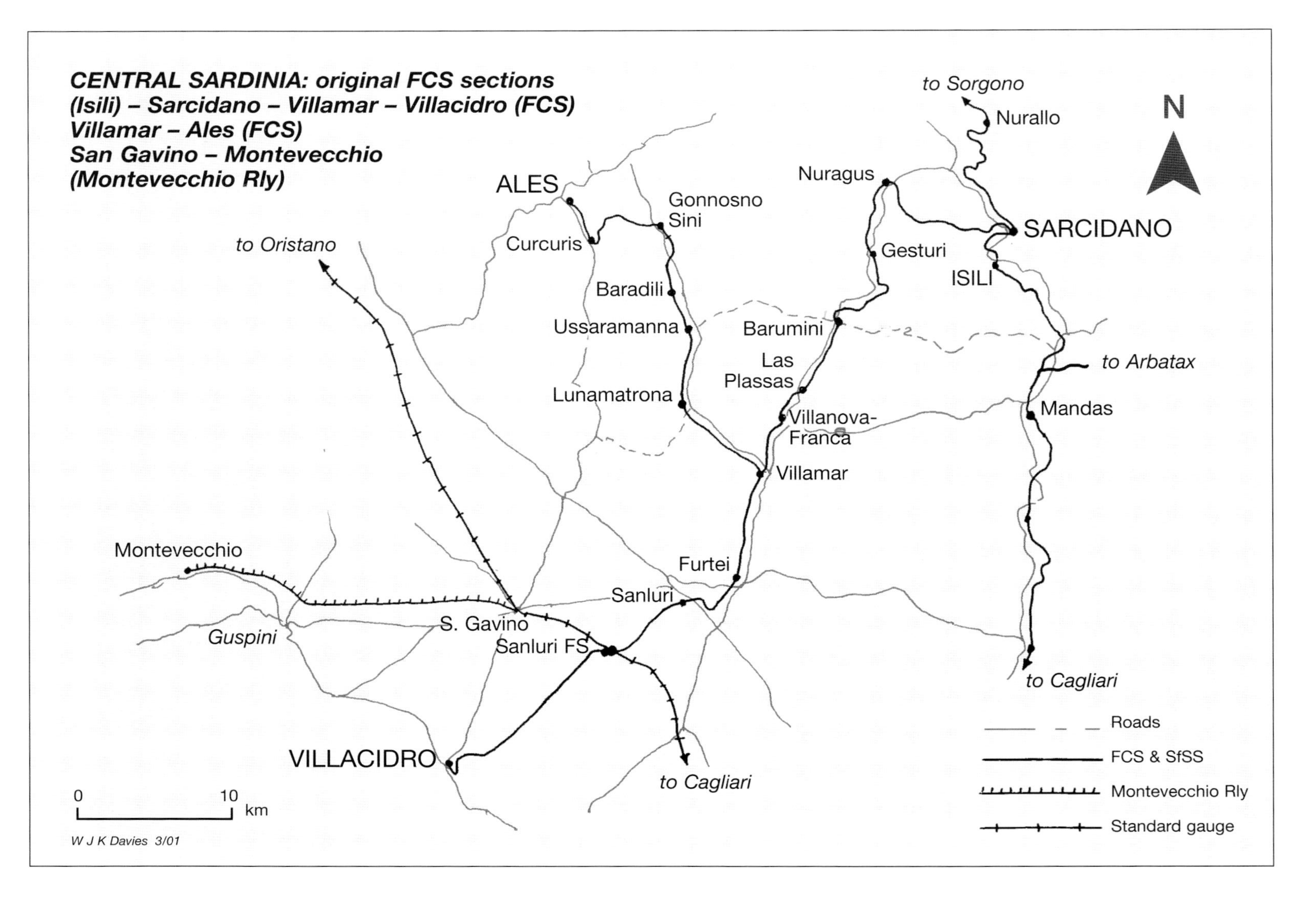

CENTRAL SARDINIA: original FCS sections
(Isili) – Sarcidano – Villamar – Villacidro (FCS)
Villamar – Ales (FCS)
San Gavino – Montevecchio
(Montevecchio Rly)
N
to Sorgono
Nurallo
Nuragus
SARCIDANO
Gesturi
ISILI
ALES
Gonnosno Sini
Curcuris
to Oristano
Baradili
Ussaramanna
Barumini
Las Plassas
Lunamatrona
Villanova-Franca
Villamar
to Arbatax
Mandas
Montevecchio
Furtei
Sanluri
S. Gavino
Sanluri FS
Guspini
VILLACIDRO
to Cagliari
to Cagliari
Roads
FCS & SfSS
Montevecchio Rly
Standard gauge
0
10
km
W J K Davies 3/01

5. FCS original lines

(Isili) – Sarcidano – Villamar – Sanluri – Villacidro
Villamar – Ales

The FCS was another example of attempts to open up the largely unpopulated interior. Occupying the so-called foothills between the Sorgono branch and the central plain, its main line ran over SFSS metals from Isili and then dropped more or less steadily from its physical junction with the SFSS at Sarcidano (6km; 416m), going first west across country to Nuragus (14km; 359m) before turning south in contact with a minor road to Gesturi (20km; 310m) and on via Barrumini (27km; 206m), Las Plassas hamlet (31km) and a halt for the remote Villanovafranca (35km, serving a hamlet up a side valley) to Villamar junction (39km; 114m). From Barramini to Villamar and on to Furtei (45km; 101m) the line closely paralleled provincial road 197; from Furtei onward it diverged to avoid a climb, to Sanluri FCS (50km) below the town, and then dropped straight down the plain to a junction with the standard gauge at Sanluri FS (56km; 60m) a good six kilometres away. From there it was an easy though generally uphill cross-country run southwest to the terminus at Villacidro (70km; 213m), with a sharp little climb at the end.

Apart from a short traverse down the upper valley of the Isca River between Gonnosno and Curcuria, the Ales branch hugged minor roads for the whole of its length from Villamar through the station (7km) for Lumamatrona and Pauli-Arbaret (both about a kilometre away) and on via the equally small hamlets of Ussaramanna (12km), Baradili (15km), Sini (18km) and Gonnosno (19km). At Curcuria (25km) it rejoined a track for its final drop into Ales (27km).

6. Ferrovie Meridionale Sarde (FMS)

Iglesias – Monteponi – Giovanni Suergiu – Calasetta

The section between Iglesias and Monteponi was originally standard gauge and operated by the Royal Sardinian railways but in 1926 was converted to 950mm gauge and made over to the new FMS. The line swung out from industrial Iglesias (199m altitude) on its own and dropped sharply along the hillside via an isolated halt called Cabitza to Monteponi town (6km; 107m) before crossing first the Monteponi Railway and then the road which both railways paralleled through a rocky gorge through Ceramica (8km; no prizes for guessing the reason for this later halt), Gonnesa (11km) and the former coal-mining town of Bacu Abis (14km, 52m) where the Monteponi once more crossed over and headed west toward the coast. There was

Very little got photographed down in the south: Here an FMS railcar traverses the double track section along the causeway from S. Antioco... (José Banaudo)

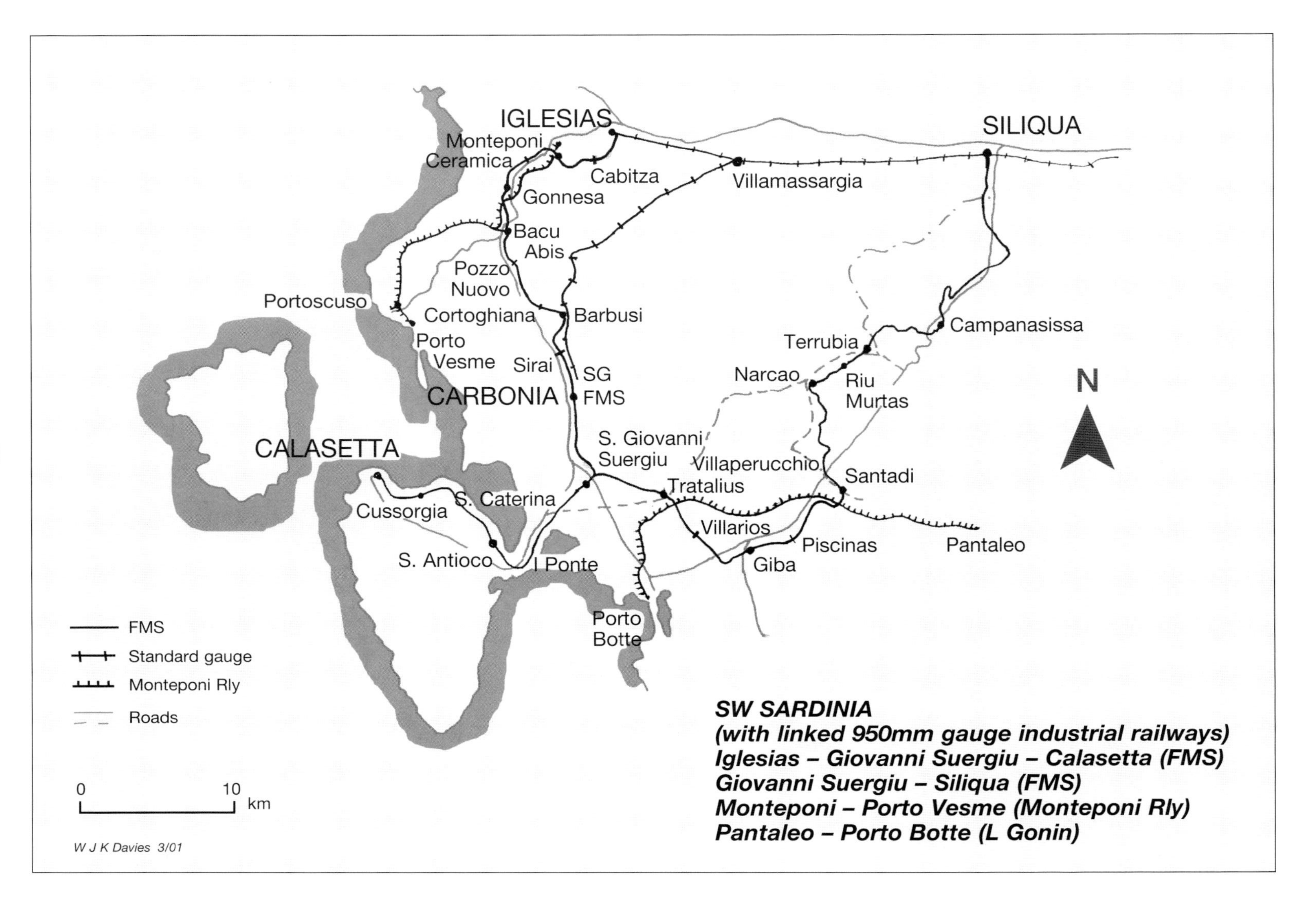

IGLESIAS
SILIQUA
Monteponi
Ceramica
Cabitza
Villamassargia
Gonnesa
Bacu
Abis
Pozzo
Nuovo
Portoscuso
Cortoghiana
Barbusi
Campanasissa
Porto
Vesme
Sirai
SG
FMS
Terrubia
Narcao
Riu
Murtas
CARBONIA
N
CALASETTA
S. Giovanni
Suergiu
Villaperucchio
Santadi
Tratalius
S. Caterina
Cussorgia
Villarios
Piscinas
Pantaleo
S. Antioco
I Ponte
Giba
Porto
Botte
FMS
Standard gauge
Monteponi Rly
Roads
0
10
km
W J K Davies 3/01
SW SARDINIA
(with linked 950mm gauge industrial railways)
Iglesias – Giovanni Suergiu – Calasetta (FMS)
Giovanni Suergiu – Siliqua (FMS)
Monteponi – Porto Vesme (Monteponi Rly)
Pantaleo – Porto Botte (L Gonin)

...and even the grimy FMS had its pleasant stretches. A railcar leaves the southern terminus at Calasetta for the largely rural run to S. Antioco port. (F PUGH)

for a time a physical link between the two railways which enabled a passenger service to operate over the Monteponi in the 1940s. Stations hereabouts were added as industry developed - a 1933 timetable for instance names only Gonnesa, Bacu Abis, Barbusi and Serbariu between Monteponi and the junction, while later ones add halts at Pozzo Nuovo, Cortoghiana, Sirai. Stops or not, the FMS continued south east down across the Flumentepido valley and up to a lowish col past what was to become the new mining town of Carbonia and the Carbonia station which originally was Serbariu, the nearest existing settlement. The FMS Carbonia station (27km) was a good half kilometre southeast of the "new" standard gauge one and from the mid 1930s the area was netted with coal sidings and transfer points; the line on from here was doubled when the coal traffic intensified. The FMS itself went on over the col and almost down to sea level to parallel the road into S. Giovanni Suergiu, its major depot and junction. (34km; 17m); originally the station was Palmas-Suergiu. Here was a depot and the island's only stretch of double narrow gauge track continued across a causeway past the minor halts of S. Caterina and I Ponte to the near-isle of S. Antioco and the identically named coal port (43km). Most freight ended here but the line ran on along the north coast past Cussorgia halt (51km) to the little port of Calasetta (55km) on its northern tip. The double track fell out of use when the coal traffic declined in the 1960s.

S. Giovanni Suergiu – Narcao – Siliqua (distances from S. Giovanni)

From S. Giovanni, the other branch of the FMS climbed into the rocky hills and valleys of the Iglesiente region. In passenger terms this was usually the through route but, unlike the coal-hauling section, it was a typical rural secondary railway, deviating from roads where gradients required or small settlements had to be served. Tratalias (5km), still on the plain, was the first station, and there followed an isolated halt theoretically serving Villarios (8km; originally Villarios-Palmas) before the line rejoined the only road at Giba (12km; originally Giba-Masainas) and followed it north east through Piscinas (15km) only to curve away in a big loop to get somewhere near the hill village of Santadi (21km; 99m). Here it crossed, and later connected with, a 950mm gauge industrial line from Pantaleo, down the valley past Santadi Basso and round the base of the hills to a wharf called Porto Botte. The FMS itself scrambled away on its own, north and then east up the Mannu valley by Meddas; the comparatively large hamlet of Narcao (30km) with its proper station; a halt serving Riu Murtas and a real station for the equally small village of Terrubia (35km). There followed a sharpish climb up the Mannu valley again to rejoin the only real road, follow it over a watershed by Campanasissa halt (42km; 287m) serving nowhere in particular and then dropping again to a standard gauge junction at Siliqua (59km; 54m) on the edges of the plain.

3XX class 2-8-0T and mixed train at Gairo, 1958. (H LUFF)

Arbatax line freight at Mandas in 1966 with a 3XX series O&K 2-6-0T. (F PUGH)

A typical SFS passenger train of the past climbs again toward Tempio with a Steam & Safaris charter in 1999; SFS 2-6-0T No. 3 and Breda coaches. (DEREK PHILLIPS)

A modern train climbing away from Nuoro, on the central system, with Breda 2-6-0T SULCIS. (DEREK PHILLIPS)

And a scene at Palau, on the northern system. The rake is typical of a passenger working at any time in the last fifty years. 2-6-0T No3 and Breda stock. (AUTHOR)

Piazza Repubblica Station, Cagliari, with a railcar of series ADe 1-20. (D TREVOR ROWE)

Billard A150D6 car and rebodied trailer at a halt on the Calvi Branch. (D Trevor Rowe)

Billard A150D6 car and trailer on a typical Ajaccio-line viaduct. (D Trevor Rowe)

A train climbing up from Lanusei, with the rolling vistas typical of the Arbatax branch. (Derek Phillips)

A modern charter train running along the Flumendosa Lake near Villagrande. (DEREK PHILLIPS)

...and a typical scheduled "Trenino Verde" working crossing a modern concrete viaduct near Rio Piatto, on the SFS line to Palau. (AUTHOR)

An evocative scene at Arbatax harbour. (DEREK PHILLIPS)

An SFS railcar and trailer climb up from Palau Marina to the reversal point with ferries and the Maddalena archipelago as a backdrop. (F PUGH)

A Bastia train leaving l'Ile Rousse; CFD 2XXX series cars in multiple. (AUTHOR)

Corsica: A ligne de Balagne shuttle, with a Renault ABH in the penultimate livery. (AUTHOR)

PART 2

Technical History

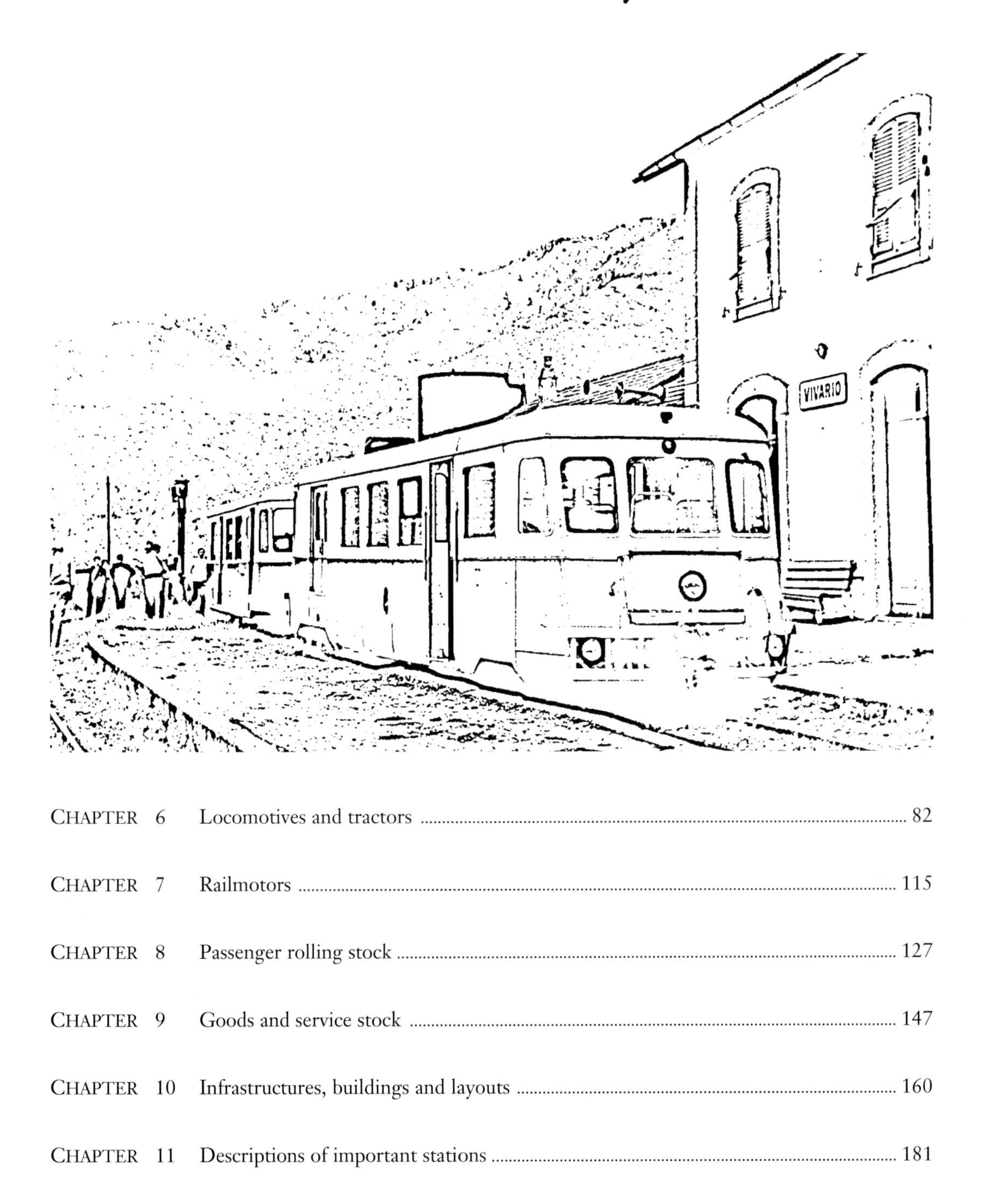

CHAPTER 6
Motive power: locomotives & tractors.

1. Introduction.

It may be interesting to compare how two such essentially similar environments saw the problem of motive power. Initially, their response was very similar. The 1880s, on the continent, were a period where narrow gauge railways had at last broken away from the early 0-6-0 designs and had realised that, for mountainous lines at least, something rather better was needed. The first attempts were simply to enlarge the trusty six-coupled type but to add leading or trailing trucks, both to take the increased weight and to help in guiding a long rigid wheelbase round the necessarily sharp curves. In Corsica, the CFD provided two very closely related series by the firm of Fives, Lille, first a set of fourteen 0-6-2T and then four very similar 2-6-0T abstracted from an order for their Vivarais network. In Sardinia the SFSS bought no less than forty-seven 2-6-0T from the Swiss firm of Societé Suisse (later Schweizer Lokomotiv u. Maschinenfabrik – SLM) in batches. When both of these designs proved somewhat underpowered, however, the islands went separate ways. The CFD in Corsica developed a standard four-coupled Mallet tank locomotive from an earlier design into their 3XX series and remained faithful to it thereafter. In Sardinia the Monteponi and SFSS concerns toyed with small quantities of four-coupled Mallet compounds and the SFSS went on to eight coupled side tanks – which were so unsatisfactory they had to be hastily rebuilt soon after delivery – before, as the FCS, settling on a final batch of powerful 2-6-2T in 1931. The original FCS, SFS and FMS decided to develop and standardise on the heavy 2-6-0T which they all bought in quantity, mainly from Breda of Milan, but including some very similar machines by Construzione Elettro-Meccaniche Saronno (CEMSA). The FMS also collected a fairly heterogeneous fleet of second-hand machines for its coal traffic but they were just what happened to be on the market at the time of need.

Indeed, systems in both islands acquired supplementary motive power at times of stress during the 1930s

The traditional shed view: Sassari SFS depot in steam days with 2-6-0Ts. (H LUFF)

and 1940s. That in Corsica was provided by the military who simply commandeered suitable locomotives from Algeria which they had already captured. In Sardinia the FMS in particular had to buy its own to cope with the coal traffic although official aid was no doubt in evidence – the majority came from ex-FS narrow gauge lines with a surplus of motive power. The second-hand bargains included, besides the ex-rack 0-6-0Ts from Sicily, 6-coupled, regauged Mallets from the Dolomites, a smaller Mallet from the mainland Arezzo – Fossato railway, and for several years even a couple of the SFSS 2-6-0T surplus to requirements. Both systems were looking for heavy haulage and it is interesting to see the differences in what they got.

So far as diesels were concerned, the Corsican system never bought them in quantity. By the early 1950s, freight traffic was in decline and it made do, first with three not entirely satisfactory diesel-electric cab units plus a couple of home-built devices on railcar bogies, and then with a purpose-built BB centre-cab machine using CFD's patented mechanical-hydraulic transmission. In Sardinia, the much more extensive FCS and SFS, in 1957, went straight for a very similar, but diesel-electric, design and bought it in sufficient quantity to last up to the present. Their choice was later confirmed in a sense by the Corsican operators who have since acquired two more BB locomotives of CFD origin for main-line traffic; it must be said that, during the SACFS regime in Corsica, a miscellaneous collection of converted 0-6-0D appeared from various French sources but these made little impact and disappeared rapidly when the concession changed. The notes below give what detail is known; appendix 1 contains the important dates.

2. Steam locomotives

a) Construction locomotives – Corsica:

State/CFD: 4 and 6 coupled locomotives by Couillet, Marcinelle & St.Leonard, Liege.
State: 0-4-0T Nos. 1-3 (Cou. 837-39 of 1886)
CFD: 0-6-0T Nos. 4-5 (St.L 812, 811 of 1889)

For the original works, the State bought three typical 0-4-0T from SA des Usines Metallurgiqes de l'Hainault, at Marcinelle, Couillet in Belgium (usually shortened to Couillet). They were delivered to Bastia in April 1886, being put to use in July, and the CFD used them mainly on the Calvi branch and working south from Casamozza. They were not suitable for revenue traffic and, after completion of their work, were laid by in bad condition. They were officially withdrawn and scrapped in 1900 without being taken into Corsican stock. Few details are available except that they were rated as 9hp.

At the end of March 1890, the Couillets were supplemented by two outside-cylinder 0-6-0Ts by the Usines St.Leonard of Liege which had been ordered by CFD for construction work on various systems as required and delivered in 1889. After working in Charente, they were transferred to Corsica and worked there, with Nos.1-3, until the beginning of 1895 when they were returned to the mainland and to the Charentes. These latter locomotives were straightforward 0-6-0T with Walschaerts valve gear and inside frames. Boiler fittings comprised a tapered, capped chimney, a cylindrical sandbox and a large dome on the boiler rear ring. Two spring-loaded safety valves were sited over the firebox and they had an open-backed cab with a typical St.Leonard curved roof. Wheelbase was only 1.900m.

b) Construction locomotives – Sardinia:

4-coupled locomotives by Henschel & Sohn, Kassel.
SFSS: 101-03. 0-4-0T. Henschel 2375-76; 2486 of 1887

These three machines were used initially in line construction. After completion of the system they were used for many years as shunters at important stations and were not withdrawn until 1958. Considering the late date, very little is recorded about these machines which, from photographs, appear to have been standard Henschel industrial locomotives of the period. PM Kalla-Bishop notes that they were briefly Nos. 1-3.

FCS/FMS: Both these concerns appear to have used their ordinary locomotives for major construction work.

SFS: This company had two Orenstein & Koppel 2-6-0T for construction work but they were subsequently taken into book stock and are noted below. They are also noted by some sources as having had a Nicola Romeo 2-6-0T second-hand in 1931 which appears also to have been taken into stock and is noted below.

c) Six-coupled "main line" designs – Corsica:

6-coupled side-tank locomotives by Fives Lille et Cie, Fives Lille.
CFD 28-41 0-6-2T (FL 2640-49 of 1886; 2707-10 of 1888)
CFD 53-56 2-6-0T (FL 2727-30 of 1891)

These two closely related series arose from recommendations by the ministerial commission described in Chapter 1 and were based on a similar design for the CF d'Hermes à Beaumont near Paris, generally enlarged to cope with the rugged terrain in Corsica. The 0-6-2Ts, which were intended for the Bastia - Ajaccio line, were conventional sidetank machines with a radial trailing truck and outside frames. They had two outside cylinders and Walschaerts valve gear, replacing the original intention of fitting Allan straight-link gear which was then popular. The side tanks were full length, smokebox doors were of the, then common, stove-door pattern. Boiler fittings comprised a simple, tapered funnel, a large, bell-mouthed dome with twin Salter safety valves, and a cylindrical sandbox feeding one pair of wheels. A rather exiguous cab shelter was provided, with front and rear weatherboards. There are variations between maker's drawings and later published dimensions which may suggest subsequent modifications - they were recognised as not being powerful enough for increasing traffic and some, at least, were later rebuilt with conventional smokeboxes which may indicate reboilering.

The four 2-6-0Ts were part of an order intended for the Vivarais network but were diverted to Corsica for use on the Calvi branch. As built they were almost identical in appearance to the 0-6-2T design except for reversal of the wheelbase; again, some later had conventional smokeboxes which suggests reboilering, and overall length is sometimes noted as slightly different from the specification.

Most of the 0-6-2Ts, along with 2-6-0T No. 56 were withdrawn in the mid 1930s, following the introduction of railcars for passenger trains and the remainder followed between 1945 and 1948.

CFD Corse: Fives Lille 0-6-2T of series 28-41. (MAKER'S PHOTO COURTESY BERNARD ROZE)

CFD Corse: Fives Lille 2-6-0T of series 53-56. (MAKER'S PHOTO COURTESY BERNARD ROZE)

SFSS: SLM 2-6-0T of the original batch. (COURTESY SULZER MARKETING AND TECHNOLOGY)

d) Six-coupled "main line" designs - Sardinia:

Monteponi Railway: 0-6-0T by Canada Works, Birkenhead and, possibly, Locomotivfabrik Krauss AG.
C1-C3: CW (213-14); 215 of 1870? Kr 1337 of 1883

The first recorded locomotives of the Monteponi Railway are three small tank locomotives of which little else is noted. C1 and C3 were still extant in the 1950s, C3 bearing the Canada Works No. 215 and C1/3 were identified by the company as CW, but C2 had been withdrawn "a long time ago". The others were scrapped on closure. It is not clear whether these came new to the Monteponi or were acquired at second-hand in the early 1880s.

0-6-0T Krauss, Munchen 1337 of 1883 is noted in the works list as delivered to "Monteponi" but there is no other data. PM Kalla Bishop suggested that it might be for the mines tramways since two small Henschel machines are also recorded as going "to Monteponi" about the same time...on the other hand it might just be locomotive C2 which has never been positively identified.

SFSS 2-6-0T by Schweizer Lokomotiv u Maschinenfabrik/Societé Suisse pour la Construction de Locomotives et de Machines
SFSS 1-9 (SLM 484-92 of 1887)
SFSS 10-30 (SLM 527-47 of 1888)
SFSS 31-38 SLM 645-52 of 1891
SFSS 39-41 SLM 773-75 of 1893
SFSS 42-47 SLM 856-61 of 1894

The orginal motive power of the SFSS was a series of no less than forty-seven 2-6-0T built by SLM Winterthur (then the Societé Suisse) between 1887 and 1894 and thus contemporaneous with the Corsican examples discussed above. They were to a standard SLM design built in differing sizes for various customers and were handsome side-tank machines with outside frames and full cabs. The original batch at least had the cab rear flush with the rear buffer beam and a large opening above the waist in the rear bulkhead; all later appear to have acquired the characteristic SLM rear bunker with the cab extended back over it and a

SFSS: Henschel 0-4-0T construction locomotive 102 oou at Cagliari in 1950s; SLM 2-6-0T behind. (H LUFF)

full cab rear-sheet. They had two outside cylinders with Walschaerts valve gear and boiler fittings comprised a plain tapered chimney, a tall cylindrical dome on the front boiler ring topped by spring-loaded safety valves, and a cylindrical sandbox between dome and cab. They were originally wood-burning and in service were fitted with large conical spark arresting chimneys until about 1914. Although no doubt "state of the art" at the time, they were significantly underpowered for the mountain sections and must have had considerable struggles, especially on the Arbatax trains. Nonetheless they survived until well after World War 2 and the FMS, always looking for cheap motive power, borrowed or leased 29-30 in 1936 and retained then until about 1940 when they were returned to the FCS.

Eight were normally allocated to the northern lines, four to Tempio and four to Alghero. Indeed eight or nine from Nos 2/4/6/18/19/20/21/27/30 and 35, were transferred to SFS control in 1947; different sources give different quantities and running numbers! By 1970, however, only four remained on the island in various states of disrepair – officially Nos. 8, 14, 36 and 43. According to the late PM Kalla-Bishop, No. 43 – which has since been restored as 43 GOITO – was actually an amalgam of Nos 5, 43 and 45; it is said that this operation led to the existence for some years of two Nos 43 – the restoree and the original stripped hulk. To add to the confusion GOITO currently bears plates 858/94 which were originally on 44 (it has been suggested that the basis of GOITO is the hulk of the old 45 – except that locomotives numbered 7, 14, 43 and 45 (with appropriate works identities) plus 46 have been recorded by enthusiasts as preserved on the mainland). An interesting fact is that the original orders were so large that SLM actually set up an Italian subsidiary in Naples to assemble them and the works plates record this as "Impresa Industriale Italiana di Construzione Mettaliche, Napoli".

FCS: 2-6-0Ts by Ernesto Breda SA, Milano.
FCS 1-7: Breda 1537-43 of 1914

For the 1915 opening, the FCS bought a series of seven large 2-6-0T by Breda of Milan. Again these were a standard design produced with minor variations in different sizes for various Italian narrow gauge lines. As built, they were – and are – chunky side-tank machines with high set boilers, side tanks extending only to the smokebox and full cabs with rear bunkers. They have inside frames and outside cylinders with Walschaerts valve gear; boiler fittings comprise a plain stovepipe, or tapered, chimney, a large dome on the front boiler ring, an oblong sandbox and twin pop safety valves between sandbox and cab; the variant chimneys may result from attempts to burn the local brown coal. They were designed for the comparatively easy FCS system and are said to have been somewhat lacking in power when used, after closure of the FCS lines, on the more mountainous sections. Nonetheless they were used up to the end of steam working and all were still in existence in 2001 although only No.5 was retained in serviceable condition. No.7 has been stuffed and plinthed near Monserrato and the remainder are dumped. Various noted discrepencies in identification suggest that boilers have been transferred from time to time, the worksplate being on the dome.

FMS: 2-6-0Ts by Ernesto Breda SA, Milano.
FMS 101-08: Breda 2145-52 of 1925.

With the early demise of the FMS, not much is recorded about these locomotives but they were very similar to FCS 1-7 and all the comments above apply; they were the heaviest and most powerful of the three 2-6-0T types according to Breda records. They had short side tanks and high pitched boilers, the rather utilitarian boiler fittings comprising a short stovepipe chimney, an ugly cylindrical dome, and cased safety valves in front of the cab.The two outside cylinders had Walschaerts valve gear and drive was to the rear axle. The locomotives were fitted with airbrakes and latterly the ancillary equipment appears to have been transferred to whichever locomotive was working, the air tanks being carried on the boiler. 101 and 106/7 were in use or reserve up to the end, mainly on inbound coal traffic. All were withdrawn and scrapped after closure except for No.101 which was intended for preservation at Iglesias. This never happened and its carcase was still rotting in the yard there as late as 2001.

Breda 2-6-0T for SFS on PW work 1970. Interestingly it is numbered 5 and named Laerru not ELSA as lists have it.
(D TREVOR ROWE)

SFS: 2-6-0Ts by Ernesto Breda SA, Milano & Construzione Elettro-Meccaniche Saronno SA (CEMSA)
SFS 1-5 Breda 2287-91 of 1930
SFS 6-11 CEMSA 947-52 of 1931

These locomotives represent the modernisation of the standard design. Like the others they have high-pitched boilers and full cabs with back bunkers but the side tanks are smaller and better proportioned, probably to keep within axleload limits. Frames are inside, with outside cylinders equipped with Caprotti valve gear which was fashionable among Italian lines at the time. The plain chimneys have, or had, spark arresters, the dome and sandbox are combined in a large rectangular housing and twin pop safety valves surmount the firebox. They are said to be the largest 2-6-0s in Sardinia but appear marginally less powerful than the others. Nos 3 and 5 are, at least nominally, serviceable at time of writing and Nos 4/6/7/11 are dumped at various points on the northern system.

SFS: 2-6-OTs by Orenstein & Koppel AG & Nicola Romeo, Saronno
SFS 12/13: O&K 11796-97 of 1929.
SFS 14: N Romeo 1922; acquired s/h 1931?

Little is recorded about the first two locomotives, noted by O&K simply as 180hp, coal-burners delivered in March 1929, although not taken on to SFS books until 1931. They were presumably used as construction locomotives and then assimilated into book stock. They did not survive to be taken over by the FdS in 1989. The only mystery is in their running numbers: Italian sources record 11797 as originally 13 with a short-lived second-hand 2-6-0T by Nicola Romeo as 14. If this is so, it seems likely that the O&K locomotive was renumbered later to avoid bad luck. Possibly superstition decreed that No.13 should be left blank since O&K records confirm that only two locomotives were ordered. The Romeo locomotive is simply listed and no other details are available.

FCS: unidentified type by Borsig of Berlin

Borsig10: occasional references crop up for a locomotive as shown but there is some confusion with FCS 202. This number has also been noted as an 0-4-4-0T. It has been suggested by Italian sources that the FCS may have acquired two locomotives directly from the Ferrovie Adriatico-Appenino (FAA) which was electrified during the 1920s and that they were this one (ex FAA 10) and the locomotive which exists as FCS 202 (qv).

e) Four-coupled Mallet compound locomotives – Corsica

One frequently used solution to the problem of providing enough power for steeply curved and graded lines was the articulated locomotive and, in France and southern Europe, the most common type was the four-or six-coupled compound locomotive to M Mallet's patents. These consisted basically of two engine components, a rear set in fixed frames driven via high pressure cylinders and a front pivoting bogie driven by low-pressure cylinders; this gave reasonable flexibility while minimising the complications of transferring high pressure steam via flexible connections. Both islands had Mallets but Corsica was the main user with no less than 22 in all plus a temporary loan of four others.

CFD: 0-4-4-0T by Societé Alsacienne de Constructions Mechaniques (SACM) at Graffenstaden

301: SACM 4285 of 1892 prototype – for Bastia – Ajaccio
302: SACM 4626 of 1895 1st series – for Bastia – Ajaccio
303-04: SACM 4627-28 of 1895 1st series – for east coast
305-06: SACM 5629-30 of 1906 1st series – for Bastia – Ajaccio
307-08: SACM 7379-80 of 1924 1st series – for Bastia – Ajaccio
309-12: SACM 7462-65 of 1927 2nd series – for east coast
313-16: SACM 7551-54 of 1930 2nd series – for east coast
317-19: SACM 7650-52 of 1932 2nd series – for east coast
351-53: SACM 7653-55 of 1932 2nd series – for Bastia – Ajaccio

These two closely related series, differing mainly in all-up weight and superstructure details, stemmed from a set of 0-4-4-0T developed for the CFD's Vivarais system but enlarged and strengthened for the conditions in Corsica. They were specifically intended for handling heavy freight traffic beyond the

CFD 0-4-4-0T Mallet 352 of the final batch in wintry conditions in Ajaccio shed. (BERNARD ROZE)

capabilities of the six-coupled machines and, even so, had to double-head on occasions. Initially SACM produced a prototype which was rigorously tested in Corsica and then batches were ordered as the system developed.

The locomotives were straightforward Mallet side-tank machines with open backed cabs, inside frames throughout and Walschaerts valve gear. Boiler fittings comprised a plain tapered chimney, a large dome on the second ring of the boiler and a cylindrical sandbox between dome and cab. Pop safety valves were mounted on the dome in the first series and over the firebox in the rest. The second series was marginally heavier and with boiler pressure increased from 12 to 13 atmospheres but no more powerful; Other dimensions were identical and differences in appearance were confined to boiler fittings and cab.

The number allocation in the final batch appears to have arisen because numbers in the 32X series had already been taken up by a modified 2-4-4-0T version for the Vivarais and Lozère systems. Initial allocations were as shown above because the French attached stock to specific concessions but in later years the whole series was used as required; wear and tear, and war damage, took their toll but six examples remained serviceable up to the end of steam working in 1954; all were subsequently scrapped.

0-4-4-0T by Sté de Construction Batignolles, type XAT
ex Tunisian Rly 25X series: built 1895, to Corsica 1944

Four of these Mallet locomotives, numbered 253, 258, 251 and 254, were brought in by the Allies in two batches during 1944 from the Tunisian railways. They were part of a larger series, most of which were transferred to the CF Algeriennes in 1922 but these appear to have remained in Tunisia. They were slightly heavier and more powerful than the indigenous ones and apparently proved very useful. After the war they were less used and were withdrawn for scrap in 1948.

Another four, identities unknown, were noted by the late PM Kalla-Bishop as brought in subsequently but no other evidence exists and none of the possibilities appear in CFA or Tunisian lists as having gone to Corsica. Since one was quoted as “158” there may just be confusion in the records.

f) Four-coupled Mallet compound locomotives – Sardinia

The Sardinian systems confined themselves to two examples for the SFSS and up to eight, mostly secondhand, for the Monteponi and Montevecchio concerns.

Monteponi: 0-4-4-0T by Borsig of Berlin and Henschel & Sohn, Kassel

The Monteponi bought two Borsig Mallets new in 1905-06 and after 1945 acquired at least four more Mallets second-hand (or, more accurately, “pre-used” by several owners) from various mainland sources. In spite of considerable efforts by both Italian and British enthusiasts, the picture is not entirely clear and the following is open to correction! The series was originally deduced by enthusiasts to be B1-6 but there is photographic evidence for the A and H variants.

A1-2: Borsig 5630 of 1905 and 6021 of 1906

Few details are available of these locomotives which are said to have been standard Borsig products of the period and bought new; both were scrapped after closure.

B3/5: Borsig 8738 of 1913 and 8096 of 1912

These two locomotives appear to have been acquired at second (or third) hand after World War 2. B3 is noted by Kalla Bishop as ex Montevecchio Railway No.4 (the Montevecchio was a Sardinian industrial line) and B5 as ex Ferrovie Adriatico-Appenine 26 (originally No. 6 of the Sangritana Rly which was subsumed in the FAA). It appears just possible that B3 was transferred to the FCS as their 202 (qv). B5 was certainly scrapped.

H6: Henschel 11674 of 1913

This was noted as ex FAA 32, ex Sangritana Rly No. 12, with a fairly complex history before coming to the island. It is noted as scrapped on closure.

SFSS: 0-4-4-0T 200 (Schwazkopf) in store at Cagliari. (K TAYLORSON)

?4: Provenance uncertain

There is said to have been a Mallet numbered 4 in the series which is logical but there are queries as to whether it was B4, another Borsig (possibly 5901 of 1906 ex FAA No.2), or H4, a Henschel (possibly 11669 of 1913). In either case it would be ex FAA Sangritana division and some sources claim this to be the current FCS 202, now in museum store at Monserrato (see below).

SFSS: 0-4-4-0T by Schwarzkopf, Berlin
200-01: Sch 4349-50 of 1909

These, again, were straightforward machines of typically German appearance, having full cabs with rear bunkers, inside frames throughout and Walschaerts valve gear. Boiler fittings originally comprised a large spark-arresting chimney, a cylindrical dome with spring loaded safety valves on the boiler centre ring and small cylindrical sandboxes fore and aft of the dome; a further pop safety valve was mounted over the firebox. They were intended as wood-burners for the mountainous lines to Arbatax and Sorgono (hence the spark-arresters). Both were used into the 1960s. No.200 was bought for preservation on the mainland and No.201 survived in a very derelict condition at Monserrato depot in 2001.

FCS 202: 0-4-4-0T, provenance uncertain

This classic Germanic Mallet tank locomotive is currently in museum store at Monserrato. Its provenance is uncertain, having according to most enthusiast records, been acquired by the FCS second-hand in or about 1962. The FCS certainly hired or borrowed FMS M30 (Borsig 7147 of 1909) about 1958 and it would seem logical that it might be passed this when no longer needed by the Government controlled FMS but a photograph of FAA 30 (its former incarnation) does not match up. The locomotive is also claimed by W Simms as Henschel 11669 of 1913 ex-Sangritana No.7. mainly on the strength of a reported "7" on a motion part but it does not display Henschel characteristics of the period. More likely is the former

FCS: the mystery Mallet in open store. Note the Borsig-pattern cylinder casings and chimney. (K TAYLORSON)

B3 of the Monteponi Railway (Borsig 8738/13) which was ex Montevecchio No. 4 and available around the right time. It does exhibit some Borsig characteristics, in particular the cab shape, cylinder casings and chimney so, failing definite identification, this is suggested as the best option. It must, however, be said that an Italian list, giving locomotive names for all systems, and generally accurate so far as it can be cross-checked, has it as Borsig 5901 of 1906, GRAZIELLA, ex FAA No. 2 and with no indication of intermediate owners. According to this theory, the FCS acquired two 0-4-4-0T directly from the Adratico - Appenine, their numbers 2 and 10, in the early 1930s and No. 10 was later either scrapped or sold-on, possibly to the Montevecchio or Monteponi. Offers are invited for a definitive identification!

FMS: 0-4-4-0T by Borsig of Berlin; secondhand
FMS M30: Borsig 7147 of 1909.

This locomotive was acquired by the FMS when desperate for motive power about 1939 and was originally No.30 of the Arrezo - Fossato railway. It was sold by them to the FC Calabro-Lucane and thence to the dealer Ing. Greco of Reggio Calabria. Greco in turn sold it to the FMS in 1939 (the M was added to differentiate it from 2-6-0T 30 ex the FCS). It was briefly loaned or hired to the FCS about 1958 and is noted elsewhere as scrapped in the early 1960s.

g) Other heavy power bought new – Sardinia

The Corsican system was quite satisfied with its Mallets and the only other machines acquired were second-hand ones brought in by the military and described below. The SFSS and FCS, however, experimented with more conventional power.

SFSS: 0-8-0T (later 2-8-0T) by Orenstein & Koppel
SFSS 300-01 O&K 5758-59 of 1914
SFSS 302-03 O&K 7721-22 of 1914

The SFSS clearly had problems with their SLM 2-6-0Ts since in 1914 they ordered two batches of two semi-articulated 0-8-0T from Orenstein & Koppel in Germany. Interestingly, in O&K records all are marked for 954mm gauge and the second pair are noted as 250hp rather than the original 225hp. All are noted as delivered in November 1914 although usually recorded as built 1915 and O&K records suggest that the first pair may have been built somewhat earlier for stock or for a customer who defaulted.

Whatever the origin, the machines, as built, were straightforward heavyweight side-tank locomotives with outside frames and cylinders and with the first and fourth axles articulated on the Klien-Lindner principle as modified by Ing. Luttermoller of O&K; this involved a rigid axle running in the normal axleboxes – and hence not disturbing the coupling rods – but with the wheels fixed to a hollow axle sleeve pivoted round the axle centre and linked by a compensating mechanism. They were fitted as new with the highly unsatisfactory Clench superheater which consisted basically of a sealed section at the boiler front through which steam was passed over the tubes and back to a secondary dome; alas it was almost impossible to keep the internal tubeplate watertight and then the thing just became a nuisance. In consequence, in 1916, they were rebuilt at the SFSS Cagliari Works, losing their Clench apparatus and, at the same time, gaining extended frames supporting a leading truck which made them into 2-8-0Ts. As such they were clearly still not entirely satisfactory since they were again rebuilt in 1926-28 acquiring proper Schmidt superheaters and also Caprotti valve gear (which one suspects replaced an original O&K design). They are said to have been the first narrow gauge locomotives in Italy – Kalla-Bishop says in the world – to be so equipped.

As finally rebuilt they are reasonably handsome machines with sidetanks extending only partway along the boiler and with a full cab with curved side sheets and a rear bunker. Boiler fittings comprise a plain tapered chimney, a small closed dome followed by a large one on which the safety valves are mounted, a rectangular sandbox. They were in use up to the late 1960s at least. In 2001, three were very derelict at Monserrato depot, No.301 being dumped reasonably complete at Mandas.

FCS: 2-6-2T by Officine Meccaniche Italiane Reggio Emilia
FCS 400-02: RE 133-35 of 1931

The most modern-looking locomotives on the Sardinian system, these three were delivered in 1931 and are claimed to be a logical development of the 2-6-0T designs. Certainly they were the most powerful and useful machines on the narrow gauge and were used throughout the Cagliari system. They have inside

SFSS O&K 2-8-0T No. 301 at Mandas, 1966. (F PUGH)

Reggiane 2-6-2T No. 402 in use for tourist trains. (AUTHOR)

frames with outside cylinders and Caprotti valve gear, drive being to the rear coupled axle. Basic boiler fittings comprise a plain, tapered chimney, a large cylindrical dome and a rectangular sandbox; twin pop safety valves are mounted on a branch pipe over the firebox. No 401 was scrapped but the other two were restored for charter trains and are serviceable at the time of writing.

h) Other locomotives acquired at second-hand – Corsica

0-10-0T by Orenstein & Koppel AG, ex CFD de la Cote d'Or
50-51 O&K 10926-27 of 1926

In 1944 the system was very short of motive power through war damage and the Allied authorities brought from Algeria two heavy 0-10-0T originally built for the CF Départementaux de la Cote d'Or in eastern France. These had been specifically designed for freight work over heavy gradients and had Koppel's patented Luttermoller articulation - the leading axle was a radial one, connected to the second axle by gearing. The other axles were coupled but the rear one had some side play, the centre one had no flanges and the ones each side of that had thin flanges... In appearance they were modern-looking side tank locomotives with full cabs and rear bunkers. Walschaerts valve gear was fitted and boiler fittings comprised a short, plain chimney, a large dome and two cylindrical sandboxes plus various ancillary equipment.

They were, apparently, thought well of by the CFDCO and were sold to Algeria on closure. In Corsican service, however, they were no more successful than their earlier Sardinian equivalents, being painfully slow, so thirsty that they had to tow a tank wagon, and not capable of very high loadings. They were withdrawn in 1954 and scrapped.

i) "Pre-used" locomotives – Sardinia

In Sardinia, the use of second-hand locomotives on public railways was confined to the coal hauling lines in the southwest and both the FMS and the Monteponi railway acquired a variety of such power from Sicily and mainland Italy.

The FMS was often hard-pressed for motive power during its coal hauling days and acquired a wide variety of stock. First were the two ex SFSS 2-6-0T (29/30) in 1936 and they were followed in 1937 by nine large 2-6-6-0T Mallets (151-59) brought in from the 760mm gauge Dolomitenbahn (Ora - Predazzo) and generally refettled and regauged by OMI Reggiane at Reggio Emilia. Two years later came a smaller 0-4-4-0T Mallet, No.30 of the Arrezo- Fossato railway, which retained its number but was prefixed M to avoid confusion with the 2-6-0Ts. Lastly, between 1939 and 1953, the FMS acquired no less than 18 ex-FS 0-6-0RT rack tanks from the FS 950mm gauge lines in Sicily. The rack mechanisms were disabled and, in most cases, removed, the rack cylinders being blanked off. They were then fitted with steel fireboxes adapted to burn the low-grade Sardinian coal and apparently proved very successful, many working up till closure of the coal mines. Subsequently, they were progressively withdrawn and scrapped, only seven being recorded as still in store by final closure of the system in 1975

In detail, the batches of locomotives brought in from the mainland were as follows:

FMS 151-59: 2-6-6-0T by Henschel & Sohn of Kassel
Hen. 14228/14203/14219/14216/14192/14217/14226/14183/14197 of 1916 in that order

These large Mallet-type locomotives were originally of 760mm gauge and built as part of a series of forty-six for the Austro-Hungarian Military Railways (Kuk Heeresbahnen) (Kuk 6001-46). They were used on various fronts but ten were allocated to the Ora-Predazzo line in the Dolomites and were taken into Italian civilian stock after the war. In 1929 the Ora line was converted to metre gauge and electrified, one locomotive being regauged for construction work and the remainder put in store until bought by the FMS in 1937. They were regauged and overhauled by OMI Reggiane at Reggio Emilia before delivery to the island. In FMS service they were initially very useful during the peak coal hauling period, being able to haul twenty loaded bogie wagons, but after the ex-Sicilian locomotives arrived they were gradually laid off and were scrapped about 1963. In the final years No.159 was hired or loaned to the FCS for shunting at Cagliari and was noted there about 1958-59.

In appearance the class were typically Henschel with Walschaerts valve gear and long side tanks with sloping front portions. Boiler fittings comprised a plain chimney, two domes (auxiliary and main) and two square sandboxes, pop safety valves being mounted over the firebox. A full cab was fitted, with a rear bunker.

FMS: up to twenty-two 0-6-0T rack locomotives by various makers ex FS narrow gauge lines in Sicily
FMS: for numbers see consolidated list in Appendix 1

In the late 1930s, the FS narrow gauge system in Sicily had already reached its peak and was starting to decline. Considerable extra kilometrage had earlier been planned, however and locomotives ordered in advance so there was a surplus of motive power. The FMS took advantage of this to buy several batches of the standard Strub-rack equipped heavy 0-6-0T originally designed for mountain work and to adapt them for coal hauling by disabling the rack mechanism and blanking off the rack cylinders. Since the FMS had fairly heavy rail and the Sicilian engines had total adhesion plus a boiler designed to supply four cylinders

R370 class 0-6-0T ex rack locomotives in store at S. Giovanni Suergiu, 1969. (D TREVOR ROWE)

they proved very useful machines and were used extensively until outward coal traffic failed. There is evidence from enthusiast records that some cannibalisation took place from time to time and the eventual quantity is not certain – 18 or 22 has been cited. Certainly in later years at least one locomotive bore the maker's details of a machine that is not recorded as having reached Sardinia, so there may have been some unidentified acquisitions; on the other hand, the company may simply have bought some spare boilers complete with fittings and workplates (which, in Italian fashion, were on the domes). They were undoubtedly cannibalised and scrapped progressively but seven at least survived to the end and were still in store on closure, together with two spare boilers. At one time an example was loaned to the FCS at Macomer, presumably for trial purposes since it is not recorded as remaining there.

In appearance, the 370 class were chunky side tanks with modified Walschaerts gear driving both sets of cylinders, the rack mechanism being mounted above the main cylinders and driving a Strub rack pinion between first and second sets of coupled wheels – the locomotives were combined rack and adhesion drive. Shortish side tanks linked to a full cab with rear bunker, and boiler fittings comprised a capped chimney and a square sandbox, followed by a large cylindrical dome on the rear boiler ring. They were fitted with vacuum and counter-pressure brakes although the latter were probably disabled in Sardinia. On the FMS the rack cylinders were blanked off and the rack gear removed; they were fitted with steel fireboxes to burn the revolting local coal and the chimneys and blast arrangements were altered accordingly.

2. Modern motive power: diesel locomotives and tractors

j) Diesel locomotives and tractors – Corsica

BB diesel-electric locomotives by Brissonneau et Lotz of Creil
401-02 BL of 1951, new to Corsica
403 (II) BL of 1951 as CP 64 for CF de Provence. to Corsica 8/63

In order to reduce dependence on steam locomotives, the CFC acquired two of a batch of ten 600hp BB locomotives being built to the order of the Ponts-et-Chaussées organisation for a number of light railways which it then controlled; the others went to the CF de Provence (4) and the Voies Ferrées du Dauphiné (4). They differed in body detail but were all double-cab machines with an all-over rectangular body having

CFC: Brissonneau et Lotz 403, ex CF de Provence. Note the different fascia with intercommunication door.
(D TREVOR ROWE)

CFC. CFD locomotives 404/5 on a double-headed goods train, showing underframe differences. (JOSÉ BANAUDO)

a luggage compartment in the centre. This separated two engine/generator rooms each containing a 300hp Renault motor and a generator set feeding motors on one bogie. They were not trouble free but gave good service until the early 1960s, being then reinforced in 1963 by an additional unit from Provence which took the number of an existing tractor (see below). Almost simultaneously 401 became unserviceable and was followed in 1966 by 402; 403 remained in reserve and occasional use until 1974. Both 402 and 403 remained in store until 1981 when they were scrapped.

BB diesel-mechanical/hydraulic locomotives by CFD Montmirail
404. CFD of 1973, ex CFD Vivarais 040-003, ex CP 403 1/74
405. CFD of 1966, new to Corsica 6/66
406. CFD of 1973 as standard gauge. converted for Corsica 1994-95

In the early 1960s CFD designed and built at their Montmirail Works a series of four 414hp tractors for various light railways – one for their Vivarais system, two for the PO Lignes de Corrèze and one for Corsica. The first three later went to the CF de Provence as 401-3, from which 403 was sent to Corsica in 1974 (since the BL 600hp locomotive was still in existence the new acquisition was renumbered as 404). It differed slightly in being originally designed for the lighter axleload restrictions on the Vivarais, having a lighter frame and narrower buffer beams; while on the CP it was ballasted with iron blocks attached to the frames. 404/5 carried out all the goods work until 1995 when an additional machine was acquired. This was accordingly (at least nominally) numbered 406 and all three are in service in 2001. In general the series are centre-cab machines, 404-05 having a Poyaud 207hp diesel under each bonnet and the CFD's patented Asynchro mechanical-hydraulic transmission. 406 is analagous but was actually built for the Swiss contractor 'Speno International' as a standard gauge machine in 1973. Speno used it to haul a rail-grinding train until this was replaced by a self-propelled unit when the locomotive was bought back by CFD. It was converted to metre gauge and sold to the CFC specifically for a project to haul wood-waste to an urban heating unit in the old locomotive sheds at Corte. In the event, the traffic did not materialise and the locomotive has seen little use except for shunting. Although of 600hp it has air brakes, not vacuum ones since it was to haul air-braked hopper wagons which are now useful only for PW work. The number has been variously recorded as BB 001 and 406. It differs visually in several respects, particularly in having no coupling rods on the bogies.

SACFS: 0-60DM tractor No 1 ex CFD du Tarn and Billard draisine 746 at Ajaccio in 1982. (José Banaudo)

Tractor No. 3 ex SE de Seine et Marne, derelict at Bastia 1976. (José Banaudo)

Second-hand tractors and locally built tractors
1: 0-6-0DM CFD of 1948, ex CFD du Tarn LT1; ex CF du Doubs 101
2: 0-6-0DM VFD of 1953, ex Voies Ferrées du Dauphiné
3: 2-6-0DM SE of 1950, ex SE Réseau de Seine et Marne

As part of its concession, the SACFS brought in several six-coupled tractors, rebuilt from steam locomotives, which it had acquired from closing lines. All were different in detail, having been rebuilt by three different firms but had a similar arrangement of an off-centre cab with the engine under a bonnet and the auxiliary equipment in a substantial "boot" and all reutilised a steam locomotive chassis, retaining the coupling rods. No. 1 was ex LT1 of the CFD du Tarn, and originally a CFD production for the CF du Doubs; No. 2 was a similar but more angular tractor built by the Voies Ferrées du Dauphiné in 1953 at Vizille on the chassis of VFD 0-6-0T No. 22, sold on to a coal mine near La Mure in 1964 and thence bought by SACFS in 1968. It was used to shunt at Bastia and was withdrawn in 1978. No. 3 was one of two machines built on Cail 0-6-2T chassis at Cosne-s-Allier by the SE for their Seine-et-Marne system which closed in 1965. They were bought by CFD for refurbishment and resale, No. 1 being sold on to Corsica in 1968 where it was numbered 3. The SACFS also intended to acquire its twin which was to be No. 4 but then decided not to do so. The machine was eventually scrapped by CFD and parts reused. The tractors were too light to be of much use and Nos. 2 and 3 were withdrawn for scrap after takeover by CFTA and scrapped in the 1980s from the dump at Borgo. No. 1 remained for some years as Ajaccio shunter and has since been rescued by the MTVS and taken to their museum, currently at Valmondois.

114: bogie DM tractor by Bastia Works

This machine was built locally in January 1955 from the running gear and motor bogie of Billard railcar 114 mated to a new frame and a most peculiar body resembling a bonneted van. The bonnet, at one end, contained the radiator and engine, the cabin consisting of a long rectangular structure housing two driving positions and including a luggage compartment at the rear end. The side "windows" consisted of naval-type portholes, whence its common local nickname of "le sousmarin" (submarine) – French enthusiasts more

Tractor 114, the "Bête de Calvi" seen from the cab end. (BERNARD ROZE)

The original tractor 403 at Ajaccio. (BERNARD ROZE)

commonly referred to it as "Le Bête de Calvi" (the beast of Calvi). It was used on passenger and light goods work on the Calvi branch although, since it was air-braked being ex-railcar, it was restricted to a maximum of four wagons; even so additional safety chains were improvised to provide security on the steep gradients! Once regular freight ceased on the Calvi branch it was retired but was still in existence, though derelict, at Casamozza in 2001.

403(1) 4wDM tractor by Bastia Works

This light tractor was built locally in 1956 using parts from Billard railcar 115 mated to a 210hp motor bogie from Billard railcar 103. It had an off-centre cab with a bonnet over the engine and a boot covering auxiliary equipment and was used as Ajaccio shunter until 1962 when it was withdrawn.

k) Diesel locomotives and tractors – Sardinia

FCS: A1 1-C-1 by Maschinenfabrik Karlsruhe

This was a 250hp centre-cab diesel with hydrostatic transmission which was borrowed from the FS in 1927 to test out the feasibility of diesel traction. It was apparently not successful and was returned very quickly.

FCS/SFS: 4wDM by Orenstein & Koppel AG, type MV4
FCS: Ln 01-05, later LM1-5. O&K 25356-60 of 1953 (not in sequence)

In 1958, the FCS bought from Carbonia colliery and regauged five four-wheeled 900mm gauge diesel shunting tractors for general use as depot shunters. They were straightforward industrial tractors with a cab at one end and the engine under an angular bonnet. Ln 01/3 (25358/6) were transferred to the SFS lines in 1962; all were taken over by FdS in 1989 and renumbered LM 1-5 (whether then or in FCS times is not certain) and most had been scrapped by 1995. In 2001 only LM 5 (OK 25359) survived as depot pet at Monserrato, named ERCOLINA, although parts of at least two others were still in existence.

FdS: O&K tractor LM5, ex Carbonia mines, at Monserrato in 1999. (AUTHOR)

FdS. BB DE locomotive of 5XX series for the SFS, in almost original condition except for roof casing. (AUTHOR)

FdS BB DE locomotive of 6XX series as rebuilt by FdS. (AUTHOR)

SFS/FCS: BB diesel electric locomotives by Ernesto Breda with electric equipment by TIBB
SFS: LDe 500-04; Breda/TIBB 5928-32 of 1958 (not in sequence); said to be originally SFS LDe 201-05
FCS: LDe 600-12/614/616; Breda TIBB 5913-27 of 1958 (not in sequence)

These related classes, which set the standard for Sardinia, were ordered for both SFS and FCS by their owning company and remain the main source of motive power for locomotive-hauled trains. The locomotives are double-ended with centre cabs and with a Breda 350hp diesel engine beneath each bonnet, driving a total of four TIBB 92kw axle-hung motors. They have vacuum (5XX) or air (6XX) brakes as appropriate and are cleared for a line speed of 70km/h making them suitable for passenger work. Recently the ex-FCS ones on the Macomer system have been rebuilt to some extent, acquiring new cabs with modified door and window arrangements and a blue/grey livery; there are minor suspension differences between the two groups, and all have acquired an unsightly casing above the cab. The ex-SFS ones, in 2001, were still in otherwise original condition and green livery with red trim.

The explanation for the odd numbering of the 6XX series appears to be that locomotives allocated to Cagliari heve even numbers and those at Macomer have odd ones...whether this just coincidentally avoids the number 613 is not clear. As at 2001, all were still officially serviceable except LDe 504 reduced to a skeleton at the former Sassari Santa Maria depot and LDe 610 similarly stripped in Monserrato depot yard.

l) Powered service vehicles: Both islands

In Corsica, two Gleismar type VTM multi-purpose self-propelled track machines analagous to those in Sardinia were purchased in 1990 and are in general use for PW work.; one has been fitted with a hydraulic crane and the other with a personnel cabin. Additionally Billard A80D 513 converted for parcels work is

CFC: Service vehicle by Gleismar, with personnel capsule and crane. (AUTHOR)

FdS: Gleismac track servicing vehicle, Macomer. (AUTHOR)

FdS: Piaggio-engined rail scooter, Monserrato 1999. (AUTHOR)

FdS: Matema railtruck in PW use at Macomer, 2001. (AUTHOR)

officially in stock as a breakdown vehicle, although noted as unserviceable in 1999. There was previously a small fleet of petrol-powered draisines or permanent way trolleys. These were introduced in 1932 with a single example from Campagne and supplemented in 1936 by six from Billard (CFD 741-46). All were boxy, 4-wheeled cars with roofs and end screens but otherwise open above the waist. They were mostly withdrawn in the 1970s.

In Sardinia, in 1960 Matema SA provided three 4-w draisines based on road pick-up truck components, one for each major section. They are essentially light rail lorries with a full-width cab and a pick-up body covered with a canvas tilt. In 1999 all were in use or serviceable. In addition, Monserrato Works at an unknown date built a light passenger draisine incorporating parts from a Piaggio scooter and in 1999 this was stored in a rather battered state at Monserrato.

In 1990, three Gleismac CF-120 multi-purpose track machines (M1223-25) were purchased by FdS. These have a steel cabin and a decked portion carrying a power-operated crane arm. They can be fitted with a variety of extra equipment including mini-diggers. (in Italy Gleismar operates under the Gleismac name).

Contractors are being used to refurbish some lines and to carry out major maintenance. They tend to bring in their own equipment from the mainland, resulting in a variety of diesel tractors ranging from regauged ex German Kof shunters to quite impressive BB machines.

FdS: SLM 2-6-0T No. 43 GOITO being steamed at Mandas, 1999 *(see Chapter 6).* (AUTHOR)

FdS: ex FCS Breda 2-6-0T No.5 SULCIS and a typical water tank, Bosa Marina *(see Chapter 6).* (AUTHOR)

FMS: 2-6-0T No. 105 at S. Giovanni. (H LUFF)

301
F.C.S.
Locomotiva Orenstein & Koppel gruppo 300
stato originario (1915)

SFSS: A painting, from a faded blueprint, of the O&K 0-8-0Ts in original condition (except for the FCS plaque!). (MUSEO FERROVIE, CAGLIARI)

FCS: ex SFSS Mallets 200-01 at Cagliari old station in the 1950s. (H LUFF)

FCS Reggiane 2-6-2T No. 402. (AUTHOR)

CFC: Brissonneau et Lotz diesel 401 in original livery, Bastia. (H LUFF)

CFC: CFD BB diesel locomotive 404, ex-CF de Provence, in service in 1998. (AUTHOR)

Bosa station with OM railbus. In the background are Miani & Silvestri coaches, including a genuine 3rd class example. (H LUFF)

FMS San Giovanni Suergiu: All the railcar types; L to R: 1935 Fiat, rebuilt Fiat, new diesel-electric car. (D TREVOR ROWE)

SFS: New diesel car and trailer (leading) at Sassari. (H LUFF)

CFC: Renault ABH car in original condition and livery, Bastia. (H LUFF)

CFC: the most modern type of railcar by CFD/Soulé. AUTHOR

CFC: De Dietrich composite coach modified in red-grey as a railcar trailer. (H LUFF)

CFC: De Dietrich 3rd class coach modified as a 3rd/luggage trailer. (H LUFF)

CFC: Typical goods stock; the fourgon has been reliveried for use with railcars. (H LUFF)

CHAPTER 7
Motive power: Railmotors

1. Introduction

As with locomotives, experiments with early railcars paralleled each other in both islands but later differed markedly. The early 1930s saw many continental secondary railways of the larger sort flirting with internal combustion power as a way of speeding up services and economising on running costs at the same time. In this case, Corsica was definitely in advance. Pre-war experiments in Sardinia were confined to FCS use of three, four-wheeled, railbuses surplus to requirements from the Calabrian system and two small series of Fiat bogie "express" cars which were used by both FMS and FCS. These latter vehicles were certainly "state-of-the art" for the period, being semi-streamlined and diesel-mechanical. The CFD in Corsica also started gingerly, with two Crochat petrol-electric devices but in 1936-37 took the bold step of commissioning two very advanced series of cars from the firm of Billard of Tours. On the other hand, postwar, the Sardinian companies bought a largely standardised design of bogie diesel-engined car, with either electric or mechanical transmission, in considerable quantity and have stuck faithfully to it, even to the extent of putting new, but very similar bodies on the original running gear when replacement became necessary; the only deviation came in 1995 when EU subsidy allowed purchase of eight modern cars with provision for conversion to straight electric drive if required - and even these are really a modernised development of the original design. Corsica started well post-war by acquiring eight modern Renault cars but then went through a period where the concessionaire brought in a motley collection of second or third hand equipment which was not satisfactory. Only in the last two decades of the 20th century has it invested in successive batches of truly modern equipment.

2. Early attempts: Corsica

CFD: Ae 51-52. B-2 petrol-electric railcars by Decauville, 1925

In 1924 the CFD was studying economic ways of reducing costs on its larger systems and bought two of the, then fashionable, petrol-electric bogie railcars for Corsica. These were actually to a design by Henri Crochat, whose business went into receivership in 1924 and was taken over by Decauville. As a result, the design was somewhat modified, emerging in December 1925 with an improved body and with the originally specified De Dion engines replaced by two Panhard 60hp ones. They were fitted out for 1st and 2nd class travel and ran express services between Bastia and Ajaccio until September 1928 when Ae 51 was badly damaged in a collision. Since one machine was not sufficient to maintain a full service, Ae 52, together with the mechanical and electrical components of Ae 51, was transferred to the CFD's Réseau des Charentes et Deux Sevres which had already received a similar car from the Réseau du Vivarais. It lasted until 1935, the components of Ae 51 being used to construct a tractor but that is another story. Meanwhile Corsica reverted to steam traction.

3. Early attempts: Sardinia

FCS: FC 1-3. 1-A diesel mechanical railbuses by Officine Meccaniche, Milan with bodies by Carminati & Toselli

In 1934, the FCS took advantage of surplus equipment built for the Calabro-Lucane system to acquire the first narrow gauge i/c engined railmotors in Sardinia. These were originally intended to be M1 15-17 of the FCL and were fairly crude, if robust, single-engined devices with a full-fronted, bus-like wooden body mounted on a standard OM lorry frame. They were single ended, using the existing turntables to be turned at each end of a journey and seated 29 2nd class passengers in forward-facing bus seats. Drive from the 100hp lorry engine was through a standard lorry gearbox with final drive by cardan shafts to the rear axle. The class was allocated to Macomer and ran many passenger services from there for the next 25 years or so. They were then withdrawn and, somewhat incredibly, all three were still derelict at Tirso in 2000.

FCS: OM railbus running the Bosa - Macomer service in 1953. (H LUFF)

4. Early express railcars: Corsica

CFD: bogie diesel-mechanical railcars by Anciens Ets. Billard of Tours
CFD: 101-06. Billard 701-06 of 1935-36; type A210D
CFD: 111-16. Billard 2001-06 of 1937 type A150D

The CFD were pioneers in the development of railcars for their narrow gauge systems and in 1934 they commissioned Billard to design for them a high capacity lightweight diesel railcar. The result was the type A210D (autorail, 210hp, diesel) a long, low double-ended car with a 210hp MAN diesel in the driving compartment at one end, two saloons (to allow for two classes if required), a toilet and a baggage compartment with another driving position at the far end. A prototype, 101, was tried out thoroughly in Corsica in July 1935 and as a result five slightly improved examples were ordered - the improvements being confined mainly to a modernised appearance with semi-streamlined ends and with a Minerva gearbox replacing the original. They were used for the express services on the central and east coast lines but had eventful careers. 101 remained in service until scrapping; 102 was destroyed by "act of war" in 1943; 103 was badly damaged by fire in 1946 and its motor bogie used to construct the first tractor 403 (qv). In May 1957 104/5 were converted to trailers for the post-war Renault cars although 105 was later reinstated for a time; 105/6 were demotored and rebodied as trailers by Garnero in 1977.

The CFD were so pleased with their acquisitions that in September 1936 they ordered nine of a smaller and lighter type, the A150D, for Corsica (6) and the Vivarais (3) which were almost directly comparable with the Sardinian Fiats described below. This was very much Billard's version of the 1930s light streamliner with a low-slung body and angled, sloping ends having ornamental radiator grills, although the lines were somewhat marred by a need to resite the radiator block when CLM engines rather than a shorter Berliet design, were fitted. Again they had two saloons, seating a total of 38 passengers and linked by an off-centre entrance lobby; one driving position was simply screened off from a saloon, the other was in a large baggage compartment that also housed the motor bogie with its CLM 6-cylinder 150hp diesel. Like their predecessors they had eventful careers, all being refitted with Renault engines from 1942-on. 116 was destroyed in 1943, 114 and 115 being withdrawn after accidents in 1956 and 1954 respectively and 113 being first rebodied by Carde in 1967 and later demotored and modified at Casamozza in 1987 to act as a control trailer at Calvi, where it still was in 1998. 111-12 continued in use until withdrawn for scrap.

CFD Corse: Billard A210D prototype at Bastia. (BERNARD ROZE)

CFD Corse: Billard A150D of the original series, running with engine at the rear, at Barchetta. (BERNARD ROZE)

FCS Fiat bogie railcar in cream/red livery in store at Macomer. (F PUGH)

5. Early express railcars: Sardinia

FCS & FMS: bogie diesel-mechanical railcars by Fiat
FCS: ABDm 40.011-13 (previously ALn 38.01-03) Fiat of 1935
FMS: ALn 201-04 Fiat of 1935

The Sardinians were more cautious, only the FCS and FMS experimenting with small quantities of a fairly standardised Fiat design for fast passenger services from Macomer and Iglesias respectively. At this time Fiat and Piaggio were very impressed with the American Zephyr lightweight streamliners and many of their products copied the sloping, streamlined ends and light construction. Some, such as those for the Calabro-Lucane, even had ribbed stainless steel bodywork but the Sardinian ones for both lines had painted steel panels. They were double-ended cars with two 80hp Fiat engines driving one axle of each bogie (1A-A1) and seated 36 passengers. They were used intensively until the late 1950s but after delivery of later cars were gradually withdrawn and stored. FMS 201-02 were locally overhauled and partially rebuilt about 1966 with rather bulbous noses recalling an earlier design. All but one of the FMS ones were scrapped after closure, FMS ALn 203 being officially "preserved" but in fact derelict at Iglesias; all three of the FCS ones still existed, derelict, at Tirso in 2000.

6. Post-war developments: Corsica

a) CFC: bogie diesel-mechanical railcars by Ets Renault, Billancourt
CFC 201-08: Renault type ABH 6 of 1949-50

This series of eight, double-ended, 300hp cars was bought specifically to upgrade express services on the main line and was capable of pulling a trailer if required. The ABH design stemmed from 1936 and seated 44 in a single saloon, flanked at one end by a toilet compartment and an engine compartment with driving position and, at the other by a small baggage compartment with a screened-off driving position; a bar could be fitted. It was a large semi-streamlined vehicle with a prominent roof radiator at one end. The series was surprisingly long-lasting, all but 208, which was withdrawn about 1968, being modernised and reengined during CFTA operation. Latterly the survivors were relegated to the Calvi - l'Ile Rousse shuttles working as "rames reversibles" with demotored Billard cars 113 and 526 as control trailers. As at 2000 five were still in existence; 201/4/6 were technically serviceable, 202/7 being withdrawn at Bastia.

b) SACFS imports 1965-on

501-04	*Billard A80D rebodied by Carde of Bordeaux*
510-13	*Billard A80D converted to parcels cars*
524-26	*Billard A150D6 refurbished by Carde*
Various	*Billard A80D series: see below and Appendix 1*

The cars acquired by SACFS basically comprised two related series of Billard lightweight bogie railcars analagous to those built new for Corsica before the war. These series were:

A80D & A80D1: The smallest double-ended car in the Billard range, this design dated from 1937 and was a low-slung vehicle with, originally, an 80hp Willeme engine sited above the bogie at one end in the baggage compartment. The body was semi-streamlined with rounded ends and passenger accommodation comprised a central saloon with off-centre entrance lobby. There were two main variants, a 2.200m wide one for the CFD's Dordogne system and a 2.400m wide body for other CFD lines. The cars were popular with operators and travelled widely after their own systems closed, as noted below. SACFS appears virtually to have cornered the Billard market, except for ex Vivarais cars. Those it already owned (mainly from the CFD du Tarn operation) were taken to Carde of Bordeaux where they were rebuilt with modified suspension and a more rectangular body incorporating a toilet compartment; four were converted for parcels work. On closure of the PO Corrèze in 1970 it also acquired a collection of cars in original condition which were brought to Corsica but not altered, except that several were demotored for use as trailers. These were hardly used and, after CFTA took over, were officially withdrawn and piled in a long heap at Borgo where they remained until scrapped in the early 1980s.

A150D6: A postwar development of the A150D already in Corsica, these were very similar but had rather more angular bodywork with sloping ends. Three, already owned by SACFS, were sent to Carde for

CFC: Renault ABH railcar 202 in reserve, Bastia 1998. (AUTHOR)

SACFS: Billard A150D6 525 ex CFD du Tarn, ex TIV, with rebodied trailer at Vivario. (D TREVOR ROWE)

mechanical improvement and internal refurbishment, including a toilet compartment, but the bodies were not rebuilt. They were used intensively and survived into the CFTA period.

Historically, the saga of the railcars imported by the SACFS in the late 1960s is crazy enough to be described in some detail. In 1962, or thereabouts, the SACFS already had at its disposal an eclectic collection of six Billard cars rendered surplus by the closure of the CFD du Tarn as recorded in Chapter 3. Basically these comprised four wide (2.400m) A80D cars already in service on the Tarn and numbered 510-13 (511-13 were ex CFD d'Indre-et-Loire 511-13 and 510 was from the CFD's Yonne network where it had been 801; SACFS thoughtfully renumbered it 510 to simplify bookkeeping and converted all four to carry "messageries"). The other two were A150D6 150hp cars which had started life on the Tramways d'Ille et Vilaine as their Nos 27 and 26, been purchased by the VFIL for their Pas de Calais lines as 24-25 and then taken over by the SACFS who added a 5 cipher to tidy things up. They then acquired similar car TIV 21 which had been passed on to the Reseau Breton as X151 and happily renumbered it 526 to fit in. A further four cars currently in store after their lines closed were then acquired - possibly originally for the Tarn - these being narrow bodied X1-2 of the Tramways de la Corrèze (originally CFD Dordogne 606/10 then CGL/VFIL 606/10) and widebodied A80D2 cars ex 803 and 705 of the CFD's Seine-et-Marne lines. These were renumbered 501-04 (logical?) and those, plus 510-13 and 524-26 were sent off to Carde of Bordeaux for major body modernisation and improvements to the suspension. On closure of the POC Corrèze in 1970, that line's collection of Billards, which were in store, became available and were sent to Corsica without modernisation or renumbering. These, in turn, comprised four wide-bodied cars ex the CFD Réseau des Charentes et Deux Sevres (31/2; 311/2 later SNCF X241-44) which had passed successively to the CF du Blanc à Argent and then the POC; and five narrow bodied cars from the CFD's Dordogne system (601/2/5/9/12) which had gone straight to the POC as SNCF 245-46/49-51 These retained their SNCF numbers and appear to have hardly been used before the SACFS had to give up. Subsequently several, namely 242-43, 245 and 249, were converted to trailers; in general the 24X group appears to have been very little used. The rebuilt 5XX series were used for some years to provide fast services and shuttle trains on the Balagne but fell out of use as the new generations of CFD and Soulé cars appeared. For some years they remained in a "graveyard" at Borgo but by 1998 only 503, 513, 242 and 245 remained in a derelict state, while 526 had been rebuilt as a control trailer for the Ligne de Balagne in 1985 and was still in service as such.

c) CFTA transfer from CFTA Somme system
X 158: bogie diesel mechanical railcar by DE Dion Bouton, type 0C1

The CFTA brought over one of their own fleet rendered surplus by the closure of the Somme system in 1972. This was a De Dion double-ended car, one of two built originally for the CF des Côtes du Nord and then acquired by the CFTA's predecessors for their Réseau Breton operation. When that closed it went to the Somme and thence to Corsica where, after running suburban services out of Bastia, it was eventually scrapped. It was a large-capacity, lightweight vehicle with a single saloon and streamlined ends, powered by a 180hp Willeme motor and seating no less than 82 passengers.

d) Railcars introduced by CFTA and SNCF
CFC: bogie diesel-mechanical railcars by CFD Montmirail
2001-05 CFD of 1975-76 type 1200.
5001-02 CFD of 1982/3, type 5000

The CFD 1200 series railcars were developments of an initial design for the CF de Provence. They are boxy vehicles with faceted ends and equipped with two underfloor 165hp engines driving through CFD's patented Asynchro transmission. Accommodation is in two saloons with views past the driver and separated by a small central baggage compartment and a toilet cabinet; Indeed three were actually delivered with 1st and 2nd class seating and numbered X1201/2/4, the others being X2003/5 from the start. All were subsequently converted to 2nd class configuration, seating 44, and numbered accordingly. From the mid-1990s on they have successively been modernised at the Casamozza Works. All are currently in existence though they have a tendency to catch fire. They can run in multiple and tend to be used mainly on the Calvi services.

The two 5000 series cars delivered in 1982/3 are an improved version of the 1200 series, with very similar appearance and accommodation but with a total of 480hp. As at 2001 they were both in service on subsidiary work.

CFC: CFD 5XXX series railcar on turntable, Bastia. (AUTHOR)

FdS: rebodied DE railcar in modern livery, Macomer 2001. (AUTHOR)

7. Post war developments: Sardinia

a) BB diesel electric railcars by Tecnomasio Italiano Brown Boveri (TIBB)
*FCS: ADe 01 -20, TIBB 5923-42 of 1957**
FMS: ADe 301-06, TIBB 6145-50 of 1959/60

These two very similar series of railcars were built by TIBB from a design for the FCS - the FMS ones differed mainly in having a slightly higher gear ratio. Both series were semi-streamlined, double-ended cars with two 165hp underfloor Fiat diesel engines driving four TIBB 44kw motors powering all axles and were capable of running on one engine; air brakes were fitted. Seating was for 15 1st class and 40 2nd class passengers and they could tow a matching trailer (qv). On closure of the FMS, its cars were reallocated to the ex-FCS lines and the combined class is divided between Cagliari and Macomer as required. They run most non-peak time services (and some of those too, in various motor-trailer combinations) and over the past few years have been undergoing a complete rebodying programme with new Licarbus monocoque bodies on the old running gear. The new bodies, largely panelled in fibreglass, are very similar to the originals but with improved windows and are all one class although the two-saloon format is maintained. The main visual difference is that rebodied vehicles have two-part windows.

* *Nine of these have works numbers duplicating those in diesel electric locomotives for FCS/SFS. Presumably someone made an error at the TIBB Works.*

b) SFS: BB diesel mechanical railcars by Fiat of Turin
SFS: ADm 51-61 Fiat of 1957

These were built for the slightly easier grades of the SFS and are a diesel-mechanical equivalent of the FCS machines – very similar in dimensions, capacity and appearance but some 4 tonnes lighter in unladen weight and were built with 150hp engines; these appear now to have been replaced with standard 165hp ones and the class is undergoing rebodying by Licarbus. The main visual difference from the diesel-electrics is the absence of roof housings for electrical equipment.

FdS: interior of rebodied railcar, Macomer. (AUTHOR)

FdS: Modern Ferrosud DE railcar of series ADe 91-98, Macomer 2001. (AUTHOR)

8. Modern variations on a theme: both islands

Both island systems have ordered really modern cars within the last ten years or so, and, oddly, enough, with very similar characteristics and in much the same quantity.

a) *Corsica: CFC: bogie diesel-mechanical railcars by Soulé/CFD*
   CFC X97051-55 Soule of 1989/92
   CFC X97056-57 CFD/Soule of 1997

This new generation of railcars was designed and built by Soulé of Bordeaux who have since been taken over by CFD. Each car has two diesel engines (2x240hp for the first five, 2x260hp Cummins for the others) and is designed to pull a matching control trailer of class XR97XX when required. The railcar has a driving position at each end screened off from the entrance lobby which is also used for luggage. At one end is a toilet compartment and a 20 seat saloon separated from a 24 seat saloon by a short passage flanked by equipment cabinets. The cars can operate alone or in multiple with various motor/trailer combinations. The two most recent are fitted with upgraded seating to TER standard.

b) *Sardinia: FdS: BB diesel-electric railcars by ABB Tecnomasio & Ferrosud*
   FdS ADe 91-98 ABB/Tecnomasio of 1995-96

This set of railcars is to a design pioneered by Ferrosud for the Calabro-Lucane's Bari network (now Appulo-Lucane) and is said to have been designed for conversion to straight electric if the Cagliari suburban electrification ever materialised. In general the layout is similar to that of the earlier cars but the bodywork is more angular. They have two Fiat 165hp diesel engines driving both bogies through four ABB 70kw motors. They are used on all three systems as required.

9. FCS General manager's saloon motor car

Restored at Monserrato museum is the rail-mounted saloon motor car formerly used by the FCS general manager; this is a 1928 two-door saloon of Fiat type 509A and, since it was not on inventory in 1933, was presumably bought second-hand.

FCS: General manager's inspection car, as restored, at Monserrato museum 2001. (AUTHOR)

10. A note on liveries

In Corsica, the CFD standard livery was a maroon shade below the waist with grey upper body and roof and this was retained well into the 1950s. The SACFS, and after them the CFTA, changed to the almost standard red below and cream above the waist, some Renaults in particular having red roofs. Some vehicles were subsequently painted in a light gloss grey with dark maroon panels and trim, and this has now been largely replaced by the CFC corporate livery – off-white base with elaborate blue trim and with the ownership displayed in full in blue on the side panels.

In Sardinia, the original railbuses were brown with grey or silvered roofs and the Fiat cars appear originally to have been silver. The FCS post-war cars were cream with red trim, the SFS ones beige with red trim. FdS has adopted a fairly elaborate corporate livery for railcars, basically grey with white upper panels and green, black and yellow trim, but not all have been repainted.

Soulé railcar 97055 at Ajaccio in modern livery. (AUTHOR)

CHAPTER 8
Passenger rolling stock

1. Introduction

Systems in both islands took very similar approaches to the provision of passenger rolling stock but with interesting differences in detail. In Sardinia the SFSS initially plumped for a mixture of four-wheeled and bogie saloon coaches with open end balconies; the CFD in Corsica had the same admixture of four-wheeled and bogie stock but initially kept firmly to side-door compartment vehicles with the occasional larger saloon-compartment incorporated in the general structure. It was not until 1920 that it delivered the first of a series of handsome metal-clad vestibuled bogie vehicles which eventually took over most main line workings. In Sardinia, the SFSS was buying open-balconied stock as late as 1913 but The FCS in 1914-15 settled on vestibuled bogie coaches with American-style semi-domed roofs. This pattern was later followed by the combined SFSS/FCS team, and both SFS and, later, the FCS bought neat metal-clad vestibuled saloons, most of which have survived to this day. There are few details of FMS stock but it is recorded as including both four-wheeled and bogie vehicles which is surprising given the late date; photographs show them as conventional wood-clad, end balcony saloons and brake coaches with deep-cambered roofs. The relevant statistics for typical years are shown in the text:

Company	*1933*		*1981*		*2000*	
	4-w	*bogie*	*4w*	*bogie*	*4w*	*bogie*
CFD	12	56	-	-	-	-
FCS/SFSS	69	52		41 in all	-	15+4 restored?
SFS	3	28	-	28	-	28
FMS	10	5	-	-	-	-

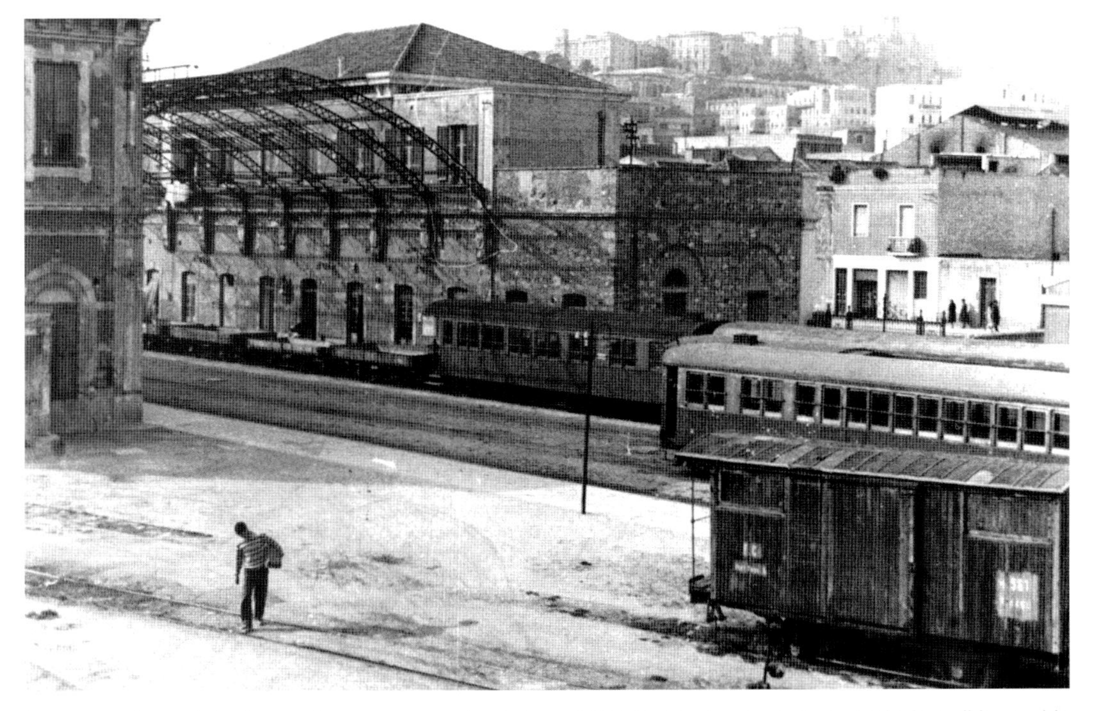

Coaches at the old Cagliari station: on the rear track is an SFSS Bauchiero composite in original condition and in front of it an FCS Breda-built composite. (MUSEO FERROVIE, CAGLIARI)

CFD 7-compartment side-door bogie coach; this is on the Vivarais but is identical to later Corsican ones. (AUTHOR)

2. Corsica: Coaching stock

The original equipment comprised a mixture of bogie and four-wheeled coaches, the latter being used mainly as reinforcement when needed. The 4-wheelers were a mixed bag - two dissimilar saloons, one with centrally placed side doors and one with an end-balcony body that included a smoking section; four, 3-compartment 1st/2nd composites and six, 4-compartment 3rd class. These two latter groups were side-door compartment vehicles, the 3rd class having windows in the doors only. They were followed by a series of bogie side-door compartment coaches on a standard 9540mm underframe and bodyshell but with varying internal arrangements; they included 1/2/3/Luggage; 1/2/3; 2/3; and all third. The original allocations and numbering were (the central line still being in two separated portions):

Bastia - Corte	4w:	2 saloons; ABv1-2; Cv1-2
	bogie	ABCv 1-4; ABCDfv 1-4
East coast	4w:	Cv3-4
	bogie	ABCv 5-8; ABCDv 5-7
Ajaccio	4w:	ABv3-4; Cv5-6
	bogie:	ABCv 9-15

later purchases 1889-91 were entirely of bogie vehicles, as under:

Calvi branch	bogie:	ABCv 16-17; CCCv 1-3
Bastia-Ajaccio	bogie:	ABCv 29-31; CCCv 16-19

These were all side-door compartment coaches with panelled bodies on a metal underframe but internal arrangements differed slightly; the original 3rd class bogie vehicles had six doors a side as shown in the drawing, later ones had seven identical compartments.

From 1920-on, the CFD started providing a modern design which was used also on their Réseau du Vivarais where survivors can still be seen. These were metal-clad, vestibuled vehicles designed for the long distance trains and with elaborate internal arrangements. They eventually comprised eleven 1st/2nd composites and nine all-thirds. The composites incorporated a deluxe saloon section, a washroom, one 1st class and two 2nd class compartments opening from a side corridor and an odd 2nd class compartment with seating arranged longitudinally (because of the bodyshell dimensions). The all-thirds had a central saloon with transverse seating each side of a gangway and, again, a compartment at each end with longitudinal seating. These were accessed from the vestibule and side corridors led to the main saloon; a lavatory was sited between this and one of the end-compartments. Various modifications took place during their careers, all but two of the composites being converted either to 2nd/3rd class (BCC) or being downgraded to have only one 1st class compartment after arrival of the express railcars. Later some vehicles incorporated postal and baggage sections, one was temporarily converted to a restaurant car and another fitted up for couchettes. From 1954, survivors were adapted as trailers for the Renault railcars and from 1958-on most were converted to flat wagons.

On delivery, these coaches were allocated and numbered as follows: (gaps are accounted for by Vivarais orders).

		AABifwy	*CCCifwy*
Bastia-Ajaccio:	1920	1601-04	1651-54
Calvi branch	1927	1605-08	1655-56
East coast	1932	1613-15	1663-66

During their lives many of the composites were modified to serve different roles. The main changes up to 1954 were:

1601/2	–	BCCifwy
1603/5	–	BCPifwy (postal compartment)
1604	–	SABifwy then BCCifwy
1606	–	BBCifwy
1607/8/13	–	ABBifwy
1615	–	convertible couchettes

After that the survivors were adapted as required by their new roles. Most became railcar trailers for the Renault cars, as under:

Passenger trailers: 1601-04, 1605, 1606, 1608, 1666
Passengers and postal: 1607, 1663-64
Sleeping van for PW gangs: 1656

After 1958, 1613 and 1652 were stripped of their bodies and reincarnated as tank wagons; twenty other coaches of all series were converted to flat wagons as Pft 1-20.

3. Sardinia: coaching stock

a) SFSS: 4w coaches

SFSS: Some details are available from inventories and archives – one problem being that the SFSS naturally abbreviated the names of its suppliers to save space and some are not easily identifiable. The company started with no less than 75, 4-wheelers, provided by the Officine Cottrau di Castellammare di Stabia (Castellammare) and in 1933 these still comprised 69 vehicles, split between the four separate systems – Cagliari; Macomer; Tempio and Alghero. In detail, they then included:

Qty:	*Type*	*No.*
4	servicio	S1,F2,G3,H4*
1	saloon	16
9	1st class	12-15;17-20
15	1st/3rd class	31/2/4/9; 40/1/2/4/6/7/8/9; 54-56
40	3rd class	101-06; 108-29; 131-38; 140/1/3/4

** probably converted from ordinary coaches*

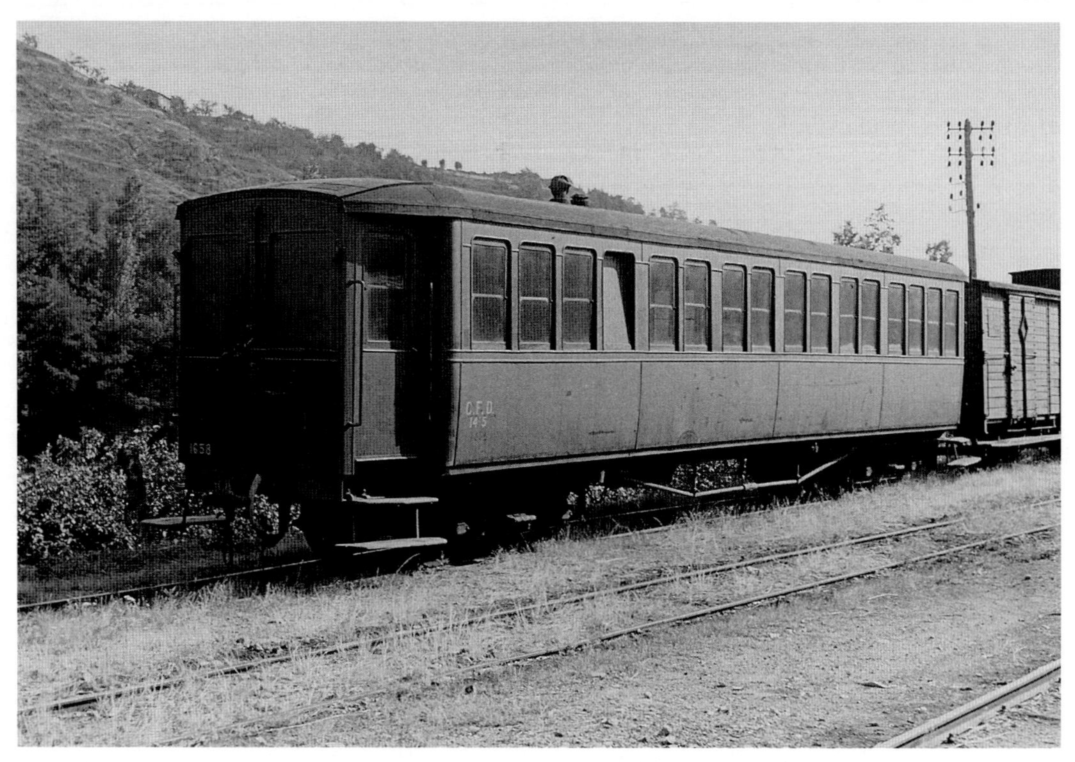

CFD 3rd class saloon coach of the De Dietrich type. This is on the Vivarais but is similar to those in Corsica. (AUTHOR)

CFD: Later pattern composite coach converted to 2nd/3rd/postal configuration. (BERNARD ROZE)

Ex SFSS 4-wheeled service coach S1 at Cagliari in 1958. (H LUFF)

From photographs of survivors in the 1950s, they were simple, end-balcony saloons, the 3rd class having only four windows a side. From a photograph of S1, the service coaches were ex-3rd class vehicles, which may explain the gaps in the 3rd class numbering.

b) SFSS: bogie coaches

By the early 1890s, when the longer lines were complete, the company had also acquired an initial series of bogie coaches from Miani-Silvestri & Co of Milan. The existing SFSS drawing shows a 1/2/3 composite and the company manufactured a complete range on a standard bodyshell so it is not certain what the original order comprised although a total of 30 is recorded. By 1933, when 2nd class had been generally abolished in Europe on minor railways the fleet comprised:

Qty:	*Type*	*No.*	*Notes*
1	saloon	1	
1	1st	201	
15	1st/3rd	221-35	some discrepancies in recording*
13	3rd	251-263	

* *examination of a 1933 inventory suggests they were originally in a 2X series and later partly renumbered.*

From drawings and photographs, these were fairly primitive-looking end-balcony saloon vehicles with matchboarded sides and with louvre ventilators above the windows. Interestingly, structural integrity was assured by a series of long coach-bolts running diagonally from top of the waist rail to bottom of the wooden solebar; these clearly were not entirely successful since some vehicles latterly had conventional truss-rods. The bogies were crude, wooden affairs without compensation. Internally the superior class(es) had compartments with side corridors or passages, the 3rd class having transverse seating in an open saloon. Some were still in use in the 1950s, most with the ventilators suppressed and with horizontal planking above the windows, and one 3rd class example survived at Monserrato depot, earmarked for preservation, in 2001. In later years all appear to have been downgraded to 2nd (nee 3rd) class but photographs clearly show ex-

Ex SFSS: Rebuilt Bauchiero composite 412 with luggage section inserted in one bay of 1st class portion. Derelict Monserrato, 1999. (AUTHOR)

Typical restored Bauchiero coach in use for charter work, 1999. (AUTHOR)

tricomposites in this condition; it seems likely that the composites were originally 1/2/3rd class demoted to 1/3 after the genuine 2nd class was discontinued and finally downgraded to 3rd when newer composites (see below) arrived.

In 1913-14, Bauchiero SA delivered a homogeneous set of 12 composite vehicles, numbered AACC 401-12. From the maker's drawing, these were all 13m-long, elegant coaches with balcony ends and wooden bodies with vertical strip cladding and elaborate brass fittings. Internally accommodation comprised a toilet compartment, two 1st class compartments with a side corridor, a single third class saloon and a second toilet cubicle. Several of these have recently been restored to what is said to be near-original condition for charter work but are now all single class; three (labelled as CC 401/6/7) are fitted out as wooden seated thirds with transverse seating for 50 in bays in a single saloon, the fourth (AACC 404) has one fewer bay of seats in a single saloon, upholstered in red plush. The restorees have a lot of ornamental brasswork and some have a rudimentary clerestory which is not original. Some of the original series were clearly substantially rebuilt during their service since there exist several derelict examples with metal cladding on the original ossature and with the balconies enclosed. At least one has had a short luggage section, with roller blind doors, installed and it seems possible that some were downgraded to 3rd class latterly.

The SFSS had the common habit of doubling letter codes for bogie vehicles so their numbers would actually be prefixed (eg) AACC for a composite and CC for 3rd class.

c) FCS original bogie coaches

The FCS, for its original lines in 1914, acquired a homogeneous set of high-quality bogie coaches from Ernesto Breda of Milan. These comprised:

Qty.	*Type*	*No.*	*Notes*
6	1st/3rd	ACf 11-16	
6	3rd	Cf 31-36	

The maker's drawings show them as elegant, vestibuled vehicles with semi-domed ends to a well-cambered roof and with vertical strip cladding on a wooden body shell. Accommodation in the composites

FCS: one of the last original FCS Breda-built 3rd class coaches derelict at Tirso, 1999. (AUTHOR)

comprised a two-bay 1st class section with its own toilet compartment and a five-bay 3rd class saloon with a separate toilet; the two classes were divided by the toilet compartments and by a side passage with no less than three doors. The 3rd class coaches had two equal-sized open saloons separated by a toilet compartment with side passage. Various survivors were still extant derelict in 1999 and, as with the Bauchiero vehicles, some at least had been reclad in metal with simplified exteriors.

d) FCS later additions

At an undetermined date, probably the early 1930s, OM Reggiane of Reggio Emilia delivered a further set of bogie coaches. If the 1933 inventory is accurate these comprised eight vehicles, either all 1sts or 1st/3rds, or possibly a mixture, numbered 500-07. These have not been definitely identified but were probably wooden-bodied vestibuled vehicles based on the FCS design (qv) though somewhat shorter and, if so, several examples with luggage sections inserted still exist derelict at various places; these certainly match three luggage vans known to have been built by Reggiane.

Finally, the FCS acquired a substantial set of metal-bodied, vestibuled, bogie coaches which are still in use in 2001. The writer has not been able to discover either the maker or date but they are said to have been acquired second-hand from the Ferrovie Circumvesuviana of Naples in 1970 and refurbished by Officine Casaralta before delivery. They are numbered in a V20.9XX series with numbers between 901 and 945; these appear to allow originally for separate number series (91X 1/3; 92X 1/luggage/3rd; 93X, 94X 3rd) and the total quantity is 16. They once clearly included 1st/3rd composites and all-3rds but the working examples are now all 3rds, with internal accommodation in a single, upgraded saloon with a toilet compartment at one end; several ex-composites exist, one or two having a small luggage section with roll-down doors inserted between 1st and 3rd class. They have Westinghouse airbrakes and roller-bearing axleboxes.

Original liveries are not known but latterly both SFSS and FCS trailer stock was painted in dual colours, dark brown below the waist and a light buff above it. The FdS has repainted the modern coaches in blue below the waist and grey above.

FCS: Former composites with inserted luggage portions, derelict at Monserrato. These are tentatively identified as from Reggiane series AACC 500-07. (AUTHOR)

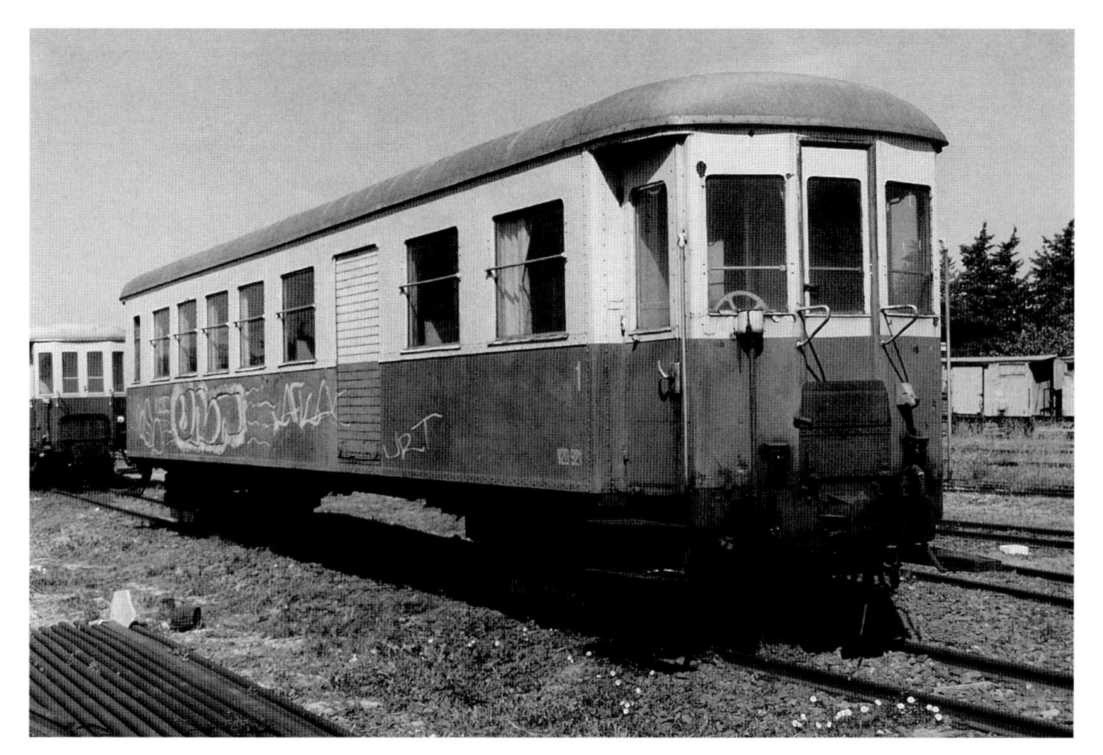

FCS modernisation: former 1st/luggage/3rd coach V20.921 in open store, Monserrato 1999. (AUTHOR)

FCS modernisation: 3rd class coach of the same batch in daily use, Macomer. (AUTHOR)

Interior of one of the coaches at Macomer, 2001. (AUTHOR)

e) SFS bogie coaches

Coming late on the scene, the SFS bought a matched set of bogie coaches with a standard bodyshell from Ernesto Breda of Milan. These were metal-clad, vestibuled saloon vehicles with wood interior trim and included some handsome composites with twin saloons divided by lavatories - one for each class; all-thirds with a lavatory compartment in the centre; third-luggage with sliding doors to the luggage section and a separate vestibule or office for the guard; and, probably, two full-luggage vans (at least there are currently two such vehicles although they may possibly be conversions).

From current numbering, which matches the quantity declared in official records, these comprised:

Qty.	*Type*	*Number*	*Notes*
9	1st/3rd composite	AC 1-9	downgraded to single class
10	3rd class	C 21-30	
7	3rd/luggage	CDU 51-57	
2	full luggage vans.	D 1-2	

In recent years 1st class has been withdrawn and at least one of the composites has been refurbished with modern drop-sash metal-framed windows in the original apertures and with modern railcar-type upholstered seating; a single toilet is placed between the two saloons which have a connecting side passage as with the 3rd class vehicles. Two third class coaches have been smartened up for charter-train work (C28-29) but not otherwise altered. Most of the remainder are currently (2001) in store at Sassari in various stages of dilapidation but CDU 57 has been transferred to Macomer, repainted in blue/grey and used as a works vehicle while CDU 51, with windows plated up, and van D2 are at Monserrato depot. D1 is based at Tempio.

SFS: A rake of coaches in almost original condition, 1958. (H LUFF)

SFS: 3rd class bogie coach as built and former composite coach AC1 refurbished as a single class vehicle with new cladding and windows, Sassari 1999. (AUTHOR)

SFS: Brake/3rd coach CDU 57, in use as a service vehicle at Macomer FdS, 2001. (AUTHOR)

FMS: Brake/3rd and 3rd class coaches in a train, Santadi, 1958. (H LUFF)

f) FMS: 4w and bogie coaches

Virtually no records are currently available of FMS passenger stock but it was noted as built by Carminati & Toselli of Milan and including ten 4-wheeled and five bogie coaches, the former being mainly for mine-workers' trains. Photographs show conventional balcony-ended vehicles with a deep-cambered roof and two-colour livery and the series includes some luggage/3rd coaches of typical Carminati & Toselli pattern. Survivors were all scrapped on closure. It is said that there were also sets of cruder four-wheelers for mineworkers' trains.

4. Purpose-built railcar trailers

Again, the French and Italian approaches were different. In Corsica Billard supplied some of their standard bogie trailers based on the A80D bodyshell and especially designed to be towed by the various types of railcar but with no control position (ie they had to be run round or shunted to the rear at each change of direction). Other than those, the system collected over the years a miscellaneous group of demotored railcars or rebodied chassis and these sufficed until the X9705X class came with matching control trailers. Sardinia ignored the problem until after the war but all types of railcar since 1957 have been provided with matching control trailers for reversible operation.

5. Corsica: trailers

a) CFC: bogie railcar trailers by Billard of Tours
CFD: 1-8 Billard Type R 210, 801-08 of 1938
SACFS: 210-12 Billard type R210, 816/8 of 1938; Nk/1949

These were purpose-designed trailers, originally for the A210D and then for the Billard A80D and A150D series and were built on a body shell matching the A80D railcar design. They had no driving positions, accommodation comprising: a large full-width luggage section over one bogie and accessed by twin folding doors; a section incorporating a half-width toilet and the "autonomous heating boiler"; transverse seating for 23-27, with an entrance vestibule in the centre. The last three seats were against the

CFC: original Billard R210 passenger trailers at Bastia, 1958. (H LUFF)

SACFS: Billard trailer 210 rebuilt on an extended frame by Carde of Bordeaux. (AUTHOR)

car end, facing inward. These cars were widely used, some being converted for parcels use by SACFS. In 2000 four, 7, 210-12, were still in book stock.

b) CFC: 104-05, bogie railcar trailers by Ets Garnero et Carros of Nice on railcar chassis

These are long, maximum capacity vehicles using the chassis, and possibly some of the ossature, from A210D railcars 105/6. They seat 44 passengers.

c) CFC: XR97XX class. bogie control trailers by Soulé of Bordeaux

These utilise the same basic body shell as the X 9705X series railcars and are designed to run with them. From the "outer" end accommodation comprises: a half-width cab for the driver with luggage space alongside; an entrance lobby; a half-width toilet; two saloons for 22 (smoking) and 32 (non-smoking) passengers; entrance lobby; full width luggage space. There is no intercommunication door.

d) Conversions from railcars

One should probably mention here the two ex-A150D railcars 113 and 526 which have been demotorised and partly rebodied to serve as control trailers for the Renault ABH cars on the Calvi - l'Ile Rousse shuttles; they retain their old numbers but are not easily recognisable as such. (see Chapter 7 for history)

e) CFC: bogie parcels trailers, various
SACFS: 242/3/6/9 ex Billard type A80D & A80D1
SACFS: 20-21 purpose-built parcels trailers by Billard of Tours

The SACFS, as noted in Chapter 3, converted four former railcars into parcels trailers. These retained the original bodyshell but had some windows blanked off and a sliding door fitted in each side in place of the original. Two, 242/3, were still in existence in 2000.

The other two vehicles were purpose-built with wooden van-type bodies for the CFD's Indre-et-Loire system, moving from there to the Vivarais and thence to Corsica in 1970. They appear to have been scrapped.

CFC: large capacity trailer R104, built on the chassis of a Billard A210D railcar, penultimate livery. (AUTHOR)

CFC: CFD/Soulé trailer of the XR 97XX type, current livery. (AUTHOR)

CFC: trailer 113 rebuilt using the carcass of Billard railcar 113. (AUTHOR)

6. Sardinia: Trailers

a) FCS/SFS/FMS: bogie control trailers by Officine Meccanica della Stanga SpA, Padova & various makers
SFS: RPm 151-58, Fiat/Stanga of 1957 (to run with ADm 5X class)
FCS: RPe 101-10, TIBB/Stanga of 1957 (to run with ADe 0X class)
FMS: RPe 351-54, TIBB/Fiat/Stanga of 1959. (to run with ADe 30X class)

These three series are very similar except in the control equipment which was designed to mate with the appropriate railcar series. They have semi-streamlined bodyshells matching the railcars and were designed for 1st/2nd class (7x1st; 40x2nd) although most if not all working survivors are now 2nd class throughout. From one end accommodation comprised: driver's full-width compartment; luggage section with roller-blind doors; 2nd class saloon; entrance vestibule with toilet compartment; 1st class compartment. Some at least are being rebodied by Licarbus SARL under the modernisation programme but others have been dumped.

b) FdS: bogie control trailers by Ferrosud/Breda & ABB Tecnomasio
FdS: RDe 901-05; Ferrosud of 1995-96

These are a modernised version of the above based on the ADe 9X series bodyshell and are said to be air conditioned although they have openable windows. As with the others they have an off-centre entrance lobby giving access to a large saloon and a small one so may have been intended for dual class use; the small saloon incorporates the section used for luggage in other series. Currently they seat 58 2nd class passengers, with two extra flap seats in the vestibule.

7. Brake/luggage vans

All brake/luggage vans were 4-wheeled in both islands and initially served the same purpose: with no continuous brakes, trains depended largely on having a specialised brake vehicle at the rear and neither the SFSS nor the FCS, nor, initially, the CFD in Corsica, provided space in their coaches for heavy luggage and small goods (messageries). The resultant vehicle was much the same everywhere, its main accommodation comprising a large compartment for cargo, sometimes with one or more livestock boxes with access from the outside for dogs and other small animals. The guard either had a corner of the main space or, in the "luxury" model, a separate compartment of his own with a desk at which he could do his paperwork. Handbrakes and, where appropriate, a brake valve were normally fitted, together with a stove for winter heating.

8. Corsica: luggage vans

The CFD provided two series of their standard four-wheeled brake/luggage vans which differed according to their period. The original set, Df 1-13; Df 20-24, were built by Ateliers de Marly and were typical late 19th century fourgons. They had all-enclosed wooden bodies with a single sliding door each side and the interior was one large space save for a full-width, half-height livestock box at one end; this had external access doors.

From 1915 on, the CFD provided their "new" variant as used on the Vivarais network. This was a long, wooden vehicle with two sliding doors each side and originally with a half-width cupola at one end and a separate guard's compartment. They were built by both Decauville and Ets De Dietrich and were numbered in the CFD's DDifv 26XX series: the Corsican ones are noted as 2618-21 and 2622-25, all by De Dietrich. They were used mainly on the express services.

9. Sardinia: luggage vans

The FMS and SFS had the advantage of continuous brakes from the start and appear to have used passenger/luggage coaches when luggage space was needed. Both the SFSS and FCS required brake vehicles to tail their trains and acquired a variety of vans for this purpose. From the few survivors there appear to have been four main series but the notes below must be taken as somewhat speculative.

FdS: rebodied trailer at Alghero S. Agustino. (AUTHOR)

a) Original SFSS stock

Built by Castellammare and Miani-Silvestri, these were numbered 301-321 in the 1933 inventory and no survivor has been identified, so their appearance is not known to the writer.

b) OM Reggiane 1905 for the SFSS

The most common surviving variety is a balcony-ended vehicle. This was a conventional guard's van with a luggage compartment and a separate section for the guard and the series was numbered from D322 to D330. D327 has been restored for use with charter trains and D325 and 330 were stored at Monserrato in 2001.

c) Ernesto Breda, Milan, for original FCS in 1914

This series of four, D 71-74, comprises fully enclosed wood-bodied vehicles with two separate internally-sliding doors each side, giving access to a luggage space and a separate guard's compartment. From observation they probably had deep-cambered roofs to match the FCS coaches but two, D72 and D74, have been rebuilt with flatter roofs on the same bodyshell. D71 survives, wheelless, in original condition at Monserrato.

d) OM Reggiane, date unknown but before 1933 for SFSS/FCS

This is a series of three vans, D 400-402. They are handsome fully-enclosed 4-wheeled vehicles with semi-domed ends to the deep-cambered roof and with vertical wood cladding. Two sets of sliding doors are fitted to each side and accommodation comprises a luggage space and a full-width compartment for the guard. Nos. D400 and D402 were serviceable at Macomer in 2001.

SFSS D 32X series luggage van as restored 1999. (AUTHOR)

FCS luggage van D71 in original? condition. (AUTHOR)

Van D72 of the same series as rebuilt. (AUTHOR)

Reggiane-built van D 400 for FCS as restored, Macomer. (AUTHOR)

10. Liveries

CFD vehicles were normally painted a medium grey with black fittings but, for some years postwar, at least some of the later series were in red and grey to match coaches and railcars. Old photographs suggest that FCS passenger vans (eg 400-03) were in the dual tone brown livery and the remainder in goods-stock grey. Currently ex FCS vehicles are grey except for 400-02 which are in the current blue and grey passenger stock livery.

CHAPTER 9
Goods rolling stock

1. Introduction

Goods rolling stock for metric narrow gauge lines was surprisingly similar all across western Europe. The vast majority of vehicles were four-wheeled, each company usually employing a standard underframe and dimensions which had the dual advantages of standardising loads and allowing easy rebuilds if needs changed. There appear to have been two major load categories, about 6 to 7 tonnes where axleloads were restricted and 10-tonnes otherwise. The typical goods vehicle, both in Corsica and in Sardinia, had laminated-spring running gear with oil or grease-lubricated axleboxes, a channel metal underframe and either a planked or metal body; the former was preferred as easier to maintain and alter. Vehicles might be totally unbraked, have a parking brake which was usually lever operated from one side, or a screw handbrake operable on the move from a seat, balcony or hut at one end. Those on lines with continuous braking were normally piped, only a small proportion actually being brake-equipped. Vacuumbraked vehicles normally had a small 'v' prefix, those with screwbrakes an 'f' prefix. Inevitably, goods stock is not so thoroughly recorded as motive power but general notes for the two islands are given below.

2. Corsica details

a) early stock

Between 1888 and 1900 the lines were steadily equipped with goods vehicles as needs expanded. Built to the early designs of the CFD and numbered in their original overall series (hence the gaps) these eventually totalled 69 vans, 65 open wagons and 74 lowsides of various types, some fitted with bolsters, together with three of the CFD's standard crane wagons. Continuous brakes were not fitted, so a large proportion of the stock had screw handbrakes. All had standard metal underframes with laminated-spring running gear, a

Not many people photograph stock: a portmanteau view of FMS equipment shows typical 3rd class and brake coaches plus the bare chassis of bogie coal container wagons. (JOSÉ BANAUDO)

wheelbase of 2.500m and a chassis length of either 5.000m or 5.500m; loading gauge was 2.200m as standard on the CFD's existing lines of Intérêt Local. They were theoretically allocated to specific concessions but in practice were used indiscriminately. The details of original stock were:

Goods vans: in the late 1880s the final all-purpose van so common on French light railways had not been finalised and the "standard" CFD goods van was a vertically planked vehicle with a single sliding door each side but no ventilation; braked vehicles had a hut raised above the roof at one end. Unusually for France, this meant that specialised livestock vans were provided, on the longer chassis and with horizontally planked sides having four oblong apertures under the eaves for ventilation; entry was via the usual sliding door on each side. Only the first order for goods vans (19-26) was unventilated.

Open wagons: These were standard vehicles of the period, with horizontally planked sides, twin hinged doors in each side and peaked ends; a fixed wooden bar ran from end to end to provide support for a tarpaulin and braked examples had an open seat overhanging the body at one end.

Lowside wagons: These were standard, wooden bodied wagons with single-plank sides arranged as twin drop-doors, while the bolster wagons had fixed sides with four stanchion sockets. Braked examples of both types had a brakesman's seat in one corner, overhanging the body as on the opens.

Crane trucks: These were the standard CFD four-wheeled crane of 4t lifting capacity with hand operated, steel jib and were built by Decauville.

Nomenclature was:

Type	*Letter*	*Running Numbers (original)*	*(supplements)*
livestock vans	E	12-17+	
goods vans:	F	19-26+; 47-54; 119-23	
ditto, braked:	Ff	7-16	17-31
open wagons:	G	61-76; 149-53	
ditto, braked:	Gf	1-20; 97-111	112-21
lowsides:	H	57-66; 92-95	
ditto, braked	Hf	21-30; 76-81	
bolsters:	I(J)	21-40; 71-85*	
ditto, braked:	If (Jf)	21-30*	
cranes:	"No."	3,6,9	

\+ *to F 12-17 and E 19-26 when reclassified by presence or absence of ventilation*

* *changed to J/Jf in 1894 to avoid confusion*

Various vehicles were modified and renumbered during their lives as was common, depending on requirements at any particular time.

b) Standard CFD stock

From 1902 onward, however, the CFD provided vans, open wagons and lowsides/bolsters to a design standard on all its later Intérêt Général systems. These utilised a standard metal frame with a wheelbase of 2.570m and a nominal chassis length of 5.500m. All had a nominal 10 tonne load capacity and were piped or fitted with vacuum brakes. The vans were dual purpose vehicles, having planked bodies with a central sliding door each side and four, vertically sliding metal ventilation flaps, two each side of the door; they were numbered in the CFD's K4XXX series, to a total of 40, of which ten had handbrakes operated from a brakesman's perch at one end. The wagons had metal-framed, planked bodies with straight ends and twin hinged doors a side and were fitted with a swinging tarpaulin bar. They were numbered in the G5XXX series and eventually totalled 185 units. Lowsides were either wood bodied (H6XXX) or metal-bodied (L8XXX) There were eventually thirty wooden ones, including twenty (Htv..) fitted with bolsters, and forty steel-bodied variants; the latter were specifically for the Porto Vecchio extension and came as part of a big reinforcement in 1930. Numbering was:

CFD standard 4-w ventilated goods van at Ajaccio. (AUTHOR)

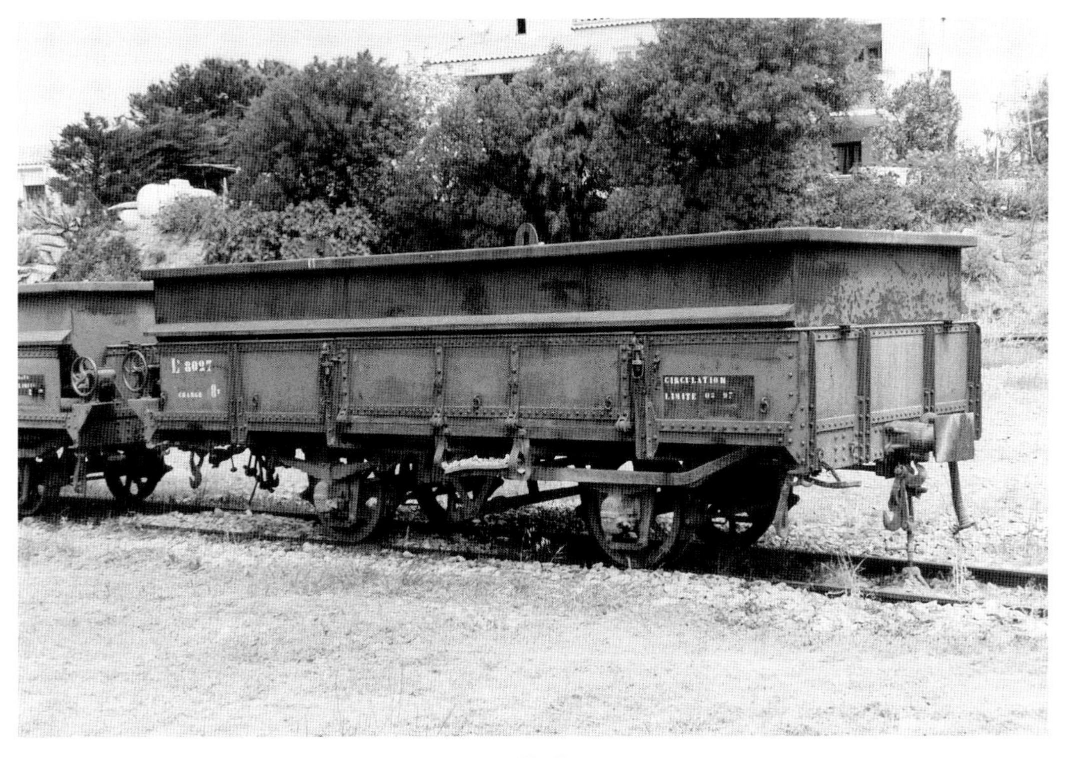

CFD steel-bodied lowside wagon converted for PW use; l'Ile Rousse. (AUTHOR)

Charge sur la traverse pivotante : 5 tonnes

CFD standard bolster wagon. (AUTHOR'S COLLECTION)

Type	*Letters*	*Running Numbers*
goods vans:	Kv	4605-24; 4640-49
ditto braked:	Kifv	4595-604
open wagons:	Gv	5541-90; 5731-80; 5801-80; 5916-21
lowsides:	Hv	6640-49
ditto, steel:	Lv	8001-40
bolsters:	Htv	6630-39; 6660-79

the coding was: f: manual brake, applicable while moving.
i: "intercirculation" - ie full-length footboard
t: traverse mobile
v: vacuum brake

c) Later additions and service vehicles

After 1954 especially, some bogie coaches were dismantled and their chassis fitted with platform bodies. A few of these are still in service for the car-carrying trains and for service use. About 1970, the SACFS brought in ten 4-wheeled hopper wagons purchased from the closing Voies Ferrées du Dauphiné, but they proved unsuitable; the main problems were wheel profiles, originally designed to allow use over tram tracks, and the fact that they had air brakes rather than vacuum. They were never modified and were stored, first at Casamozza and then at Ponte Nuovo until they were scrapped in the 1980s. Later some more hopper wagons were acquired in the 1990s from mines in the Orne for use in the abortive Corte heating project but these also had air brakes and, when the project failed, were laid aside.

In general PW work is carried out using former goods wagons and bogie coach underframes converted to flat wagons. There are also two Gleismar self-propelled permanent way vehicles equipped with light cranes and other devices, together with a single converted Billard car (513) which is currently out of use (see Chapter 7).

CFC: Former bogie coach underframe converted for car carrying. Note the neat use of a former loading bank as a dock. (AUTHOR)

3. Sardinia

No full original stocklists of the Sardinian systems are currently available so the following notes are compiled largely from a later inventory plus observation and photographs. At their peak, around 1936, the combined systems had approximately 820 goods vehicles which figure probably included luggage vans but not bogie coal container wagons for the FMS, said eventually to total 250. By 1981 the total was down to 590 and in 1996 the FdS is recorded as having 539 – most of which have now been sidelined or scrapped following the discontinuance of freight traffic.

For the most part, goods stock appears to have been four-wheeled and of a pattern also used by various mainland systems, notably the Calabrian-Lucanian system. Little detail is available about FMS stock but the other systems are better documented and the notes below refer to them.

Goods vans: The most common surviving type dates from SFSS days and has a wooden body with narrow, vertically planked cladding and with a single sliding door each side. Suppliers are noted as Miani-Silvestri, Casaralta and Castellammare. Most have rather crude ventilation arrangements consisting of narrow barred apertures under the eaves, covered when required by bottom-hinged planked flaps and Miani, at any rate, classed these as livestock wagons. Most are unbraked but there are examples with the frame extended at one end to carry a balcony and pillar handbrake; in this case the roof, which may be cambered or an inverted V, is extended over the balcony. Again, average dimensions are: length over chassis 5200mm (nominally 5230); wheelbase 2500mm; width 2190mm (nominally 2100) with a tare weight of between 4500kg and 5000kg and a load limit of 6 tonnes; the class letter prefix is M and vehicles of this type noted were numbered in the M5XX series. Casaralta provided 20 vacuum-fitted vehicles (Mcfv 1-20) which have not been positively identified. There are also examples of a different body with one or more vertically sliding flaps each side and unusual twin sliding doors; both metal and horizontally planked bodies of this type are in use and there are unbraked and braked variants, the latter having one end balcony. Those seen are numbered in the M1XX (braked) and M11X series (unbraked), have a tare weight of about 4900kg and

SFSS: Braked and unbraked Miani - Silvestri goods vans. (AUTHOR)

FdS: Braked, steel bodied goods van by Breda, probably for original FCS. (AUTHOR)

SFS: standard braked goods van Fv 120 at Tempio Pausania. (AUTHOR)

a 6-tonne load and are generally similar in dimensions to their earlier equivalents. Along with the metal-bodied wagons noted below they may represent a later purchase, possibly by the FCS. The metal-bodied ones were certainly built by Breda who supplied the original FCS and were originally Gf 101-10 and G 111-20, later reclassified as M. The SFS had its own distinctive van series of which several examples still exist, prefixed F or Fv and numbered in a 1XX series. They were probably built by Breda and have average dimensions of length 5500mm; 2300mm width and wheelbase 2800mm (unbraked version)

Open wagons: Two main varieties exist, those with wooden bodies and some metal-bodied equivalents; All have twin hinged doors in the centre of each side and have trapezoidal raised ends. Braked variants have a narrow hut at one end, supported on a frame extension and controlling a pillar handbrake. Standard letter prefix is N and all wooden ones seen were in the N7XX series (braked). Again inventories suggest that various makers were involved with original numbering running into the 800s; Breda is noted as providing 10 braked and 5 unbraked metal versions, probably for the FCS, and these were numbered Nf 301-10 and N 311-15. Basic dimensions and load were as for closed vans.

Lowsides: All those noted are of a type standard throughout Europe, with metal frames, laminated-spring running gear and platform bodies with low metal or plank dropsides and either fixed or drop ends. As with other varieties, both braked and unbraked versions exist. Standard letter prefix for both lowsides and bolsters is P and those seen were in the P9XX series (lowsides) and P10XX series (bolsters). There are also examples of a P 1-1X series built by Bauchiero. All are of similar dimensions to other goods vehicles. In general SFS vehicles appear to have two-piece wood dropsides, ex SFSS/FCS ones have single, full-length wood or metal dropsides.

Hopper wagons: These are of two main types. There exist a number of four-wheeled bottom-discharge hopper wagons with metal bodies on what appear to be standard chassis. More common are long wheelbase platform wagons with a central rectangular hopper compartment discharging sideways within the wheelbase. These are in general use for PW work and appear to have been rebuilt locally from other types of goods vehicles – numbering includes examples from the 1X and 8XX series, now prefixed "P" and underframe fittings suggest they once had side bracing bars.

FdS: Steel-bodied, braked open wagon by Breda, probably for original FCS. (AUTHOR)

FdS: Braked, steel-bodied lowside Pfb3, one of a batch built by Bauchiero (AUTHOR)

FdS: Purpose-built hopper wagon, of unidentified origin. (AUTHOR)

FdS: Braked, ballast hopper wagon on frame of former open wagon. (AUTHOR)

Tank wagons 1: CFC cylindrical tank wagon, possibly on a former wagon frame. (AUTHOR)

Tank wagons 2: FdS Mv4 rectangular tank, probably on a former wagon chassis. (AUTHOR)

FdS transporter bogies (rollbocke) at Macomer, 2001. (AUTHOR)

Service stock: as with all Italian minor lines operating through remote territory, substantial numbers of water tank wagons were provided to carry drinking water to outlying stations. A total of 13, by Castellammare and Miani-Silvestri plus one from Bauchiero, are recorded in 1933 with numbers scattered in the 9XX series (prefixed Pfc). From observation, these were mainly normal cylindrical tanks on the standard chassis. There were also at least a few rectangualar tanks on similar chassis but these appear to have been converted from goods vans or wagons; M4, based at Bortigiadas, is typical. The FCS also had several rail-mounted cranes, two being recorded in 1933 as U 1102-03. One was derelict at Olmedo in 2001, another is at Monserrato Museum.

Rollbocke: The Macomer – Nuoro line and industrial sidings at Sassari latterly used rollbocke, or transporter bogies, to convey standard gauge goods vehicles and several pairs, of conventional design, still exist at Macomer and Sassari. Various facilities exist also at Macomer and various stations.

Bogie vehicles: A single example of what may have been a larger series existed at Monserrato in 2001. This had a planked, lowside body with a tall brakehut at one end. Its origin is not known but it may be a rebuild on a coach underframe.

The FMS acquired a considerable number – 250 is the usual figure quoted – of bogie coal container wagons. These consisted of a long steel chassis carrying five metal coal tubs which could be lifted off at S.Antioco and discharged directly into ships. Some had brakesman's huts at one end.

As late as 1997-98 Cometi SA have delivered a series of heavy-duty platform wagons with pivoting stanchions, presumably for maintenance use, together with matching goods vans. They appear to see little use but each Division appears to have been allocated four bogie lowsides and two bogie goods vans, one of which has a guard's compartment. They are painted light grey with no visible identification. A typical vehicle is 12m long overall, with a chassis length of 10.500m, a tare weight of 15 tonnes and a 25 tonne load capacity.

FdS Cometi bogie lowside stanchion wagon. (AUTHOR)

FdS Cometi bogie vans; the nearest one included a guard's section. (AUTHOR)

Exact numbers of goods stock are difficult to ascertain at this late date unless or until the relevant stock inventories become available. PM Kalla Bishop gives the following figures for original stock of the FMS and SFS and of the combined FCS/SFSS in the mid 1930s:

	Vans	*Wagons**
FCS/SFSS	194	366
FMS	20	60 (later 250 bogie coal containers)
SFS	45	88

** KB says "open wagons" but this almost certainly includes bolsters and lowsides*

In 1981, after closures but with freight traffic still operating, the official overall figures for goods stock were:

FCS:	428
SFS:	162 (this would include ex FCS stock on the northern lines).

They suggest that very few additions, if any, took place during the intervening years. Currently, much stock has been scrapped and that remaining is either derelict, used for service purposes or "restored" for museum use.

Service vehicles: Most PW and rebuilding work is carried out using former goods vehicles either unchanged or modified for particular purposes.

CHAPTER 10
Infrastructure: Standard layouts and buildings; signalling; track; engineering works

1. Introduction

Because of the variety of companies involved, and the length of time the railways have been in existence, the notes in this chapter can give only a general picture; there are many exceptions to the norm. In addition, as is always the case with living railways, small modifications are constantly taking place. Except where noted, comments apply to both islands.

2. Station layouts

In general, continental railways recognised three categories of intermediate stopping place: stations, which would have full traffic facilities; compulsory halts (halte; fermata) which normally had passenger and parcels facilities plus, sometimes, a siding for wagonload goods; request stops (arret or facultatif; facultativo) which might have minimal passenger facilities in a convenient crossing-keeper's cottage or else consisted simply of a rail-level platform and a nameplaque. One category could easily metamorphose into another as traffic demand changed and, in recent years, there have also been modifications dictated by the need to economise (or alternatively, by availability of EU funding!). Appendix 2 tries to record some of the changes.

The "standard" layout for a station in western Europe provided a running loop away from the station building, plus a dead-end siding into a goods shed/loading dock; this enabled any station to be used for passing trains in an emergency. The French were slightly unusual in preferring what was, in effect, a loop siding next to the station building. This allowed easy shunting in both directions at some cost in passenger convenience but really required an extra loop for crossing trains, especially since the "siding" often incorporated a vehicle weighbridge. The original sections in Corsica, designed to normal "Intérêt Général" requirements, overcame this by separating goods facilities entirely but they were not typical. This section covers standard layouts and buildings. Examples of larger stations with special features in both islands are in Chapter 11.

a) Standard layouts: Corsica

The Corsican system had two distinct patterns of standard wayside station – those on the Bastia – Ajaccio line, and as far as Ghisonaccia on the east coast; and "the rest". The differences arose from the original planning.

Bastia – Ajaccio: This was designed by State engineers using the rules then in force for secondary railways of Intérêt Général. The standard intermediate station thus had a two-storey station building, usually with single storey wings; a separate toilet block; and a goods shed with raised loading dock completely separated from the station house. The running line had a loop with mid-platform and the goods shed a separate loop with headshunts as in standard gauge practice. Halts normally had a loop, possibly with an additional siding and a loading dock. Their station house tended to be smaller and there was rarely a goods shed.

Calvi and Porto Vecchio lines: These were designed from the start by the CFD and incorporated their standard practice. They normally had a two-storey station house with adjacent goods shed but the loop-siding often had an additional crossover and passing stations had an additional loop off the running line. A stopping place classed as a halt would have a small station house with separate toilets and a loop-siding, sometimes with a loading dock.

b) Standard layouts: Sardinia

The notes below are from observation: from photographs, it seems likely that the FMS and original FCS lines were very similar but it is now over twenty-five years since the last one was lifted and unless official layout diagrams are discovered it is hard to be certain. The companies differed in detail.

Standard pattern of intermediate stations & halts: Corsica and Sardinia

CORSICA: Ponts et Chaussées

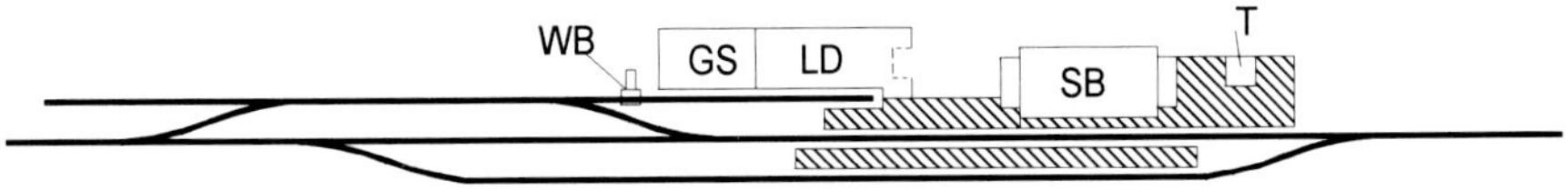

CORSICA: CFD

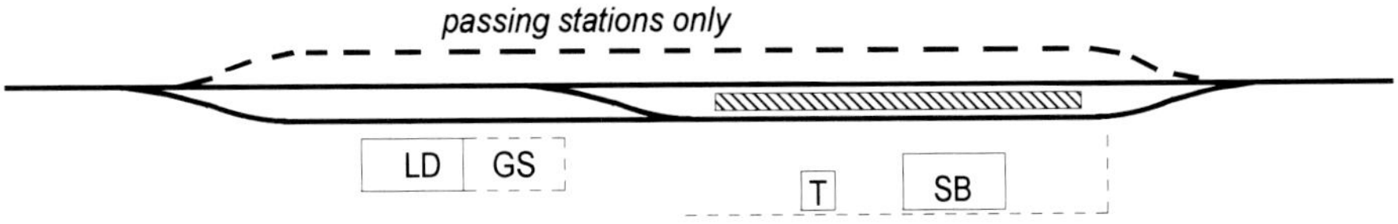

CORSICA: halts

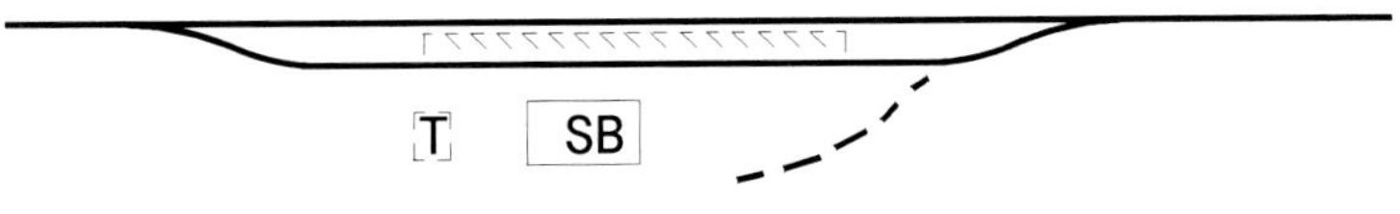

SARDINIA: SfSS/FCS

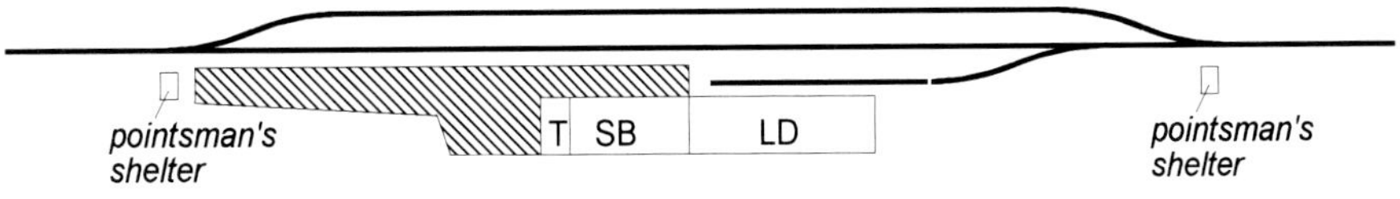

SARDINIA: SFS

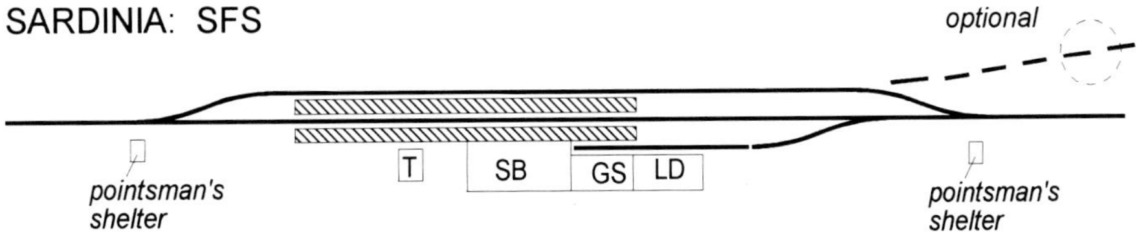

SARDINIA: all companies halts

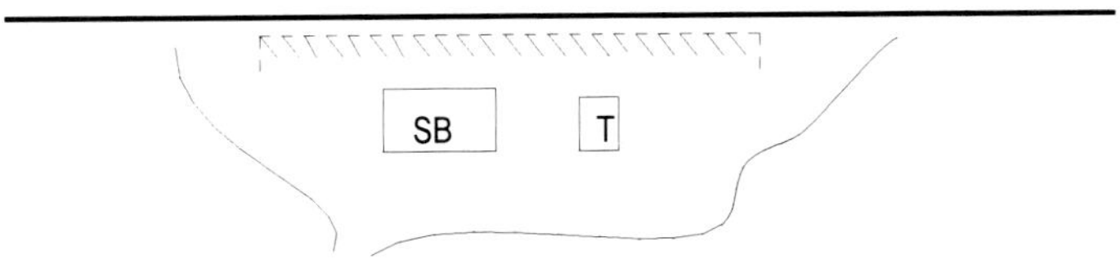

W J K Davies 6/01r

SFS: The standard intermediate stopping places are of two main types, with minor variations. One classed as a station (stazione) normally had a 2-storey station building with attached goods shed and loading dock, served by a siding off a loop; the siding normally had a loading gauge and, usually, a vehicle weighbridge. There was a separate toilet block. Some stations have a turntable on an extra spur; these are likely to have locomotive watering facilities. A halt (fermata) usually had a small 2 storey station building, sometimes with a siding and open loading dock. Sometimes these were purpose-built two-door houses with dedicated "railway" rooms, sometimes the standard ganger's cottage.

SFSS: A station had a 2-storey station building with loading dock, loop and siding, sometimes with turntable. Some have a separate toilet block but more usually the toilets are incorporated in one end of the main building. Some stations have, or had, a wooden goods shed or an awning over part of the loading dock; the traces can be seen on end walls of many station houses and the wooden structures were probably removed to save maintenance costs after freight traffic ceased. Some stations, particularly on the Cagliari – Mandas and Macomer – Nuoro lines, were modernised in the 1950s and these tend to have rather blockish brick and concrete buildings of the period with a matching goods shed attached. A halt had a small two-storey building, sometimes a crossing-keeper's cottage; occasionally a siding or a loop adjacent, particularly when in the middle of a long single track section.

FMS and original FCS: Not recorded.

3. Buildings

a) Lengthman's and crossing keeper's cottages

Most light railways operating through remote territory originally coped with general track surveillance and minor repairs by employing lengthmen who each oversaw a specific section of track ranging from 1km

Typical lengthman's cottage on most island lines. (AUTHOR)

The more elaborate double-fronted version favoured by the SFS. (AUTHOR)

up to about 5km depending on circumstances. Since the person clearly needed to live "on the job", particularly to carry out regular track inspections, the company normally supplied living accommodation on his "length". Typically, in both islands, this was a one up, one down brick or stone cottage, possibly with a kitchen annexe at the side or rear and with a combined store and outside toilet block nearby in a patch of garden. In Sardinia, the SFS, coming late on the scene, felt compelled to provide something slightly better for its Sassari – Palau line, hence the (almost) palatial double-fronted residences still existing, if generally derelict. It is noteworthy that, where possible, they are sited on a knoll or rise above the track so that, at some cost in extra walking, the occupant can survey a wide slice of his territory. Unusually they had quite elaborate coloured decoration to the frontage and traces of this are still visible.

Quite often, especially near towns, the lengthman's cottage was combined with that needed at level crossings of public roads; the theory was that the lengthman's wife or family could operate the crossing and even, occasionally, act as halt keeper if it became a designated stopping place. In most rural districts the crossing was either unprotected or guarded by removable chains when required, the keeper warning traffic with red and green flags. Latterly the more important crossings in both islands have been controlled by automatic flashing lights and, often, half or full-barriers.

b) Station houses

Away from main line junctions, most rural railways expected the station staff to live above the job and, in both Corsica and Sardinia, tended to provide a dual-purpose 2-storey building with railway facilities – possibly plus a kitchen – on the ground floor and living accommodation above, graded according to the station's importance. Toilet facilities were normally in a separate hut, either common with those for public use or in a lockable cubicle in the same building; the SFSS differed in preferring to site toilets within the main station building at one end. In the remoter parts it was common to have a well, or even a small water tower; otherwise water was brought regularly in a tank wagon. In most smaller stations, railway accommodation included a hall-cum-waiting area, a parcels and small-goods counter with a hand weighing

The "standard" stationhouse almost everywhere was a three-doored affair. This, at Tortoli, shows one of the few remaining wooden goods sheds of the SFSS. (AUTHOR)

machine; a booking office and an office for the stationmaster; the two latter could be combined and often contained the railway telephone and signalling apparatus. Larger stations might, in addition, have 1st and 3rd class waiting rooms and sometimes a bar or buffet; a lamproom was often tacked on to one end of the main building. Halts usually had no more than one room, at most, dedicated to operational purposes.

c) Goods facilities

Simplest goods facility was just an open loading bank, usually ramped at one end and placed beside a subsidiary track. Halts often had this, any perishable items being held by the station staff. Stations might have just this arrangement - the SFSS was very fond of it - or link it to a proper goods shed with a raised loading platform, often in a gated yard. The Corsican lines and the SFS favoured this latter arrangement. It was common for the goods shed to be adjacent to the main building for ease of use but important places might have it separated, in its own yard and often with an extra siding for wagonload traffic. It was common to site a simple weighbridge and a loading gauge either on the goods spur (Sardinia) or on the loop-siding (Corsica).

d) Locomotive and stock servicing

The Europeans did not favour running tank locomotives bunker first since they were often designed with a leading truck to ease progress round the curves - so the simplest facility was just provision of a turntable spur to allow for short workings. This was a peculiarly Sardinian feature, the Palau line, for example, having no less than 4 otherwise standard wayside stations thus equipped with turntables. The SFSS often used metal-decked turning plates which appear to have been designed to take the early 2-6-0Ts. The next stage up was to provide a one or two road locomotive shed (or, in the case of Calvi, a quarter roundhouse) together with coal and water and an inspection pit. Then came the serious locomotive changing point (eg Tempio Pausania or Corte) which had substantial first-line servicing facilities for a small fleet of locomotives. Finally there was the full-blown depot, with locomotive and stock sheds, workshops and

The FMS version of a station house, at Narcao. (JOSÉ BANAUDO)

The large-pattern of SFSS stationhouse, at Lanusei, showing toilets in the main building. (AUTHOR)

Simple locomotive facilities: taken from the shed entrance this shows a typical turntable and associated facilities. (AUTHOR)

A more substantial intermediate shed with water tower and coaling facilities, Seui, Sardinia. (AUTHOR)

various offices. In Corsica this was at Bastia, in Sardinia at Cagliari (SFSS/FCS); Sassari (SFS); and S. Giovanni Suergiu (FMS). The original FCS does not appear to have had a major depot but, given its ambitions, may have relied on the SFSS Works at Cagliari until it took them over!

4. Infrastructure

a) Track and engineering works

The original intention in Corsica was to provide the then "standard" track for metre gauge, consisting of 20kg/m Vignoles rail on wooden sleepers but the Ministerial Commission thought otherwise. Their recommendation, duly carried out everywhere except on the final stretch from Ghisonaccia to Porto Vecchio, was for 21.865kg/m bullhead rail "type anglais" and "as used on the London Metropolitan" and mounted in chairs on oak or pine sleepers; the Porto Vecchio stretch got Vignoles flat-bottom rail on metal sleepers and all subsequent relaying has been in flat-bottomed rail: currently most track, following extensive relaying by CFTA in the late 1970s, is 39kg/m on wood or concrete sleepers with modern rail fastenings.

In Sardinia, flatbottomed rail on wood sleepers was the norm from the beginning but in comparatively light track – generally 21kg/m in short 9m lengths on the early lines,laid on wood sleepers and often ballasted with local stone which lay in abundance in the surrounding fields. Both SFSS and the original FCS were laid to this standard and the FMS (23.5kg/m) and SFS (25kg/m) only marginally improved on it. The 1950s relaying was done mainly in 39kg/m rail in 18m lengths and the recent EU funded realignment has been in even heavier rail, largely on wood sleepers and fastened via bolts or clips on metal baseplates. The "category 2" lines have been generally resleepered and upgraded but not extensively relaid although considerable stockpiles of material (presumably bought with capital funding) are sited at intervals along the routes.

Engineering works, because of the terrain, were and are very impressive in both islands. For the record, Corsica at its peak had no less than 43 tunnels totalling some 13.2km and 76 bridges or viaducts (defined as greater than 10m span). In both islands, tunnels are like mountain tunnels everywhere, mainly rock lined with neat masonry portals. Original bridges and viaducts seem to be almost equally divided between multi-arch masonry structures and masonry-arched approaches to metal girder spans. For high or long spans

Girder bridge of SFSS pattern. (AUTHOR)

Viaducts 1: Small viaduct (over 10m) on the SFS line from Palau. (AUTHOR)

Viaducts 2: The Corsican equivalent, a typical masonry structure. (D TREVOR ROWE)

Two hits at once: A tall viaduct on the Bortigiadas spiral with a typical tunnel mouth beneath. (AUTHOR)

these are most commonly of the truss girder pattern, with the track either on top (favoured in Corsica) or running through the girders; some of the Sardinian examples of this type are said to have replaced lighter, bow girder structures during the 1950s modernisation. More recently, particularly on the Sardinian stretches financed by EU funding, much use has been made of modern reinforced-concrete structures which are sometimes of considerable length. These EU funded realignments have also led to considerable cuttings and embankments where once the line would have contour-chased with minimal earthworks.

b) Water tanks

The most common variety on all lines was a rectangular metal tank either on a stone base containing the pumping equipment or on a steel frame with a stone or brick pumphouse adjacent; a very few have cylindrical tanks, in one case horizontal. Water cranes might be attached to the tank or free-standing by the platforms. Because of length of section and availability of watercourses, the Sardinian mountain sections in particular also had a number of tanks sited in plain line away from stations.

A typical rectangular water tower with pump-house underneath and water crane. (AUTHOR)

A typical Sardinian disc signal, here allowing an FMS railcar to go through. (JOSÉ BANAUDO)

Modern signalling on the Alghero branch, clearly anticipating something more than the odd railcar crossing. (AUTHOR)

c) Signalling

Corsica used the standard signalling for lines of Intérêt Général, with pivoting discs or chequerboards as appropriate. So far as can be determined, in Sardinia the standard advance warning signal for stations was a pivoting metal disc with attached lamp to provide indication at night. Points were normally hand-operated by a member of station staff using flag signals, tiny shelters often being provided beside the point: these are frequently still in existence and even in use.

In Sardinia, as part of the 1950s modernisation, most of these discs were replaced by two-aspect colour lights and important stations had their point work connected to a central, chain-operated groundframe sited near the stationmaster's office. The colour light signals on mothballed lines appear to have been abandoned presumably because stations no longer have operational personnel. They are in use only on the commuter sections which are fully protected. Road crossings on many sections have been fully automated, with full or half-barriers and flashing lights, the train being warned by a flashing light centred on a yellow-black chequerboard.

Standard 1950s ground frame for a loop and siding station, Sardinia. (AUTHOR)

SFSS: Old 4-w coach, C46, at Macomer in dual tone brown, 1953. (H LUFF)

SFSS: Miani & Silvestri former tricomposite as 2nd class coach, Macomer, 1953. (H LUFF)

SFSS: Bauchiero 1st/3rd composite in fairly original condition, Macomer 1953. (H LUFF)

FMS: Bogie coal container wagons. (H LUFF)

A fairly elaborate masonry viaduct on the SFS line, with a diesel-hauled charter train; original pattern of locomotive.
(AUTHOR)

2-6-2T and train on a typical truss girder span on the Arbatax line, showing mountain scenery.
(AUTHOR)

Breda 2-6-0T No. 3 and train on a modern concrete viaduct. (AUTHOR)

A reminder of the olden days: A Cagliari bogie car on Route M pauses at the old FCS Monserrato station in 1966. (F PUGH)

Calvi terminus, as refurbished by SNCF, with a reversible shuttle at the platform. (AUTHOR)

Ajaccio terminus, with CFD/Soulé cars. (AUTHOR)

Archazena: A standard SFS layout, complete with decoration, as refurbished; for a mothballed line the track is of high quality. (AUTHOR)

Sorgono terminus: a large-type SFSS station building as restored for tourist use. (AUTHOR)

Orroli, on the Arbatax line, is a typical SFSS wayside station in a rural setting. (AUTHOR)

A 1950s rebuild of a station on the Nuoro line, with No. 5 at the platform. (AUTHOR)

Typical of the relationship between an island railway and its hill towns. 2-6-2T 402 brings a charter train into Lanusei beneath the serried ranks of dwellings. (DEREK PHILLIPS)

CHAPTER 11
Comparison of typical large stations in the two islands

To record all variant station descriptions is not possible in the space of this book but it may be of interest to compare typical ones in the different companies. To provide valid comparisons, they are listed by category.

1. Major termini: Bastia (Corsica) and Macomer (Sardinia)

Regrettably the original Cagliari terminus of the SFSS is long gone and does not appear to have been recorded in detail. The next best is probably Macomer on the central section since it has various things in common with Bastia – the Works area has been considerably revised; there is a long spur going off to a transhipment point even if that is a railway one rather than a harbour; it looks after a self-contained system.

In Corsica, Bastia was the original terminus of both the east coast and central lines and was also site of the main workshops and stock sheds. It was entered from a tunnel in a very steep hillface and, as built, the line led straight to no less than five parallel loop roads with the goods shed and loading dock on their eastern side. Immediately in front of the tunnel a facing point gave access to a five-road carriage shed, two roads of which were served by a traverser – and limited to 4w stock. A long loop off this access line served the big station building on the east of the site and also a triangle running across the station forecourt and linking to the harbour branch which ran down through the town. The locomotive running shed and the extensive workshops were off to the west and served by a long loop. At some time after the war, a temporary plastic "shed" resembling a huge garden cloche was erected in the eastern part of the site and served by sidings off the platform roads. In the late 1970s this layout was drastically altered when the whole north and east end of the site was sold off for urban development. The works yard was greatly truncated and reduced to the status of running shed and first line maintenance, the workshops being transferred to Casamozza.

Bastia in 1970 with the original layout. (D TREVOR ROWE)

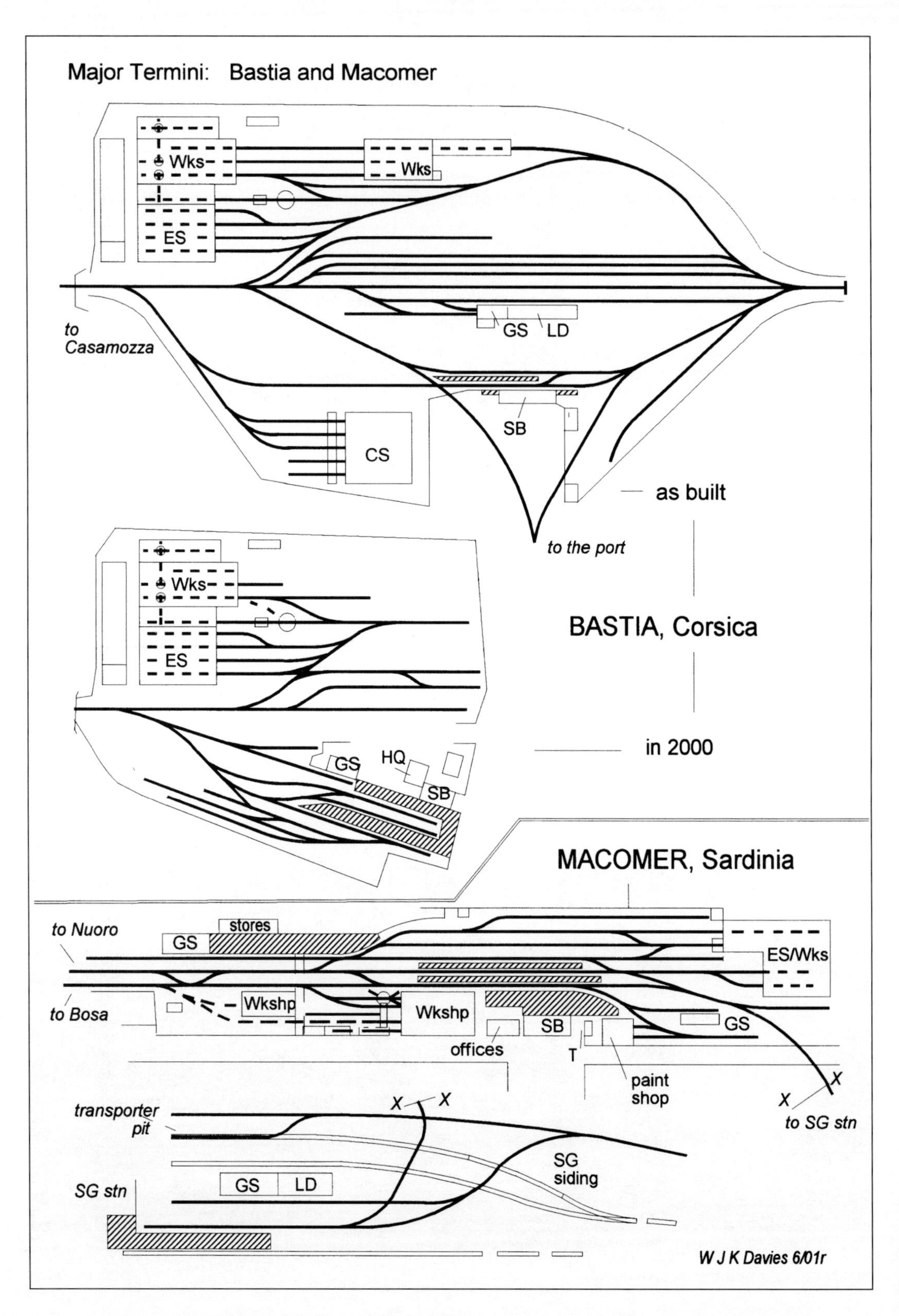
Major Termini: Bastia and Macomer
Wks
Wks
ES
to Casamozza
GS
LD
SB
CS
as built
to the port
BASTIA, Corsica
Wks
ES
GS
HQ
SB
in 2000
MACOMER, Sardinia
to Nuoro
stores
GS
ES/Wks
to Bosa
Wkshp
Wkshp
SB
GS
offices
T
paint shop
transporter pit
X
X
X
X
to SG stn
SG siding
GS
LD
SG stn
W J K Davies 6/01r

Bastia in 1998, after "urbanisation". (AUTHOR)

Aspects of Macomer (1): the modern stocksheds and goods shed; the link to the SG station curves off centre rear. (AUTHOR)

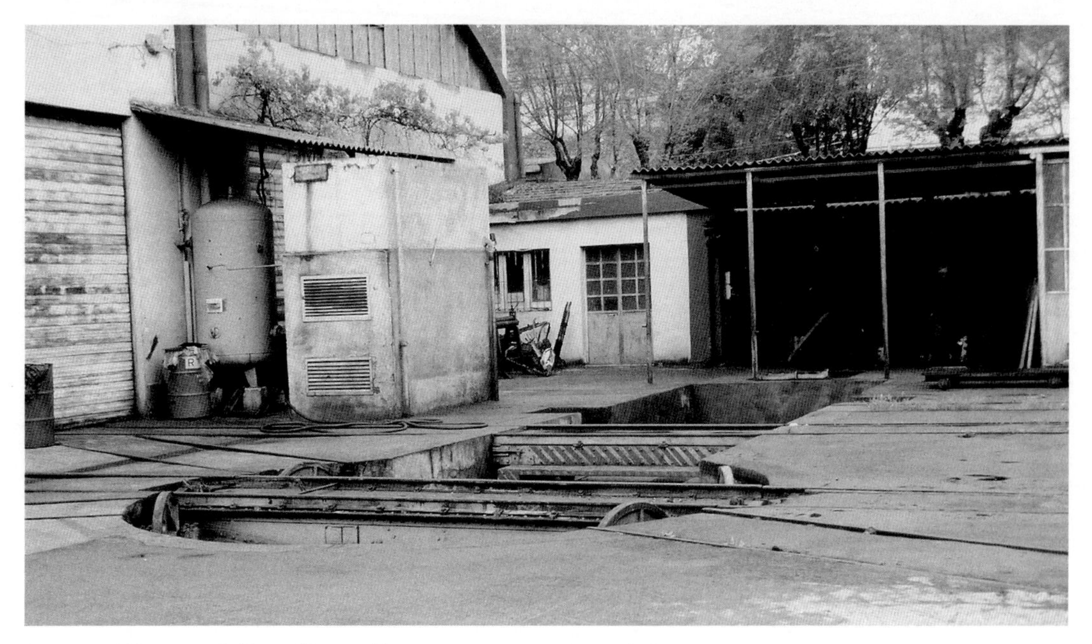

Aspects of Macomer 2: The odd turntable cum traverser at the workshops. (AUTHOR)

The harbour branch disappeared and a new station building, headquarters offices and goods shed were built roughly on the site of the old carriage shed but with the buildings all to the west of the main line. Three dead-end platform faces replaced the original through loop line, this being possible because of the use of double-ended railcars and control trailers.

Macomer is, by contrast, on a long thin site with the buildings strung out along it. The Bosa and Nuoro lines come together a few hundred metres before the station and run in past a long refuge siding, on the left, and a succession of stores and workshops on the right. These include the main erecting shop with an odd combination of turntable and traverser for access. The main station buildings, with their platforms, front five loop lines and, on the road side, face across a small square and down a street to the standard gauge station about two hundred metres away. The station site now terminates in a bank of 1950s-style stock sheds and maintenance facilities, replacing the originals, with a spur off to a now disused goods shed and a headshunt to the paint shop. From in front of the stocksheds, a long, sharply curved siding drops away to cross a road, turn through 180 degrees and end in a bay platform at the SG station. It also gives access to an SG/NG goods interchange yard which includes a pit for loading standard gauge wagons onto transporter bogies.

2. Intermediate servicing points: Corte (Corsica); Tempio Pausania and Seui (Sardinia)

Very few if any British secondary railways needed substantial intermediate facilities, although, of course some big-company lines did (Machynlleth was an example). Many continental lines, however, needed somewhere that was capable of acting as a sort of intermediate terminus, being able to house a substantial fleet of locomotives which were often changed at such points in a long run, and also capable of undertaking at least first line maintenance and minor repairs. Both Corte and Tempio Pausania were excellent examples of this, and both, interestingly, started life as outer termini. Seui was on a smaller scale and was always a through station but had the same basic purpose.

Corte was terminus and centre for the original section from Bastia for a number of years while the difficult task of joining up to Ajaccio was continued. Its real importance came once the line was complete since the length and gradients required trains usually to change locomotives and, often, to take a pilot engine to help them over the very difficult terrain. Hence there was a big stock yard with locomotive sheds

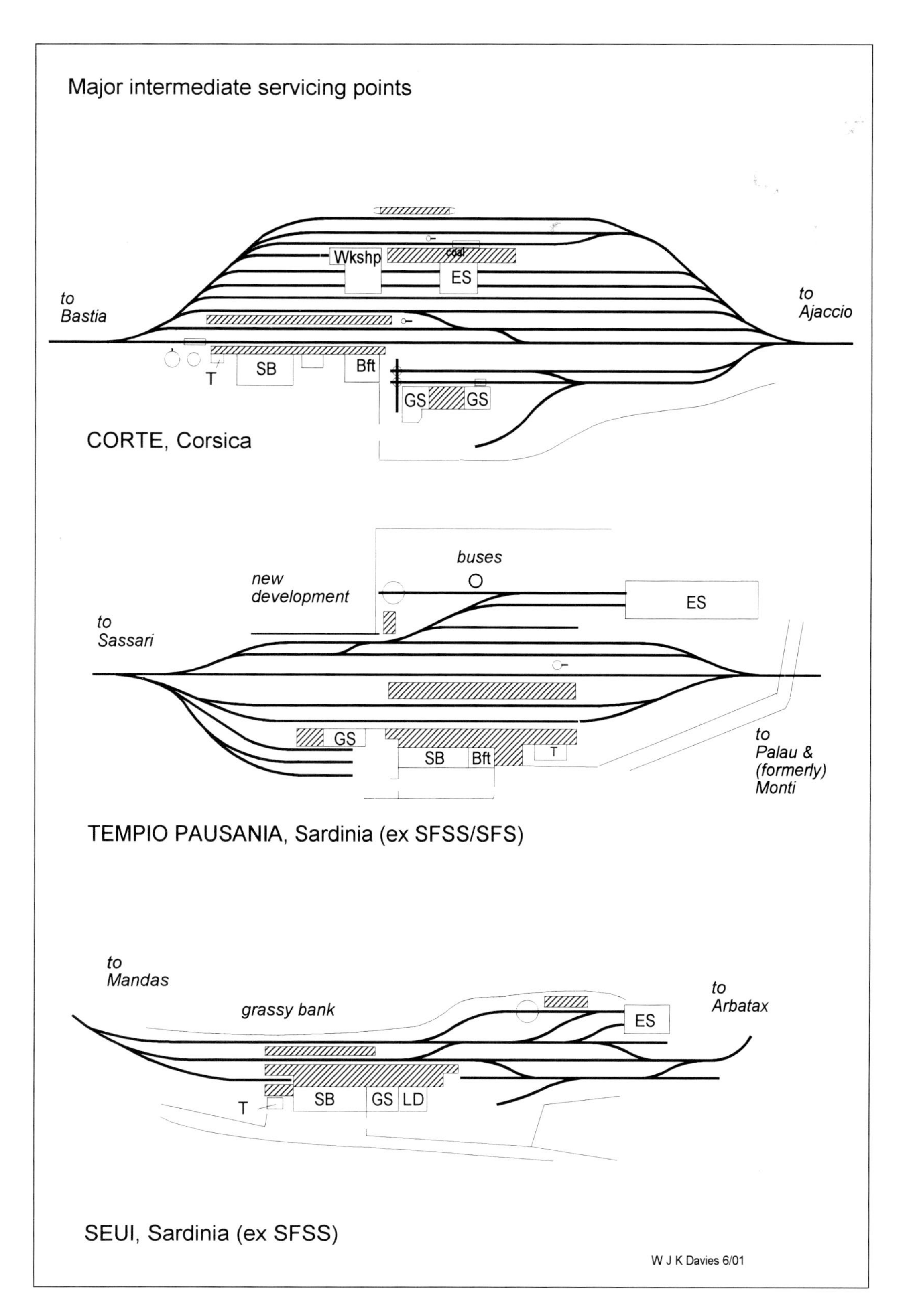
Major intermediate servicing points
to Bastia
to Ajaccio
Wkshp
coal
ES
T
SB
Bft
GS
GS
CORTE, Corsica
buses
new development
to Sassari
ES
GS
SB
Bft
T
to Palau & (formerly) Monti
TEMPIO PAUSANIA, Sardinia (ex SFSS/SFS)
to Mandas
grassy bank
to Arbatax
ES
T
SB
GS
LD
SEUI, Sardinia (ex SFSS)
W J K Davies 6/01

A typical big Corsican station; Corte in its heyday. (COURTESY JOSÉ BANAUDO)

Seui, as "touristified" for Trenino Verde use, with the old goods facilities converted to passenger use. (AUTHOR)

and a small workshop. Corte is the old capital of the island and important in its own right so its traffic facilities were also substantial. The big passenger station building had a separate buffet block and there was a proper goods yard with a loop, three sidings and wagon turntables, together with the usual weighbridge; unusually the goods shed consisted of two enclosed portions with an open dock between.

Tempio Pausania was originally just the terminus of the short SFSS branch from Monti. Once the SFS arrived, however, it had much the same function to fulfil as Corte, being a natural staging point on the long haul between Sassari and Palau, serving what was certainly the biggest settlement for kilometres around and also being railhead for a wide district. While slightly simpler than Corte it also has a large station building, with refreshment facilities, a separate goods yard and a two-road locomotive shed with a turntable spur. There are also divisional offices for railway staff and indications on the ground suggest that, when the Monti branch was operative and steam traction the norm, the layout was more extensive.

Seui, midway along the Mandas – Arbatax line, was always on a smaller scale but had the same basic features – a two-road locomotive shed with first line servicing facilities and a turntable, a large station building and extra provision for handling goods. In FCS days it was a normal terminus and starting point for short workings both eastward and westward and it is interesting to note that "trenino verde" charter trains also tend to use it as a changeover point for locomotives so it has to some extent regained its former importance.

3. Outer termini: Calvi (Corsica), Sorgono and Nuoro (Sardinia)

These represent differing approaches to the same requirement – railhead of a fairly long branch, which therefore requires at least first line stock storage and servicing facilities together with adequate provision for goods traffic. Two are inland termini; **Calvi** happens to be by the seaside but is not a marine terminus. As to facilities, Calvi is an example of having to fit these into an awkward site, hence the quarter-roundhouse occupying a corner where a conventional oblong shed would be awkward. Originally the main platform area was rather messy, with typical French half-buried track and skimpy mid-platforms but it has

Nuoro, looking to the dead-end, with goods shed on the left. (AUTHOR)

Branch Termini: Corsica and Sardinia

CALVI, Corsica

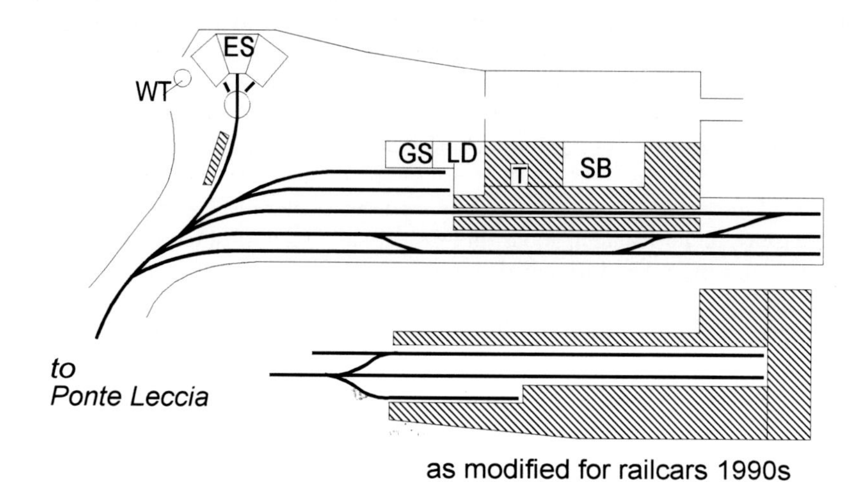

SORGONO, Sardinia

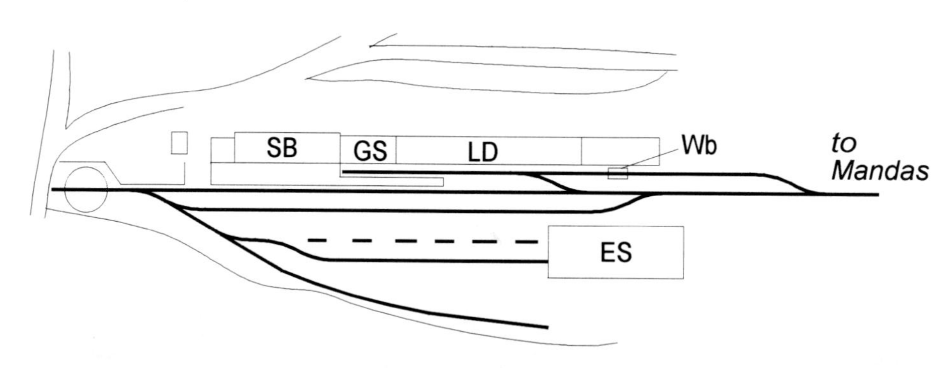

NUORO, Sardinia

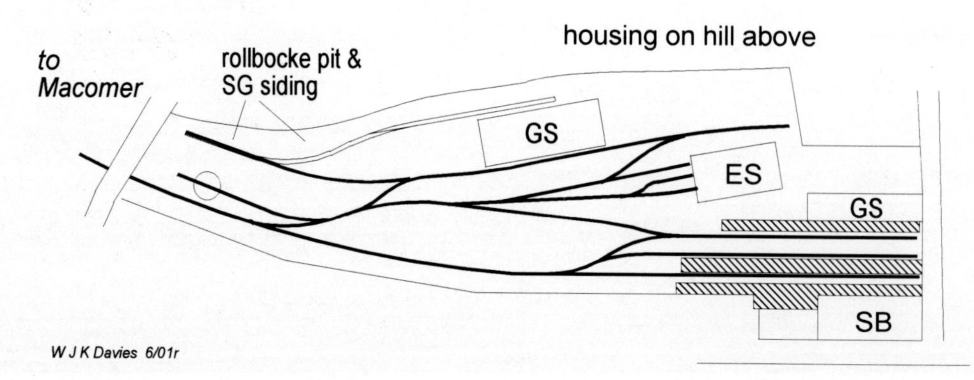

recently been reorganised as part of a general refurbishment; the use of push-pull sets in particular has led to simplification of layout and provision of a short bay in which the spare set can be parked. The depot layout, however, is now something of an embarrassment and only a single track is usable so stock sits in the open.

Sorgono, on the other hand, was about as typical a long-branch terminus as you can get. The goods facilities were tidily separated alongside a nearby road, there was a big two-road shed that could contain both locomotives and stock and the main line ended neatly in a turntable.The station building was a large, two-storey affair and had separate toilets by the station entrance. In recent years, the shed has been largely converted to service buses and only one road is retained for emergencies.

Nuoro is different again. The present station was built in the mid-1950s when the line was cut back to allow urban development and the architecture is of that period with a large, flat-roofed station building and three platform faces. Again the stock shed, being designed in the diesel era, is multipurpose although retaining facilities for steam working. It is interesting to see how all the facilities have been shoehorned into a restricted site, even though they include a turntable spur, a transporter pit and a long standard gauge siding to serve one side of the big goods shed.

4. Reconstructions: Casamozza (Corsica); Alghero S. Agustino; Bosa Marina (Sardinia)

These reflect approaches to three different problems. **Casamozza** (Corsica) is an excellent example of change of use. Originally a junction, the station building was damaged in the war and replaced by a "traditional" two-storey erection in a post-war austerity finish, while the existing goods shed was retained. In 1953 the junction was removed, making the original transfer sidings between coastal and central lines redundant. Hence, when it was decided to move the main workshops here, there was an available tract of land and modern industrial buildings have been erected with a more logical layout than in traditional works; one is fitted out to deal with mechanical overhauls, the other is designed for bodywork repair and refurbishment.

Alghero S. Agustino is again an answer to physical changes in a system. After the SFS took over the Alghero line in 1947, the old Alghero Porto and Sassari Santa Maria depots were eventually closed and their

The modern station building at Alghero S. Agustino, with gantry signal controlling the dead-end sidings. (AUTHOR)

Typical station reconstructions: Corsica and Sardinia

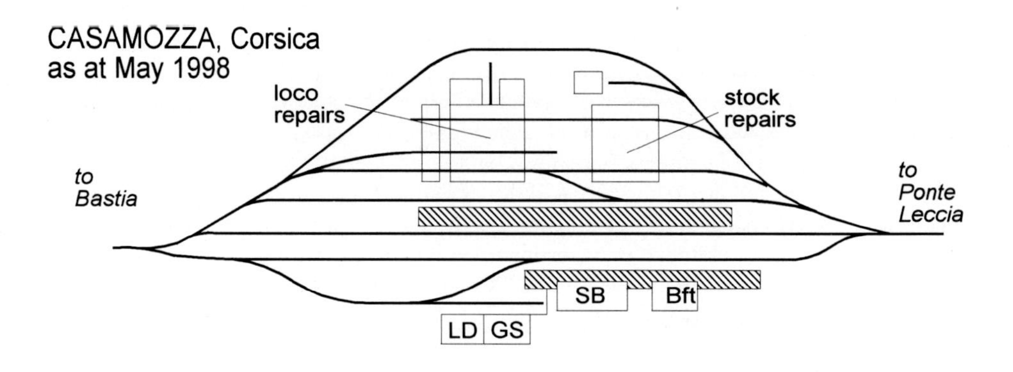

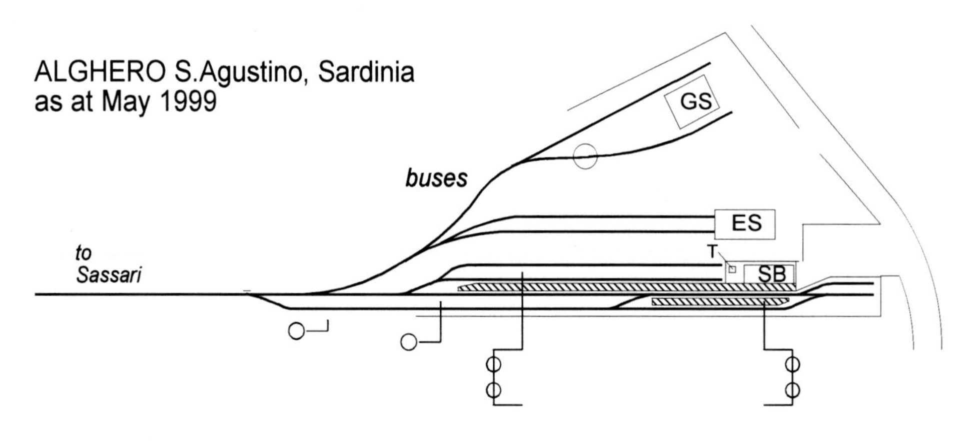

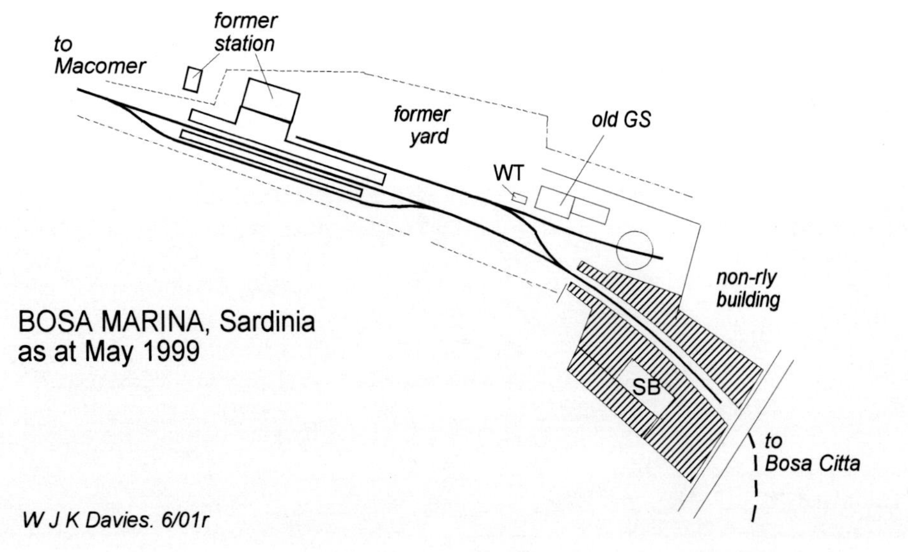

The "new" tourist station of Bosa Marina, looking to the dead end. (AUTHOR)

duties assimilated into Sassari SFS works. Some years later, the original terminus at Alghero port was closed and the line cut back to S. Agostino on the outskirts of town. This required a proper terminus and Alghero S. Agostino is the result. There is plenty of space for the servicing elements - two road stock shed; separate goods yard adjoining the road - but the original line and its passenger facilities, in a large 1950s building, are more restricted. This has meant the unusual provision of a siding at the dead end, to take a single railcar trailer, and a crossover partway down the long loop to ease shunting for different lengths of train (these can vary from a single railcar in off-peak periods to a five-coach locomotive hauled train or a multiple railcars-trailers combination in the rush hours). Recent EU aid has also led to modernisation of the station building and toilet block and to the provision of colour-light signalling with overhead gantries; a notable feature is the one opposite the station building which appears to control entry into the dead-end sidings.

Bosa Marina (Sardinia) is basically an improvisation when the original terminus at Bosa Citta, with its facilities for servicing and storage, was abandoned. The Bosa - Macomer line has been closed to regular traffic for some years but there was a need to service tourist and charter workings. Hence the old Marina station, which was a standard wayside station with goods spur, is now disused but its trackwork has been retained and a turntable installed on the former goods shed spur. A new single storey passenger building with wide platform space has been provided alongside the coast road to serve tourist purposes.

Ponte Leccia, Corsica, showing main building and buffet. (AUTHOR)

5. Junctions: Ponte Leccia (Corsica); Tirso; Mandas (Sardinia)

These are all examples of substantial junctions and have certain items in common, namely a fair sized locomotive shed with accoutrements such as coal, water and inspection pits, plus a selection of stock sidings for spare vehicles or transfer purposes. Equally, each has its own character derived from its particular purpose. **Ponte Leccia** was clearly a staging point where passengers in particular might spend some time before catching a train on and also served a local community since, as its name suggests, it was a river crossing point; it had a purpose-built buffet building and generally good passenger facilities. On the other hand **Tirso** was out in the country and just a convenient point for a branch serving isolated settlements but, unusually, with links to the standard gauge in two directions and with an important town (Nuoro) in the third; again, it originally had a bar in which waiting passengers could drown their impatience. A slightly odd

Tirso, looking to Nuoro, showing 1950s style buildings and the storage sidings. (AUTHOR)

Typical junction stations: Corsica and Sardinia

PONTE LECCIA, Corsica

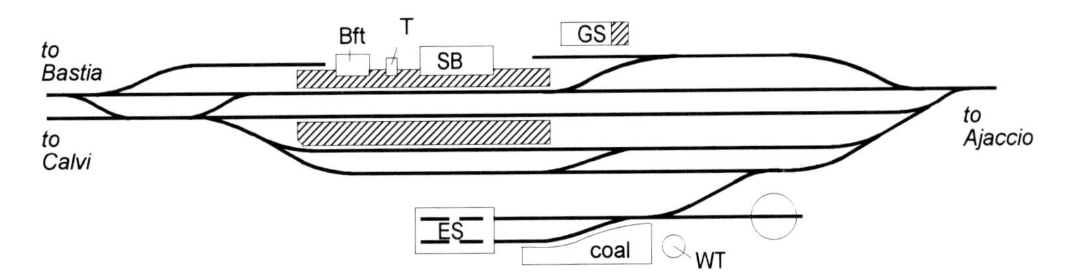

TIRSO, Sardinia

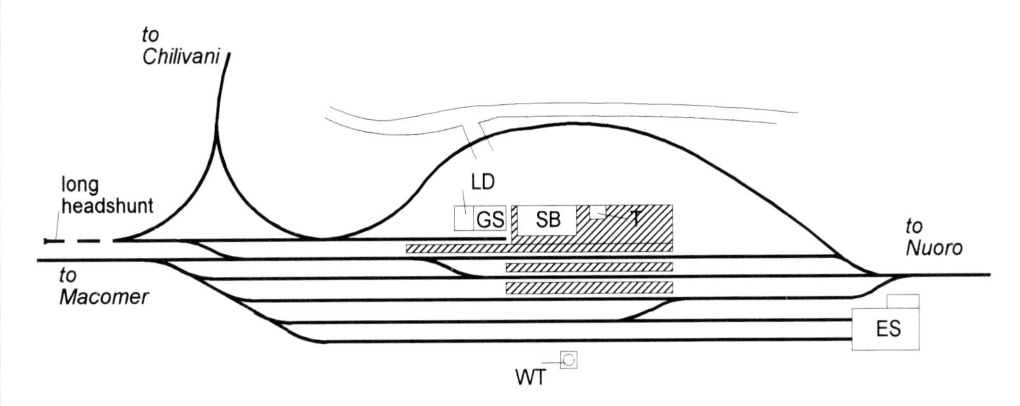

MANDAS, Sardinia

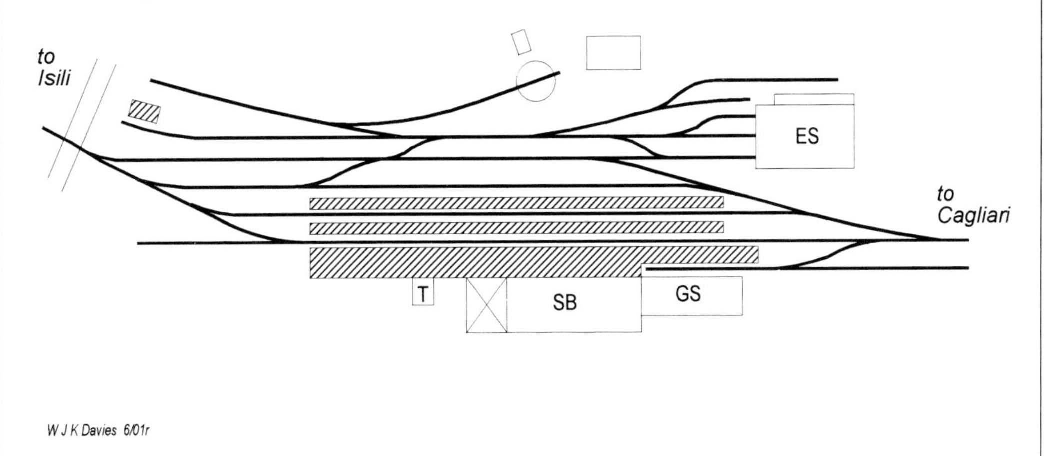

W J K Davies 6/01r

Mandas, to the south, with 1950s building and original locomotive shed. (AUTHOR)

feature, which appears original, is that the branch junction is arranged so that branch trains must reverse in and out of the station; there is a triangle (which appears to have substituted for a turntable) but it links onto the goods headshunt. **Mandas** is different again in that it was operationally at the junction of two branches, to Sorgono and Arbatax, which had through services but it also, with Isili, served as outer terminus for some Cagliari services, now its major function. As with a number of ex-FCS stations, the big two-storey station building, with its attached goods shed, appears to be a 1950s reconstruction, as is the separate toilet block. The long locomotive shed and offices are clearly original. A mildly interesting feature is the small shed, presumably for PW trolleys, sited beside the turntable.

6. Downgraded seaside termini: Ajaccio (Corsica); Palau; Arbatax (Sardinia)

Quite a few long branches, on both islands, ended at ferry ports and all had their individual ways of serving these. With the changing patterns of traffic – in particular the almost universal use of roll on-roll off ferries – their role has changed.

Ajaccio, Corsica: Ajaccio is the prefecture of the Département of Lower Corsica (Corse-du-sud) and, as the terminus of the original line, its station was correspondingly important. Alone of the three described here it had the "traditional" terminal arrangement of tracks ending in a concourse with the station building across the end of track and with the port connection leaving the station area as a siding through the goods yard. The large, three road locomotive servicing shed and long goods shed reflected its importance. Here the change to railcars and decline in traditional goods traffic has led to abandonment of the harbour branch and rationalisation of station tracks. The locomotive shed is almost disused and the goods shed is used largely by associated road services. On the other hand a "new" goods traffic has developed to carry road vehicles between the major termini and thus cut out journeys over the still tortuous roads; an end-on car loading dock has been built to foster this traffic.

Palau, like Ajaccio, is a ferry port, although mainly for local island ships and services to Corsica. The main station, however, was up in the town area and arranged as a normal through station with buildings along one side and a small locomotive depot and turntable opposite. The harbour branch runs on to a long headshunt with a steeply graded reversal down to a dead end by the quay, with a trailing point leading to a

Downgraded termini: Corsica and Sardinia

AJACCIO, Corsica

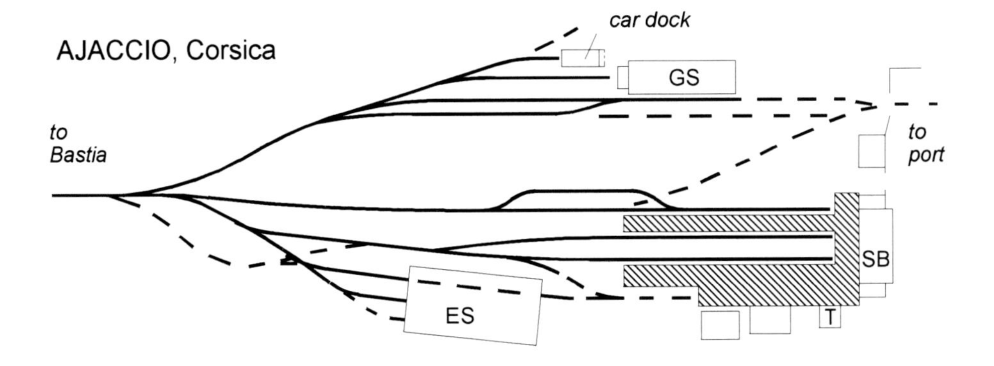

PALAU, Sardinia

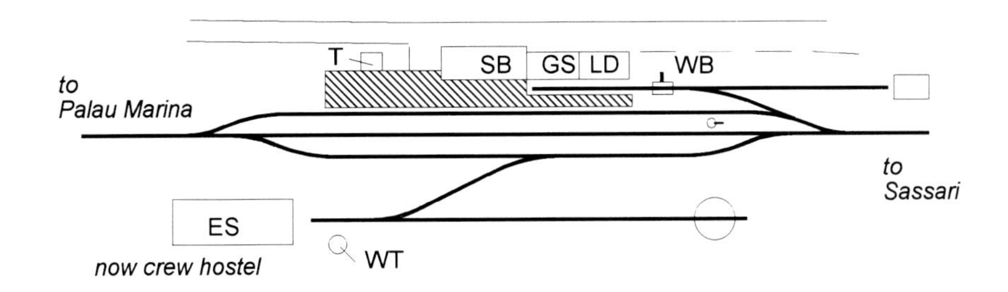

ARBATAX, Sardinia

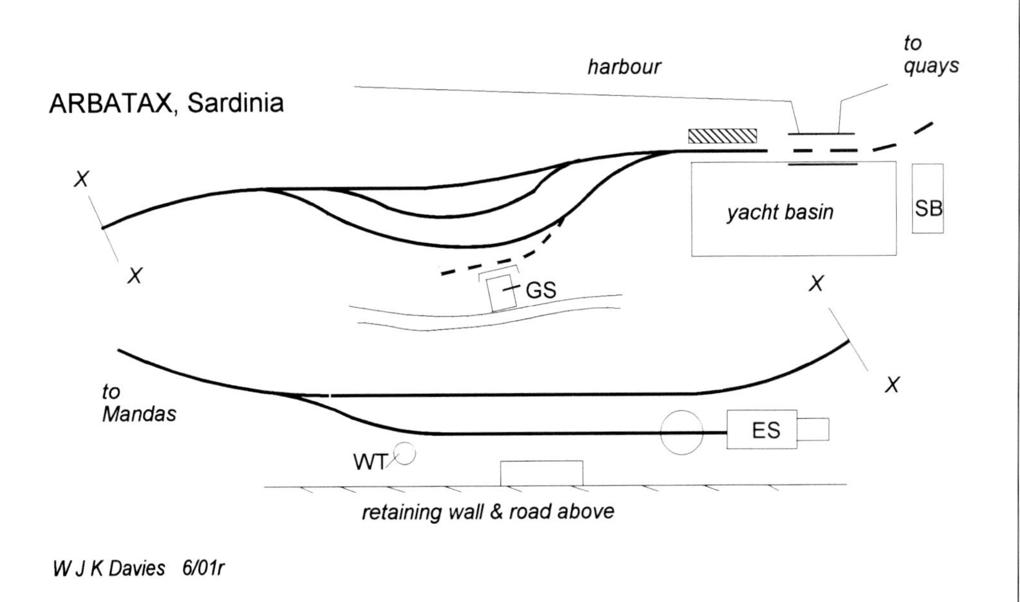

W J K Davies 6/01r

Arbatax as it now is; station building in background. (AUTHOR)

goods shed spur. In more spacious days it was presumably a source of transfer traffic but is currently retained for charter and tourist trains. Apart from these the branch is disused and the old locomotive shed at the main station has been converted to crew accommodation.

Arbatax is as nearly a linear terminus as one can get and an interesting example of how to use a long, narrow site bounded on one side by the sea. First come the locomotive servicing facilities fitted between a corniche road and the shore and consisting simply of a long siding leading to a one road shed with turntable; departmental offices and dormitory are in a long narrow building up against the retaining wall. Round a bend is, first, a three-loop "marshalling yard" which appears once to have had a siding to a goods shed and then a single line which once led across a bridge and past a station building which is at right angles to the track. The line formerly ran on to sidings along the quays but is now truncated at a concrete platform just before the bridge. As with Palau, the line is now disused except for seasonal tourist and charter train workings.

7. Intermediate stations that have changed functions: l'Ile Rousse (Corsica); Tortoli and Isili (Sardinia)

l'Ile Rousse, on the Calvi branch where it meets the sea, was clearly once a standard wayside station of Intérêt Général type but has now been modified to meet its new role of through station for Bastia workings and effective terminus for a quite intensive service of passenger shuttles during the high season. Hence the running loop has been widened and lit to provide a substantial platform for loading and unloading trainfuls en-masse, while a repaved platform has been retained in front of the station building for through trains. Since at an absolute peak there could conceivably be three trains present (through, outgoing shuttle, incoming shuttle) a stock siding has been provided to store a "spare" set - remembering that both shuttles and through trains are reversible so do not need to run round. The goods loop and facilities have been retained but appear to be used for storing PW equipment. The whole affair has been generally smartened up to make a good impression on tourists.

Stations that have changed their function

I'Ile Rousse, Corsica

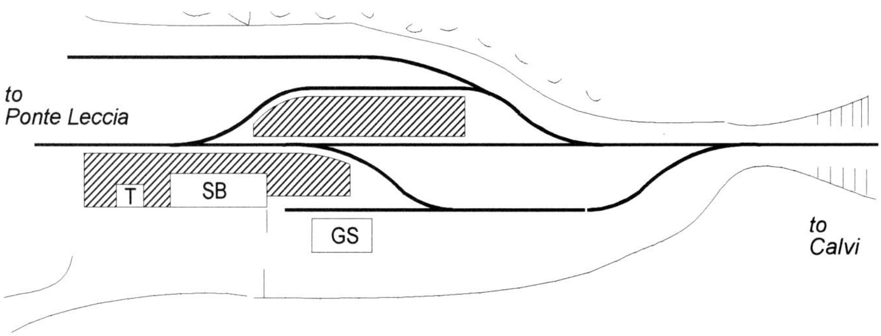

to Ponte Leccia

T

SB

GS

to Calvi

Tortoli, Sardinia

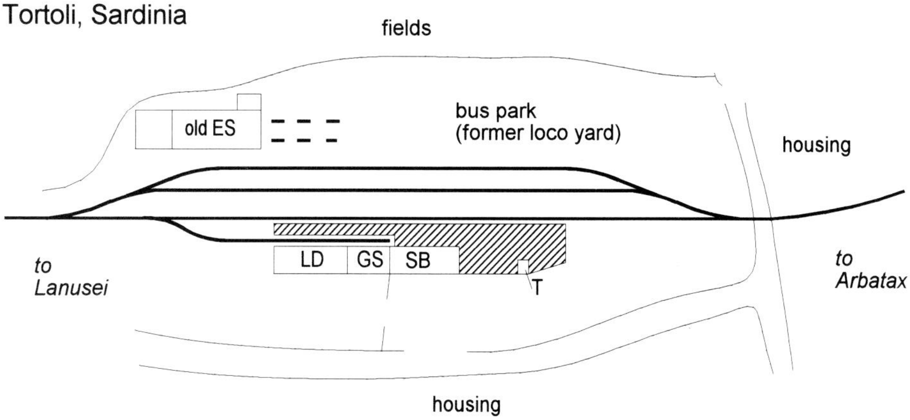

fields

old ES

bus park (former loco yard)

housing

to Lanusei

LD GS SB

T

to Arbatax

housing

Isili, Sardinia

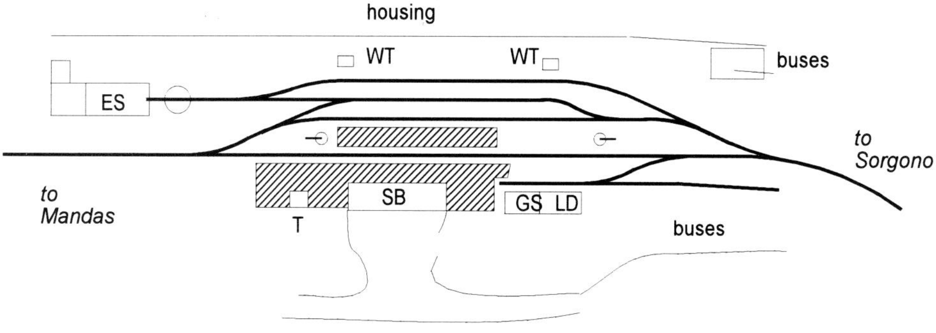

housing

WT

WT

buses

ES

to Sorgono

to Mandas

T

SB

GS LD

buses

W J K Davies 6/01

The former locomotive shed and layout at Tortoli. (AUTHOR)

Tortoli was clearly once the major end-servicing point on the Arbatax line when steam traction was the norm - indeed pre-war it was Tortoli-Arbatax. Now it is simply another station on a mothballed branch, what servicing facilities are needed being provided by the small shed at Arbatax (qv). The exact layout near the shed is not clear but presumably included sidings and a turntable. The main building is interesting in still being in the dressed stone used on this section of line – it has not been refurbished with painted stucco, courtesy of the EU. Another interesting feature is one of the few surviving SFSS wooden goods sheds still intact.

Isili: Furthest north of the 1950s refurbished stations on the Cagliari - Sorgono line, Isili still retains much of its former structure although now it is terminus for only a few southbound trains rather than acting as terminus for the original FCS lines as it did from 1915 to 1958. The elaborate watering facilities and multiple loops presumably date from that period, as may the, now disused, locomotive shed; it is difficult to see any other reason for them with Mandas so close. Part of the yard has been taken over by buses and the main buildings are of the "blockhouse" vintage typical of post-war refurbishment.

PART 3

Appendices

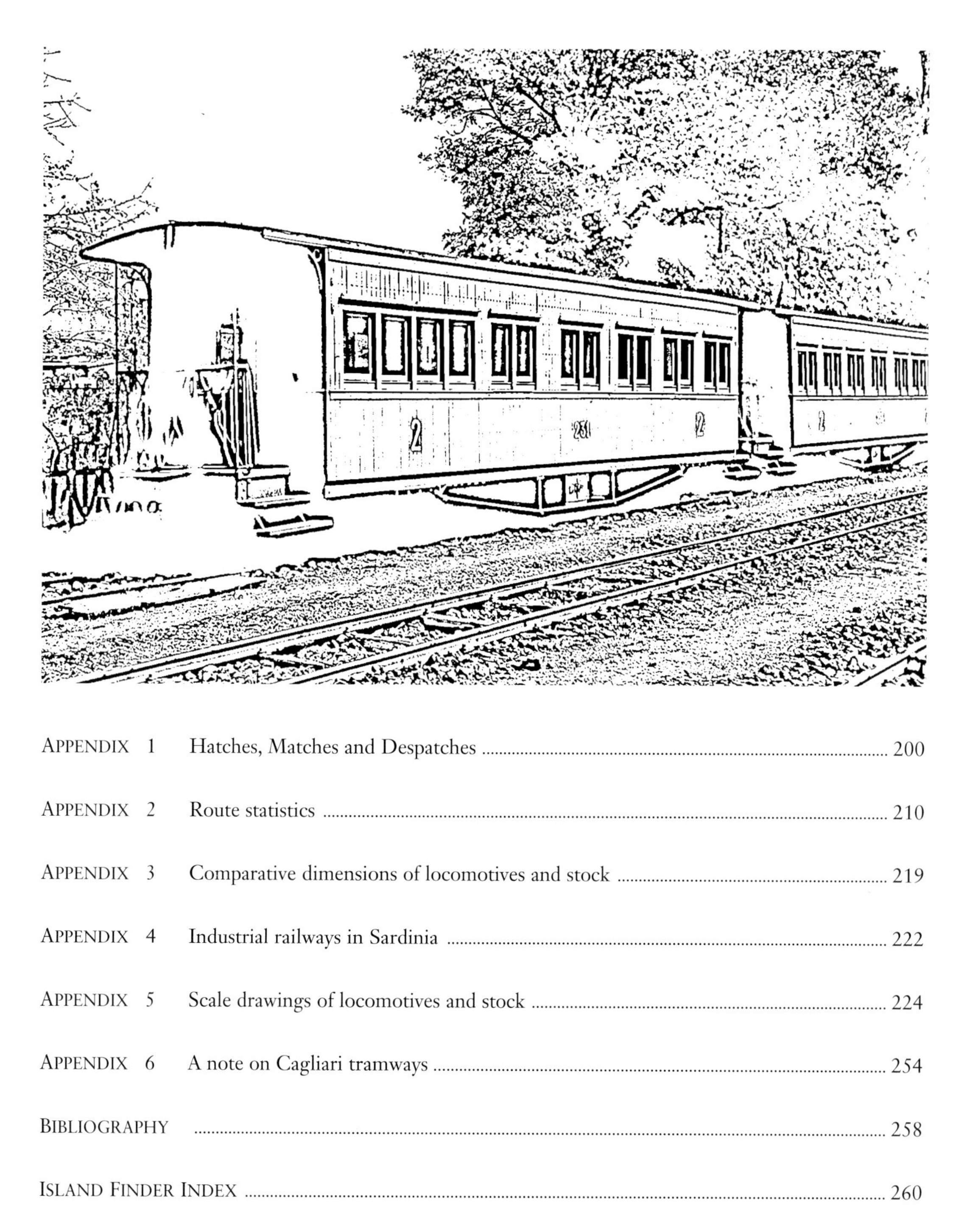

APPENDIX 1

Hatches, Matches and Dispatches

Data on the comings and goings of locomotives and powered rolling stock in both islands (position as at 2001 for those still in existence).

It should be noted that the Sardinian lines appear to have little compunction about swapping frames and boiler assemblies between locomotives if overhauls so require. Since a common Italian practice was to put the maker's plate on the steam dome, this can result in running numbers and works numbers being out of sequence. Some enthusiast records, in later years particularly, reflect this.

Columns show *(a)* running number
(b) Works number
(c) Year of manufacture
(d) notes, including withdrawal/scrapping

a) Steam locomotives

Corsica (note: withdrawal date is that struck off charge. scrapping dates vary)

(a)	*(b)*	*(c)*	*(d)*	
ETAT/CFD 0-4-0T by Couillet				
1	837	1886	construction work	wdn c.1900
2	838	1886	"	wdn c.1900
3	839	1886	"	wdn c.1900
CFD 0-6-0T by St.Leonard, Liege				
4	812	1886	constr: ex Charentes	to mainland 11/95
5	811	1886	"	to mainland 11/95
CFD 0-6-2T by Cie Fives-Lille				
28	2640	1886*	for Bastia-Corte.	wdn 1932
29	2641	1886*	"	wdn 1932
30	2642	1886*	"	wdn 1932
31	2643	1886*	"	wdn 1932
32	2644	1886*	"	wdn 1932
33	2645	1886*	"	wdn 1937
34	2646	1886+	for Bastia-Ghisonaccia	wdn 1937
35	2647	1886+	"	wdn 1937
36	2648	1886+	"	wdn 1945
37	2649	1886+	"	wdn 1937
38	2707	1888	for Ajaccio-Bocognano	wdn 1947
39	2708	1888	"	wdn 1947
40	2709	1888	"	wdn 1937
41	2710	1888	"	wdn 1948

*delivered 12/87 + delivered 02/88

(a)	*(b)*	*(c)*	*(d)*	
CFD 2-6-0T by Cie Fives-Lille				
53	2727	1891	for Calvi-Ponte Leccia	wdn 1947
54	2728	1891	"	wdn 1947
55	2729	1891	"	wdn 1945
56	2730	1891	"	wdn 1937

CFD 0-4-4-0T by S.A.C.M.

301	4285	1892	for Bastia-Ajaccio	wdn 1945
302	4626	1895	”	wdn 1948
303	4627	1895	for Bastia-Ghisonaccia	wdn 1945
304	4628	1895	”	wdn 1947
305	5629	1906	for Bastia-Ajaccio	wdn 1948
306	5630	1906	”	wdn 1945
307	7379	1924	”	wdn 1945
308	7380	1924	”	wdn 1950
309	7462	1927	for Bastia-Ghisonaccia	wdn 1950
310	7463	1927	”	wdn 1954
311	7464	1927	”	wdn 1945
312	7465	1927	”	wdn 1950
313	7551	1930	for Solenzara extn.	wdn 1954
314	7552	1930	”	wdn 1950
315	7553	1930	”	wdn 1954
316	7554	1930	”	wdn 1950
317	7650	1932	for Porto-Vecchio extn.	wdn 1954
318	7651	1932	”	wdn 1954
319	7652	1932	”	wdn 1950
351	7653	1932	for Bastia-Ajaccio	wdn 1954
352	7654	1932	”	wdn 1950
353	7655	1932	“	wdn 1950

CF Corses: locomotives acquired or borrowed at second-hand 1944

0-4-4-0T by Ste de Construction Batignolles, type XAT

253	n/k	1895	from Tunisian Rlys 1944.	scr 1948
258	n/k	1895	”	”
251	n/k	1895	”	”
254	n/k	1895	”	”

0-10-0T by Orenstein & Koppel AG, for CFD de la Côte d’Or, France

50	10926	1926	from Algerian Rlys 1944.	wdn/scr 1954
51	10926	1926	from Algerian Rlys 1944.	wdn/scr 1954

Sardinia

No.	*Works No.*	*Year*	*Notes as at 2001*	
0-4-0T by Henschel for construction work.				
101	2375	1887	ALESSANDRO VOLTA.	scr.
102	2376	1887	CRISTOFORO COLOMBO.	store 1958. scr
103	2486	1887	GALILEO GALILEI.	scr
SFSS: 2-6-0T by SLM Winterthur; originally named as shown				
1	484	1887	ICHNUSA:	scr.
2	485	1887	SARDEGNA:	to SFS 1947; wdn. c 1960
3	486	1887	MONTI:	scr
4	487	1887	TEMPIO:	scr
5	488	1887	ITALIA:	dere. Cagliari 1966; scr

6	489	1887	ISILI:	to SFS 1947; wdn c.1960
7	490	1887	SASSARI:	dere. Cagliari 1966; scr
8	491	1887	ALGHERO:	dere. Mandas 1973; scr
9	492	1887	MACOMER:	scr
10	527	1888	BOSA:	scr
11	528	1888	IGLESIAS:	scr
12	529	1888	LACONI:	scr
13	530	1888	LANUSEI:	scr
14	531	1888	NUORO:	to Ing. Di Giacomo, Rome
15	532	1888	ORISTANO:	scr
16	533	1888	OZIERI:	scr
17	534	1888	PORTO TORRES:	scr
18	535	1888	TERRANOVA:	to SFS 1947; wdn c.1960
19	536	1888	TORTOLI:	to SFS 1947; wdn c.1960
20	537	1888	ROMA:	to SFS 1947; wdn c.1960
21	538	1888	NAPOLI:	to SFS 1947; wdn c.1960
22	539	1888	MILANO:	scr
23	540	1888	TORINO:	scr
24	541	1888	FIRENZE:	scr
25	542	1888	VENEZIA:	scr
26	543	1888	GENOVA:	scr
27	544	1888	PALERMO:	to SFS 1947; wdn c.1960
28	545	1888	LIVORNO:	scr
29	546	1888	BOLOGNA:	to Ing. Di Giacomo, Rome (2)
30	547	1888	PADOVA:	to SFS 1947, then to Ing Di Giacomo. (2)
31	645	1891	TIRSO:	scr
32	646	1891	FLUMENDOSA:	scr
33	647	1891	ADDA:	scr
34	648	1891	TICINO:	scr
35	649	1891	BISAGNO:	to SFS 1947; scr
36	650	1891	PO:	dere. Macomer 1973; scr
37	651	1891	TEVERE:	scr
38	652	1891	VOLTURNO:	scr
39	773	1893	RENO:	scr
40	774	1893	POLCEVERA:	scr
41	775	1893	MAGENTA:	scr
42	856	1894	PASTRENGO:	scr
43	857	1894	GOITO:	restored, serviceable (1) (3)
44	858	1894	SANTA LUZIA:	? dere. Monserrato 1973; scr
45	859	1894	PALESTRO:	sold to Ing. Di Giacomo (3)
46	860	1894	S. MARTINO:	scr? (noted as sold to Rome)
47	861	1894	MONTEBELLO:	scr

(1) probably a combination of two or more locomotives; 5, 43 and 45 have been cited as contributors. 43 noted as derelict 1966.

(2) loaned or hired to FMS 1936-40

(3) there is some confusion; locomotives sold may be combinations fitted with appropriate plates. GOITO currently bears plates 858/94

SFSS: 2-8-0T (previously 0-8-0T) by Orenstein & Koppel

300	5758	1914	Monserrato. derelict and dismantled

301	5759	1914		Mandas. open store/derelict
302	7721	1914	ROMA.	Monserrato. derelict and dismantled
303	7722	1914		Monserrato. derelict and dismantled

SFSS: 0-4-4-0T by Schwarzkopf

200	4349	1909		sold to Ing Di Giacomo after 1973
201	4350	1909		Monserrato. derelict and dismantled

SFSS: 0-4-4-0T by Borsig, s/h

202	??		??	Monserrato. preserved; see text (1)

(1) has been given as GRAZIELLA, Borsig 5901 of 1906 ex FAA and as Henschel 11669 of 1913 ex Sangritana Rly, and as M30 of the FMS and as ex-Montevecchio No.4. See ch 6 for discussion.

SFSS or FCS: 0-4-4-0T by Borsig (alternatively noted as 2-4-0T)

10	8106	1911	? ex FAA No. 10, possibly for FCS construction (or came later s/h? This may be a red herring but it has also been suggested that the FCS acquired two ex FAA Borsig mallets in the 1930s, FCS 202 being the survivor.

FCS: 2-6-0T by Breda. originally named as shown

1	1537	1914	MARMILLA:	Sorgono. derelict
2	1538	1914	TREXENTA:	Mandas. derelict
3	1539	1914	ARBOREA:	Mandas. derelict
4	1540	1914	SARCIDANO:	Macomer. derelict
5	1541	1914	SULCIS:	Macomer. serviceable as FCS 5 SULCIS
6	1542	1914	PLANARGIA:	Mandas. derelict
7	1543	1914	GIARA:	Cagliari (Pirri). plinthed at roundabout

FCS: 2-6-2T by OM Reggiane (1)

400	133	1931		Monserrato. under restoration 2001 (1)
401	134	1931		scr c.1997 (1)
402	135	1931		Monserrato. serviceable

(1) according to enthusiast records, boilers (& plates) of 400/1 were exchanged at some point.

FMS: 2-6-0T by Breda

101	2145	1925		used to 1975. derelict Iglesias 2001
102	2146	1925		oou Iglesias 8/72 as 2147. scr.
103	2147	1925		oou Iglesias 8/72 as 2149. scr.
104	2148	1925		oou Iglesias 8/72 as 2146. scr.
105	2149	1925		oou Iglesias 8/72 as 2148. scr.
106	2150	1925		reserve S. Giovanni 8/72 as 2150. scr.

107	2151	1925		reserve Iglesias 8/72 as 2151. scr.
108	2152	1925		oou Iglesias 8/72 as 2152. scr.

SFS: 2-6-0T by Breda (1-5) and CEMSA (6-11). formerly named, as shown

1	2287	1930	ADRIANA:	scr
2	2288	1930	ALBA:	scr
3	2289	1930	WALLY:	Sassari. restored as NULVI (1)
4	2290	1930	MARZIA:	Tempio. derelict
5	2291	1930	LAERRU:	Sassari. restored (1)
6	947	1931	SASSARI:	Sorso. stored under cover
7	948	1931	OSILO:	Olmedo sidings. dismantled
8	949	1931	MARTIS:	scr
9	950	1931	GUILIANA:	scr
10	951	1931	NULVI:	scr
11	952	1931	TEMPIO:	Tempio. derelict

(1) at 8/5/01 a locomotive numbered 3 and bearing names WALLY and NULVI was officially serviceable; one numbered 5 and bearing names ELSA and LAERRU was in open store. No.5 was in service with the name LAERRU (a local town) in the late 1960s.

SFS: 2-6-0T by O&K (12-13) and N. Romeo (14)

12	11796	1931	SORSO:	scr
13	11797	1931	PALAU:	scr (1)
14	?	1922	PERFUGAS:	wheel arr. probably 2-6-0T. scr. (1)

(1) given in some lists as 14. Italian sources give 14 as by Nicola Romeo, Saronno, 1922, used for construction work from 15.10.31. If so, this locomotive was presumably second-hand.

Batches acquired at secondhand

FMS: 2-6-6-0T by Henschel & Sohn, Kassel

151	14228	1916	Kuk 6046; ex Ora - Predazzo 1937		oou by 1945.	scr c.1962
152	14203	1916	Kuk 6021; ex Ora - Predazzo 1937		"	scr c.1962
153	14219	1916	Kuk 6037; ex Ora - Predazzo 1937		"	scr c1962
154	14216	1916	Kuk 6034; "	"	"	scr c1962
155	14192	1916	Kuk 6010; "	"	"	scr c1962
156	14317	1916	Kuk 6035; "	"	"	scr c1962
157	14226	1916	Kuk 6044; "	"	"	scr c1962
158	14183	1916	Kuk 6001; "	"	"	scr c1962
159	14197	1916	Kuk 6015;	"	"	scr c1962 (1)

(1) loaned to FCS Cagliari c. 1959 for unknown period.

FMS: 0-6-0T by various makers, ex FS Sicily, rack tanks.
all numbers prefixed R370. (the FS class No.)

R370	*Works No.*	*Year*	*Manufacturer*	*Notes*
01	321	1908	CEMSA (1)	ex FS 1953 scr c.1962
03	323	1908	CEMSA	ex FS 1939 "
04	324	1908	CEMSA	ex FS 1953 "
05	325	1908	CEMSA	ex FS 1939 "

06	326	1908	CEMSA	ex FS 1940 "
07	475	1913	CEMSA	ex FS 1940 "
14	524	1915	CEMSA	ex FS 1940 "
15	525	1915	CEMSA	ex FS 1939 "
21	637	1921	N Romeo (2)	ex FS 1939 "
26	642	1921	N Romeo	ex FS 1939 dere by 1966. scr after 1973
31	647	1921	N Romeo	ex FS 1939 dere by 1966. scr after 1973 (4)
32	648	1921	N Romeo	ex FS 1939 dere by 1966. scr after 1973
36	652	1921	N Romeo	ex FS 1940 scr by c.1962
037	017	1928	O Terni (3)	ex FS 1953 dere by 1966. scr after 1973 (4)
038	018	1928	O Terni	ex FS 1939 dere by 1966. scr after 1973 (4)
039	019	1928	O Terni	ex FS 1939 dere by 1966. scr after 1973 (5)
043	023	1928	O Terni	ex FS 1939 dere by 1966. scr after 1973 (5)
047	027	1928	O Terni	ex FS 1940 scr c.1962

(1) actually Const. Mecanniche de Saronno (CMSA), predecessors of CEMSA

(2) Nicola Romeo SA, Saronno. Nicola Romeo took over the CMSA Works, a subsidiary of Esslingen, at Saronno during the first world war; it became CEMSA about 1925.

(3) SA Odero-Terni, La Spezia

(4) enthusiasts records suggest these are amalgams of different locos; 31 with parts of 038; 037 with parts of an unidentified loco CEMSA 476/13; 038 with parts of 21

(5) enthusiasts notes suggest Odero Terni wks nos were actually in 61X/91X range but these latter are misreadings. For example, in 1972 the seven complete survivors bore boilers as follows:

26	642/21 N Romeo
31	018/28 Odero-Terni
32	no identity
37	no identity
38	637/21 N Romeo
39	019/28 Odero-Terni
43	023/28 Odero-Terni

Some sources also suggest that four others were acquired in 1953 .If so, no details are available and none survived to the end. The attribution is dubious and it is tentatively suggested these may have been spare boilers for the existing machines, complete with worksplates on their domes.

Tranvie della Sardegna (Cagliari): 0-6-0 Tram locomotives by Krauss

1	2806	1893	presumably scr.
2	2807	1893	"
3	3040	1894	"
4	3041	1894	"
5	5377	1905	GIOVANNI MERELLO. scr
6	6955	1914	ROMA. scr.

Monteponi Railway

The stock of this railway is still not entirely known. After World War II, several Mallets were acquired from the mainland and, apparently, the nearby Montevecchio industrial line. The following is what is known or deduced:

C1 0-6-0T	by Canada Works, Birkenhead 213? of 1870
C2 0-6-0T	either Canada Works 214/70 or Krauss 1337/83
C3 0-6-0T	definitely Canada Works 215/70
A1 0-4-4-0T	Borsig 5630 of 1905 new
A2 0-4-4-0T	PORTOVESME. Borsig 6021 of 1906 new
B3 0-4-4-0T	R CATTANEO Borsig 8738 of 1913 ex Montevecchio No.4
B4 or H4: 0-4-4-0T	provenance indeterminate, possibly ex Sangritana
B5 0-4-4-0T	CAMPO PISANO Borsig 8096 of 1912 ex Sangritana
H6 0-4-4-0T	Henschel 11674 of 1913 ex Sangritana

all the ex Sagritana locos came via other sources. The late PM Kalla-Bishop also identified 0-4-0Ts Henschel 1209-10 of 1881 as going to Monteponi but without any other data – possibly for mines use? All Monteponi locomotives were scrapped after closure except possibly one transferred to the FCS (see text)

b) Details of i/c engined locomotives, tractors and railcars

Corsica: diesel locomotives

CFC: diesel-electric locomotives by Brissonneau et Lotz

401	1951	wdn 1963. scr.
402	1951	wdn 1966. scr c.1981
403(II)	1951	ex CF de Provence 1963. wdn 1974. scr. 1981

CFC: diesel hydro/mechanical locomotives by CFD Montmirail

404	1963	ex CFD du Vivarais; ex CF de Provence 1974. in service
405	1966	new to CFC; in service
406	1973	to CFC 1994. reb from SG by CFD. in service

CFC; diesel-mechanical tractors by Bastia Works

403(I)	1956	ex rcars 103/115. wdn 1962. scr.
114	1955	ex rcar 114. dere. Casamozza 2001.

SACFS: diesel mechanical tractors

1	1948	ex CFD du Tarn LT1 1966? wdn c. 1981. to MTVS Valmondois
2	1953	ex Voies Ferrées du Dauphiné T13 1968. wdn 1978 & scr.
3	1950	ex SE Réseau de Seine-et-Marne 1968. scr.

Corsica: railcars

CFD: bogie petrol-electric railcars by Decauville/Crochat

Ae 51	1925	damaged 09/28 & remains sent away.
Ae 52	1925	tr to CFD Charentes 1929.

CFD: bogie diesel-mechanical railcars by Billard of Tours

No.	*Works No.*	*Year*	*Notes*
101	701	1935	scr
102	702	1936	destroyed by act of war, Bastia 1943

103	703	1936	burnt-out 08/46 and scr.
104	704	1936	demotored 05/57. scr.
105	705	1936	demotored 05/57; reb as R104 in 1977
106	706	1936	demotored & reb. as R105 in 1977.
111	2001	1938	scr after 1973.
112	2002	1938	wdn 1973 and scr.
113	2003	1938	reb.Carde 1967; demotored 1987. reb. as control trailer XR113
114	2004	1938	scr. after accident 1956
115	2005	1938	scr. after accident 1954
116	2006	1938	destroyed by act of war, Casamozza 1943

CFC: bogie diesel-mechanical railcars by Renault

201	-	1949	in use Calvi 1998
202	-	1949	oou Bastia 1998
203		1949	wdn & scr.
204		1949	in reserve Calvi 1998
205		1950	wdn & scr.
206		1950	in use Calvi 1998
207		1950	oou Bastia 1998
208		1950	wdn & scr by 1980.

SACFS: bogie diesel mechanical railcars by Billard of Tours
(see text for full provenance)

501	1018	1938	ex TC 07/67, reb Carde. scr
502	1020	1938	ex TC 01/67, reb Carde. scr
503	1033	1948	ex CFD S&M 10/66, reb Carde. dere. Casamozza 1998
504	1030	1940	ex CFDT 08/66, reb Carde
510	1004	1937	ex CFDT 05/66, reb Carde as parcels car. scr
511	1007	1937	ex CFDT 03/66. reb Carde as parcels car. scr.
512	1008	1937	ex CFDT 07/66. reb Carde as parcels car. scr.
513	1023	1938	ex CFDT 06/66. reb. as above. PW vehicle 1998
524	2030	1947	ex CFDT 05/66. refurb. Carde. scr.
525	2029	1947	ex CFDT 12/65. refurb. Carde. scr
526	2028	1947	ex RB 06/69. refurb Carde. reb. as control trailer XR 526 in 1985
241	1001	1937	ex POC 1970. all wdn c1977
242	1002	1937	ex POC 1970. demotored. oou Bastia 1998
243	1003	1937	ex POC 1970. demotored. scr.
244	1009	1937	ex POC 1970. scr.
245	1012	1937	ex POC 1970. demotored. oou Bastia 1998
246	1015	1938	ex POC 1970. scr.
249	1019	1938	ex POC 1970. scr. ? demotored?
250	1011	1937	ex POC 1970. scr.

CFTA: bogie diesel-mechanical railcar by De Dion Bouton (cl OC1)

158	153	1937	ex CFTA Somme 1972. scr.

CFC: bogie diesel-mechanical railcars by CFD Montmirail

X2001		1975	orig X 1201. in service 2001
X2002		1975	orig X 1202. in service 2001
X2003		1975	in service 2001
X2004		1976	orig X 1203. in service 2001

X2005	1976	in service 2001
X5001	1981	in service 2001
X5002	1982	in service 2001

CFC: bogie diesel-mechanical railcars by Soulé and CFD Soulé, Bordeaux

X 97051	1989	in service 2001
X 97052	1989	as above
X 97053	1989	as above
X 97054	1992	as above
X 97055	1992	as above
X 97056	1997	as above
X 97057	1997	as above

Sardinia: diesel locomotives

FCS: diesel locomotive by Maschinenfabrik Karlsruhe AG

A1	?	1927	loaned for trial by FS and returned 1928

FCS: diesel-electric locomotives by TIBB/Breda (TIBB plates)

LDe	*Wks No*	*year*	*notes*
600	5913	1958	serviceable Cagliari
601	5915	1958	serviceable Macomer
602	5914	1958	serviceable Cagliari
603	5916	1958	serviceable Macomer
604	5917	1958	serviceable Cagliari
605	5918	1958	serviceable Macomer
606	5923	1958	serviceable Cagliari
607	5919	1958	serviceable Macomer
608	5920	1958	serviceable Cagliari
609	5921	1958	serviceable Macomer
610	5922	1958	stripped hulk, Monserrato
611	5924	1958	serviceable Macomer
612	5925	1958	serviceable Cagliari
614	5926	1958	serviceable Cagliari
616	5927	1958	serviceable Cagliari

FCS: diesel-mechanical shunting locomotives by Orenstein & Koppel (ex 900mm gauge; Carbonia Collieries, 1962)

LM 1	25358	1953	to SFS LDn 1, 1962. scr after 1973.
LM 2	25357	1953	scr. (1)
LM 3	25356	1953	to SFS LDn 2, 1962. scr after 1973.
LM 4	25360	1953	scr. (1)
LM 5	25359	1953	serviceable Monserrato (1)

(1) noted as originally Ln 01-03, renumbered by FdS?

SFS: diesel-electric locomotives by TIBB/Breda, 1958

500	5928	1958	in service Sassari
501	5932	1958	in service, Sassari
502	5930	1958	in service, Sassari
503	5931	1958	in service, Sassari
504	5929	1958	derelict Sassari S. Maria

Sardinia: Railcars

FCS: 4w railbuses by OM Milan/Carminati & Toselli

FCS 1	1934	derelict Tirso 1999
FCS 2	1934	derelict Tirso 1999
FCS 3	1934	derelict Tirso 1999

FCS: bogie diesel-mechanical railcars by Fiat, 1935? (1)

40.11	1935	derelict Tirso 1999
40.12	1935	derelict Tirso 1999
40.13	1935	derelict Tirso 1999

(1) originally numbered ALn 38.01-03. some sources note them as 40.01-03

FCS: bogie diesel-electric railcars by TIBB/OMS/Fiat 1957

ADe 01-20. TIBB 5923-42 of 1957 in sequence

All in use, some being rebodied, 2000 (except ADe 06, parked derelict at Tirso, apparently in original (burnt-out) condition). Class split between Macomer and Cagliari as required.

FMS: bogie diesel-mechanical railcars by Fiat, 1935

ALn 201	1935	dere. S. Giovanni 1973. scr. (1)
ALn 202	1935	dere. S. Giovanni 1973. scr. (1)
ALn 203	1935	derelict Iglesias 2001
ALn 204	1935	dere. S. Giovanni 1973. scr.

(1) rebuilt by FMS in 1960s

FMS: bogie diesel-electric railcars by TIBB/OMS/Fiat

(all to FCS c.1975)

ADe 301	6145	1959	in service
ADe 302	6146	1959	serviceable, Macomer 1999
ADe 303	6147	1959	dere. Monserrato 1998
ADe 304	6148	1959	store Monserrato 1998
ADe 305	6149	1959	dere. Macomer 1998
ADe 306	6150	1959	dere. Monserrato 1998

SFS: bogie diesel-mechanical railcars by OMS/Fiat

ADm 51-61 of 1957, no obvious works nos. All in service 1998.

FdS: bogie diesel-electric railcars by Breda(Ferrosud)/ABB Technomasio

ADe 91-98 Ferrosud/TIBB 1995-96 Wks nos in late 73XX-74XX range

All in use 2001, split between Cagliari, Macomer and Sassari as required.

APPENDIX 2
Route Statistics

Official lengths, opening and closure dates for Corsican and Sardinian narrow gauge lines.

Introduction

The problem with recording the details of stopping places is that many over the years have been added or deleted, or simply changed and some are now just unstaffed halts - plus, unless old plans lurk in archives, many are now closed and their details forgotten.

This appendix tries to:

- list opening and closing dates, together with route lengths.
- list stations as recorded at their peak, with official timetable kilometrages where these are available and accurate ones where known. In general whole numbers are timetable ones which are usually rounded up to the nearest kilometre. Those with a decimal component are normally from working timetables or civil engineering sources.
- provide basic information on station facilities.

Columns in the summaries give: section; rounded km; opening date; closure date.

Corsica: total length 360km plus c2km harbour branches at Bastia & Ajaccio

Bastia – Casamozza – Ponte Leccia – Ajaccio (157km) central portion built from both ends

Bastia – Casamozza – Ponte Leccia – Corte:	74km	01.02.1888
Ajaccio – Bocognano:	41km	01.12.1888
Bocognano – Vizzavona:	09km	14.07.1889
Vizzavona – Vivario:	11km	09.10.1892
Vivario – Corte:	22km	03.12.1894

Stations and halts:

Km	*Place*	*Notes*
00	BASTIA	terminus; originally major works and depot
01.7	Lupino	commuter halt
05.6	Furiani	station
09.6	Bigulia	station; current commuter terminus
16.2	Borgo	halt
18.3	Lucciana	halt
21.0	Casamozza	former junction and water point; workshops
25.6	Prunelli	halt
29.6	Barchetta	stn. former buffet
39.1	Ponte Nuovo	station
46.7	PONTE LECCIA	junction; former buffet and water point
54.6	Francardo	station
61.0	Omessa	halt
65.2	Soveria	station
73.8	Corte	major servicing point, buffet, shed
82.1	Poggio Riventosa	station
85.1	Venaco:	station; watering point
89.8	Vecchio	halt

95.9	Vivario:	station; watering point; buffet
102.8	Tattone:	station; watering point
106.7	Vizzavona:	station; watering point (1)
116.3	Bocognano:	station; watering point; buffet
123.5	Tavera:	station
126.8	Ucciani:	station; watering point
136.0	Carbuccia	station
144.9	Mezzana:	station; watering point
148.9	Caldaniccia	station
151.8	Campo di Loro	halt
157.4	AJACCIO:	terminus, buffet, locomotive shed, water.
158.0	Ajaccio port (terminus of harbour branch)	

(1) unusually, passengers were specifically allowed to break their journeys here on notifying the station staff.

Ponte Leccia – l'Ile Rousse – Calvi 73.3km (detail distances from Bastia)

Ponte Leccia - Palasca:	29km	10.01.1889
Palasca - Calvi:	44km	15.11.1890

52.7	Pietralba	halt
65.3	Novella	halt; former station
75.1	Palasca	halt; former station and watering point
82.8	Belgodere	halt; former station
88.1	Le Regino	halt; former station and watering point
98.1	L'Ile Rousse	station; shuttle terminus
106.3	Algajola	halt, former station
108.6	Sant Ambroggio	halt
115.5	Calenzana-Lumio	halt, former station
120.0	CALVI	terminus; former sub-shed and water point

Casamozza – Ghisonaccia – Porto Vecchio: 129km (detail distances from Bastia)

Casamozza – Folelli	11	01.02.1888	01.07.1953
Folelli – Tallone	36	01.02.1888	08.09.1943
Tallone – Ghisonaccia	17	17.06.1888	08.09.1943
Ghisonaccia – Solenzara	25	15.09.1930	08.09.1943
Solenzara – Porto Vecchio	40	21.09.1935	08.09.1943

21.0	CASAMOZZA	junction, buffet, now workshops
24.2	Arena-Vescovata	station
c29	St Pancrace:	halt
31.9	Folelli-Orezza	station; briefly terminus
40.3	Padulella	halt
46.8	Prunete-Cervione	station; watering point
53.7	Alistro	halt
59.0	Bravone	halt
67.6	Tallone	station
73.2	Aleria	station; watering point
78.9	Puzzichello:	halt
85.3	Ghisonaccia	former terminus; watering point
91.7	Prunelli-Pietrapola	station

97.3	Gavone:	halt (sometime Cavonne)
102.8	Pont du Travo	station (alternatively Ponte do Travo)
105.6	Solaro:	halt
109.9	Solenzara:	temporary terminus; water point
120.7	Favone-Conca:	halt
126.3	Figa:	station?
134.4	Ste-Lucie:	station
135.1	Lecci:	halt
150.9	Porto Vecchio:	terminus; sub-shed, watering point

Sardinia

Note: for Sardinia the "standard" wayside station layout comprises a loop with a siding serving a loading dock and possibly a goods shed detached from a two-storey station house. Places retaining these tracks are classed below as stations, those with only a running line as halts unless specifically noted in timetables as request stops only. Whole-figure kilometrages are from timetables but correlate well with map calculations and indications still visible on some buildings.

A. Societa Italiana Stade Ferrate Secondarie della Sardegna (SFSS) (599km)
Note: in practice the lines were eventually classified as shown in the detail descriptions below.

Consolidated opening/closure dates, as conceded, in chronological order.

Cagliari – Mandas – Sorgono (165km) and the detached Northern lines (75km)

Cagliari – Mandas – Isili	81	15.02.1888		(1)(2)
Isili – Sarcidano – Meana Sardo	47	01.04.1889		
Meana Sardo – Sorgono	37	03.11.1889		
Monti – Luras – Tempio Pausania	40	15.02.1888	21.07.1958	(6)
Sassari – Alghero	35	01.04.1889		(1)(3)

Bosa – Macomer – Nuoro (112km) & Chilivani – Tirso (79km)

Bosa Citta – Tresnurages	20	26.12.1888	15.06.81	
Tresnurages – Macomer – Tirso	55	26.12.1888	1995-97 (T-M)	(1)(4)
Tirso – Orotelli	15	25.01.1889		(1)
Orotelli - Nuoro	22	06.02.1889		(5)
Chilivani - Ozieri	9	10.02.1891	31.12.1969	
Ozieri - Tirso	70	01.04.1893	31.12.1969	

Mandas – Arbatax (159km) and Gairo – Jerzu (9km) built from both ends simultaneously

Mandas – Nurri	23	01.04.1893	
Nurri – Villanovatulo	11	16.11.1893	
Villanovatulo – Ussassai	59	20.04.1894	
Arbatax – Gairo	62	01.04.1893	
Gairo – Ussassai	4	16.11.1893	
Gairo – Jerzu	9	16.11.1893	14.09.1956

SFSS Northern lines: station details.

Sassari – Alghero (c.3km shortened by realignment; in brackets)

0	Sassari:	terminus; junction with SG, depot and works
01	Sassari Sta. Maria:	former FCS station and depot, now closed
06	Molafa:	halt, former station
08	"Rifornitone"	request stop
11	San Giorgio	station, replacing old station
15(13)	Arcone	halt
23(20)	Olmedo	station
28(25)	Mamuntanas	station
30(27)	Punta Moro	halt (opened since 1952)
33(30)	Alghero	San Agustino: now terminus, sub shed, watering point, TT
34	San Giovanni	halt; now closed
35	Alghero Porto	former terminus, now closed

Pre-realignment CE kilometrages for Alghero line (FCS) from Alghero S. Agustino to Sassari are available and are given here to show general correlation with timeteable distances.

0.000	Alghero S. Agostino
2.741	Punta Moro
4.758	Mamuntanas
9.868	Olmedo
17.757	Arcone
19.772	San Giorgio
24.680	Molafa
29.478	Sassari Santa Maria
32.078	Sassari SG station

Monti – Tempio Pausania (operated from Tempio)

00	Tempio Pausania	terminus; water; depot.
09	Nuchis	request stop for FCS; station
11	Luras	station (junction to SFS)
13	Calangianus SfSS	station
25	"Rifornitone"	request stop; added after 1933 and 1952
33	Piras	station
35	Telti	request stop; added between 1933 and 1952
40	Monti	junction station (SG)

Central system

Macomer – Bosa Citta (CE kilometrages where displayed)

00.000	Macomer FCS:	terminus; depot; works
06	Bara:	request stop; loading siding
13.568	Sindia:	station; closed
25.441	Tinnura:	station; closed: originally Suni

28.374	Tresnurages:*	station; watering point
37	Magomadas	not original; Nigolosu in 1952
41.462	Modolo	station; not original
46.032	Bosa Marina:	now terminus; water and servicing point
48.100	Bosa (Citta):	former terminus; abandoned.

* latterly, as railhead, Tresnurages-Magomadas-Cuglieri

Macomer – Nuoro (TT distances prior to realignments)

00	Macomer FS:	terminus; junction with SG. depot and works
06	Birori:	halt
09	Bortigali:	station
14	Silanus:	station
17	Lei:	station, formerly halt
21	Bolotana:	station
26	Tirso:	station; 2 loops; storage sidings; former junction with Chilivani branch; water point. Former buffet
31	Iscra:	station; 2 loops; SG transfer siding; halt before 1950s
41	Orotelli:	station
44	Oniferi:	station
55	Prato Sardo:	station
58	Rifornitone	halt? not in later TTs
61	Nuoro:	terminus; sub-shed; water point and SG transfer siding;TT noted as 63km prior to 1950s

Chilivani – Tirso:

00	Chilivani	terminus; junction to SG.
09	Ozieri	station
12	Vigne	halt
24	Pattada	station
30	Budduso	station
37	Osidda	station
47	Benetutti-Nule	station
54	Bultei	station
57	Anela	station
62	Bono	station
67	Bottida	station
69	Burgos-Esporlatu	station
74	Illorai	station
79	Tirso	junction station; water; shed.

SFSS southern system:

Cagliari – Monserrato – Mandas – (Isili)

As opened. Noted km imply recent shortening by c. 7-8km and distances in brackets are working timetable distances from Piazza Repubblica as at 2001)

00 (00.0)	Cagliari FCS	terminus, works, buffet
02	S. Benedetto	halt
06 (04.6)	Monserrato-Pirri	station; correspondence with tramway. Now Pirri

(06.4)	Monserrato	new station 1968
09	Selargius:	halt; not in current timetable
12 (10.4)	Settimo San Pietro:	station
21 (18.3)	Soleminis:	station
24 (22.0)	Dolinova-Serdiana:	station; 2 loops
35 (31.0)	Donori:	station, formerly Donori-Pimentel
?	Piscanali:	halt, out of use by 1950s
?	Onigu:	halt, out of use by 1950s
44 (40.7)	Barrali-Pimentel:	station
51 (47.3)	Senorbi:	station; sidings, turntable
55 (50.5)	Suelli:	station
62 (57.4)	Gesico-Siurgus:	station, now Gesico; originally a halt
69 (65.3)	Mandas:	junction; shed; watering point; TT

Cagliari suburban section as at 2001 (formerly c 1km further to Cagliari FCS)

00	Piazza Repubblica	terminus
01	Puccini:	passenger halt
02	Mercali	passenger halt
03	Vesalio	passenger halt
04	Citta Mercato Mar:	passenger halt
05	Pirri:	halt; former station
06	Redentore:	passenger halt
07	Monserrato:	station; depot and works

Mandas – Isili – Sorgono (97km: short portion in common with Arbatax line)
CE distances from Mandas; 1933 TT distances given in brackets

00		Mandas	
04.400		Serri	station
12.200	(13)	Isili	station; TT water; formerly FCS terminus
17.501	(18)	Sarcidano**	station, TT, former junction
21.881	(23)	Nurallo	station
	(29)	Cignoni	request stop by 1952
36.716	(38)	Laconi	station
	(44)	Funtanamela	request stop by 1952
	(48)	Ortuabis	station; now derelict
59.059	(60)	Meana Sardo	station
75.135	(76)	Belvi-Aritzo	station
79.705	(81)	Desulo-Tonara	station
90	?	Illare	halt
95.310	(97)	Sorgono	terminus; shed and water; TT

Mandas – Arbatax (continuation of kilometrage from Cagliari as "main line")
original CE distances from Piazza Repubblica

88.341	Orroli	station
?	Strintaxou	request stop? since 1952
93.227	Nurri	station; TT
103.824	Villanovatulo	station; watering point
116.400	Betilli	request stop; water and refuge siding
122.981	Esterzili	station

127.163	Sadali-Seulo	station
140.480	Seui	station; water; sub-shed; TT
151.500	Anulu	request stop; passing siding
162.271	Ussassai	station
166.518	Gairo	station; former junction; shed and water; TT
178.668	Villagrande	station
183.???	Arzana	station; TT
194.822	Lanusei	station; TT, shed and water
197.758	Elini-Ilboso	station
209.221	Sella Elecci	halt with loop; water; not original
221.558	Tortoli	station; orig Arbatax-Tortoli
228.000	Arbatax	terminus; TT and water.

Gairo – Jerzu

00	Gairo	junction
06	Osini-Ulassi	station
09	Jerzu	station; terminus

SFSS notes:

* now reduced by recent realignments
** FCS timetables give 6km to junction
(1) shortened by realignments in 1990s, exact extent unknown
(2) cut back c1km at Cagliari 1968
(3) cut back c.2km at Alghero from harbour to San Agostino
(4) Tresnurages - Macomer closed to regular traffic c.1995 and stretch Bosa Citta - Marina mothballed
(5) cut back c.700m at Nuoro c.1955
(6) Monti - Luras only

Ferrovie Complementari della Sardegna (FCS original lines): 91km

Sarcidano – Villamar – Villacidro	64	21.06.1915	01.07.1956
Villamar – Ales	27	21.06.1915	01.07.1956

(for timetable purposes distances were calculated from Isili as shown)

00	(Isili)	SFSS station; FCS terminus
06	Sarcidano	junction; locomotive shed
14	Nuragus	station
21	Gesturi	station
27	Barumini	station
31	Las Plassas	halt
35	Villanovafranca	halt
39	Villamar	junction station; water
45	Furtei	station
50	Sanluri FCS	station
56	Sanluri FS	junction station; water
70	Villacidro	terminus; sub-shed; water
00	Villamar	junction station; water
07	Lunamatrona	station
12	Ussaramanna	station

14	Baradili	station; halt by 1952
18	Sini	request stop
19	Gonnosno	station
25	Curcuris	station; halt by 1952
27	Ales	terminus; sub-shed; water

Ferrovie Meridionale Sarde (FMS) (114km)

Siliqua – Narcao	29	23.05.1926	1969
Narcao – San Giovanni – Calasetta	51	23.05.1926	1973-75
Iglesias – San Giovanni	34	23.05.1926	1969-75

00	Iglesias	junction; terminus; depot
03	Cabitza	station; request stop by 1952
06 (05)	Monteponi	station
08	Ceramica	request stop
11	Gonnesa	station
14	Bacu Abis	station; coal loading point
16	Pozzo Nuovo	not original. request stop by 1952
19	Cortoghiana	halt; station by 1952
21	Barbusi	station, later halt
24	Sirai	request stop
26	Carbonia	station; water; coal loading point
34	S. Giovanni Suergiu	junction station; depot; water
37	S. Caterina	halt
42	S. Antonio Ponti	halt (later I Ponte)
43	Sant 'Antioco	station; port
51	Cussorgia	station
55	Calasetta	terminus; port.

00	Siliqua	station; SG junction
17	Campanasissa	halt (later request stop)
24	Terrubia	station
26	Rio Murtas	request stop
29	Narcao	station
37	Villaperucchio	halt; not original.
38	Santadi	station
44	Piscinas	station
47	Giba	station (originally Giba-Masainas)
51	Villarios-Palmas	request stop
54	Tratalias	station
59	S. Giovanni Suergiu	station, junction. originally Palmas-Suergiu

Strate Ferrate Sarde (SFS) (150km + 11km running powers)

Sassari – Sorso	11	12.05.1930	(1)
Sassari – Tempio Pausania	91	16.11.1931	
(Tempio) – Luras – Palau Marina	48	18.01.1932	

Sassari – Sorso (as at 1999)

00	Sassari SG	
01	Maria di Pisa	after 1952. halt
03	Roda Quadda	halt, former station
06	Crabulazzi	after 1952. halt
07	Funta Niedda	halt, former station
11	Sorso	terminus; water; former shed; TT.

Sassari – Nulvi – Tempio Pausania – Palau

00	Sassari	terminus
06	Filighedou:	halt
11	Achettas:	halt. after 1952
17.8	Osilo:	station, watering point
26.3	Fenosu	halt, former station
34.7	Nulvi:	station; terminus of regular working
45	Martis	station; watering point; TT
54	Laerru	station
59.0	Perfugas	station; watering point
63.4	Cochinas	halt, former station
67.6	Scala Ruia	station; watering point
81	Bortigiadas	station; watering point
87	Aggius	halt; loop
91	Tempio Pausania	major station; water, locomotive sheds, TT
100	Nuchis	halt, siding, former station
102	Luras:	station; former junction; watering point
103	Calangianus	halt; originally request stop
111	S. Leonardo	halt
115	Rio Piatto	probably closed by flooding
120	S. Antonio di Gallura	station
128	Oddastru	halt; siding; former request stop
?	Capichera?	request stop, later halt
132	Caldosa	request stop, later halt
136	Arachzena	station; watering point
144	Surrau	halt; lengthman's cottage
149	Palau	station; former engine shed, water; TT.
150	Palau Marina	terminus, halt

SFS notes:

(1) shortened from this by realignments in recent years

General notes

The Palau line beyond Nulvi, the Arbatax branch and the Isili – Sorgono line have no all-year round service but have had scheduled tourist trains in summer since about 1997 and are used in spring and autumn for special charters. Bosa – Macomer is currently used only for charters. This situation is subject to change.

Monteponi Railway

This industrial line did carry passengers at certain periods and was linked to the FMS. It comprised a main line from Monteponi to Portoscuso, (18km, opened 05.1871) and an extension to Portovesme (3km, opened 03.79) with a later link to the FMS near Bacu Abis. It was closed completely in 1963.

APPENDIX 3

Comparative dimensions of motive power and rolling stock: Corsica and Sardinia

1. Locomotives and tractors

NB: Sardinian locomotives taken from field notes so subject to wear (eg on tyres) and measurement error: data on some locomotives is not available.

a) Locomotives bought new: Six coupled locomotives

owner	CFD	CFD	SFSS	FCS	FMS	SFS	FCS
numbers	28-41	53-56	1-47	1-7	1-8	1-14	400-02
type	062T	260T	260T	260T	260T	260T	2-6-2T
length (mm)	8150	8050	6350	6700		7730	8300
width (mm)	2500	2420	2400	2100		2450	2460
height (mm)	3470	3400	3400	3700		3630	3580
c/wheels (mm)	1000	1000	900	1000		960	1000
wbase (total)	4300	4300	4050	2400		4440	6200
wbase (rigid)	2400	2400	2250	2400		2600	2400
tare (kg)	22300	22700		22300	30600	28700	
w/o (kg)	28700	29500		29300	40300	37930	
cyls -stroke	460	460	350				
(mm) -dia	350	350	330				
pressure (atm)	10	10	12	13			12
t/e (kg)	3662	3662					

b) Typical heavier motive power (Mallets, 2-8-0T and 0-10-0T)

owner	CFD	CFD	CFT	FMS	SFSS	CDCO
type	0440T	0440T	0440T	0440T	280T**	0100T
Nos.	301-08	309-19 351-53	253/58 251/54	M30	300-04	50-51
length (mm)	9020	9020	9473*	9600*	8650	9240**
width (mm)	2400	2400	2400	2430	2420	2350
height (mm)	3400	3450	4060	3630	3640	3300
c/wheels (mm)	1010	1010	1010	1050	900	900
wbase (total)	4670	4670	5270	5000	6090	3850
wbase (rigid)	1400	1400	1700	1500	2900	2810
tare: (kg)	26800	28000	31800	25000		37584
w/o (kg)	34000	35400	40300	32000		48000
cyls -stroke	500	500	500	500		450
(mm) -dia	280/425	280/425	300/460	290/450		450
pressure (atm)	12	13	12			13
t/e (kg)	4650	4650	7600	4850		-

* as rebuilt   ** o b/beams

2. Comparative details of railcars and diesel locomotives.

All dimensions exclude jutting out steps and buffer/couplers

a) Comparative details of diesel main-line locomotives

Owner:	CFC	CFC	FCS
Nos:	401-03	404-05	LDe 501-04**
Wheels:	Bo-Bo	Bo-Bo	Bo-Bo
Drive:	DE	DMH	DE
hp:	2x300	2x207	2x350
Motors:	4x120kw	n/a	4x92kw
Length:	12300	9810	10000
Width:	2200	2500	2400
Height:	3560	3750	3300
Wt tare:	46000	32000	33800
Wt w/o:			34700

** LDe 6XX similar

b) Comparative details of diesel tractors

Owner:	FCS	CFC	CFC	CFC	CFC
Nos:	LM1-5	403(I)	114	1-2	3
Wheels:	B	B	B-2	C	C1
Drive:	DM	DM	DM	DM	DM
hp:	30kw?	210	50	180	180
Length:		8000	8000	7000	6300
Width:		2400	2400	2000	2250
Height:		3000	3000	3000	3100
Wt tare:		13000	13000	18000	21000

c) Comparative details of railmotors bought new
(full details of FCS and FMS pre-war Fiats are not currently available)

	Modern cars		*Post-war cars*		*Pre-war express cars*		*Early cars*		
Owner:	CFC	FdS	CFC	CS**	CFC	CFC	FCS	CFD	FCS
Nos:	X95051-7	ADe 91-8	201-08	ADe 01-20	101-06	111-16	40.X	AE51-52	1-3
Wheels:	B0-B0	Bo-Bo	B-2	Bo-Bo	B-2	B-2	B-2	B-B	1-A
Drive:	DM	DE	DM	DM	DM	DM	DM	PE	DM
hp:	2x177kw	300	300	2x165	210	150	2x80	2x60	100
Motors:	n/a	4x44kw	n/a	4x44kw	n/a	n/a	n/a	4	n/a
Seats:	40+4	51+2	44	55	42+16	40+2	24+6	32	29
Toilet:	yes	yes	yes	yes	yes	no	yes	no	no
Baggage:	yes	no	yes	no	yes	yes	no	yes	no
Length(mm):	17710	17310	20090	16750	16750	13440	14930	12800	8170
Width:	2499	2470	2500	2400	2400	2400		2500	2500
Height:		3480	3770		2740	2745		3200	3050
Bogie Ø	1200	11600	13690		13050	9360		8600	n/a
Bogie w/base:	2300	2100	2200		2680*	2400*		1800	4200
Wt tare (kg):			26000	27000	22600	12250		20000	6600

* motor bogie
** SFS cars similar but with mechanical transmission and, originally, 150hp engines

3. Comparative dimensions of typical rolling stock

a) Typical bogie coaches

Dimension	CFD	CFD	SFSS*	SFSS	FCS	SFS
Number	CCCv 1-3	CCC165X	AACCy4XX	CC251-63	Cf7-12	C21-31
Length o/bb:	9540	13500	13000	11125	13710	13000
Width o/all:	2300	2600	2500	2450	2420	2460
Height o/roof:	3300	3200	3225	3355**	3375	3280
Bogie Ø:	5400	8800	8300	6755	8900	7850
Bogie wbase:	1400	1600	1600	1400	1800	1600
Wheel dia:	680	670	700	720	720	720
Seats:	51	60	12+31	54	64	52
Tare wt:	9660	14750	13500			16000

* as originally built
** to top of prominent lamp housings

b) Luggage vans

Dimension	CFD	CFD	SFSS	FCS	FCS
	Df 1-13	DDifv 26XX	Df 321-30	Dfv 71-74	400-02
Length o/bb	5940	8040	6700	5850	6000
Width o/all	2200	2400	2180	2450	2380
Height o/body	2900	3450*	2950	3295**	c3150
Wheelbase	2500	3700	2500	3000	2700
Wheel dia	720	720	650	720	650
Tare wt kg	5000	7000	5000	6000	7040

* to cupola
** as running now

c) Goods vehicles: (typical vans and open wagons)

		Vans			*Wagons*		*Lowsides*	
Dimension	CFD	CFD	FdS	CFD	CFD	FdS	CFD	FdS
	E/F	K	M53X	G	Gv	N3XX	H	P
Length o/bb	5500	5500	5200	5500	5500	5200	5500	5250
Width o/all	2200	2290	2180	2200	2292	2120	2300	2200
Height o/body	2900	3163	2950	2540*	1965	2160	1130	1320
Wheelbase:	2500	576	2600	2500	2570	2600	2576	2500
Wheel dia:	680	720	720	680	720	720	720	720
Tare wt: (ave)	3750	5600	4750	3650	4600	5550	3050	5190
Load kg	10000	10000	6000	10000	10000	6000	10000	6000

* fixed tarpaulin bar

APPENDIX 4
Some notes on industrial railways in Sardinia

The writer does not claim any expertise in the history of Sardinian industrial railways of narrow gauge; the following notes are compiled from available sources and offered only as a starting point for serious investigators – although it may well be too late! Apart from the Monteponi Railway, which is described elsewhere, the main industrial users appear to have been:

a) San Leone iron mines (760mm gauge actual, with a nominal gauge of 800mm to rail centres): This was the first industrial railway in Sardinia, being opened for traffic on 17 March 1864 according to PM Kalla Bishop. It ran from Maddalena, on the south coast some 8km to the west of Cagliari, north and then west into the hills for about 15km to iron workings at San Leone; it was later extended about another 7km south-west up the valley of the Gutturu Mannu stream to a locality known as Casa is Pauceris. At that time it was operated by MM Petin and Gaudet and achieved some prominence as being one of the first continental narrow gauge lines to use steam locomotives. These were crude 6.6-tonne 0-4-0Ts by Schneider Creusot hauling simple metal-bodied tubs running in plain bearings and are said to have been very hard on what, from Ledoux' 1874 description, was clearly light and primitive trackwork comprising bulb-headed rail (simple champignon) on a variety of experimental sleepers. Their unsatisfactory performance may well have been the reason why the trains are reported to have been mule-hauled in later years. PM Kalla Bishop records the line as later in the ownership of Luigi Gonin who also owned a neighbouring line noted below and suggests it was used to transport firewood after the iron ran out. It is said to have been extended to Cagliari and to have closed "in the 1920s" although the track of the line as far as Maddalena was still marked on post 1945 maps.

b) Porto Botte – Pantaleo (950mm gauge): This was in the Iglesiente region east of S. Giovanni Suergiu. It is said by Kalla-Bishop to have originally run only to Punto dette Nicolo Carru, to have been opened on 23 November 1887 and, at least latterly, to have been used by Luigi Gonin to carry firewood to a wharf at Porto Botte. Approximately 28km long, it is said to have been worked by steam locomotives (so far unidentified) and crossed the FMS near Santadi and again near Tratalius – enthusiasts noted that it eventually made a junction at the Santadi crossing and the line on to Porto Botte appeared abandoned. It is noted as "still in existence" in the early 1950s although it is not clear if there was any traffic at that time.

c) San Gavino – Montevecchio (950mm gauge): The Montevecchio railway, owned by the Societa Montevecchio, was built west from San Gavino station, north of Sanluri on the standard gauge, through Guspini to lead mines in the western hills at Montevecchio. It was substantially built, about 15km long, was opened about 1903 and worked by steam locomotives from the start. For some time it appeared in the official lists of passenger carrying railways and maps show stations marked at San Gavino, Guspini and Montevecchio but no details are known. It closed in the 1950s after a metalled road was completed to Montevecchio in 1956. Some (uncertain) details are recorded about the stock which definitely included Krauss 0-6-0T 4880 of 1903 and Borsig 0-4-4-0T Mallet 8738 of 1913 (Montevecchio No.4). It has also been credited with a further 0-4-4-0T by Schicau (sic) AG of Elbing in Germany but this appears to depend entirely on two assumptions – a one-line reference in Wiener's "Articulated Locomotives" to locomotives having been supplied to "the Sardininan 0m.954 gauge lines" with a footnote attributing the supplier as "Schichau at Elbing"; and an interpretation that, since this appeared in no public railways lists, it must have been for the Montevecchio. Given that Wiener's minor references are not always accurate in any case this may be considered dubious. Kalla Bishop also deduced the existence of another 0-6-0T on the logical grounds that a No.4 implied at least four locomotives but there is no supporting evidence for this.

d) Nurra Mining Co (950mm gauge): A short-lived line said to have existed between 1916 and the mid 1920s at a location about 9km west of Porto Torres on the north coast. Virtually nothing appears known about this system except that OM Reggiane delivered four 0-6-0T (OMR 38-41 of 1916), two of which were later sold to the railways in Italian Somaliland in 1926-27. A best guess is that it was constructed to meet the wartime demand for minerals during the 1914-18 period and failed when the market receded postwar.

e) Porto Torres – Muragadu Quarry (gauge unknown): Kalla-Bishop notes this as being about 5.5km long, owned by Ing. Filippo Gamba and opened on 29 June 1888. It is said to have been locomotive-worked but closed before the end of the 19th century; a post-1945 map shows a "tramway" extending southwest from Porto Torres for several km, with a longer branch to a location called Canaglia some 20km away but it is not clear if this is the same item.

Otherwise there were three internal works systems which are noted briefly:

f) Bacu Abis Collieries (600mm gauge): Two Hunslet 4-6-0T of British War Department type were supplied post-1918 by dealer Glauco Greco. They were Wks Nos. 1298 (LROD 2326) and 1303 (LROD 2333) of 1918 ordered under requisition Egrail 262 and delivered to the Italian front. Nothing further definite is known.

g) Carbonia Collieries (900mm gauge): These had an internal system and the only motive power recorded are the five Orenstein & Koppel B diesel tractors 25356-60 of 1953 which eventually went to La Ferrotranviaria for regauging and allocation to their FCS and SFS lines. They went when the collieries closed about 1960 but what happened before they came?

h) Monopoli Stato, Saline di Sardegna (600mm gauge): The Cagliari saltpans operations had – and still have – an extensive internal system serviced by a wide variety of small diesel tractors. There were apparently two main types, up to 29 by Jenbacher Werke, Austria between 1953 and 1962 and up to 20 by Officine Ing. Greco of Reggio Emilia (who may have been dealers) between 1964-65.

APPENDIX 5

Scale drawings of typical locomotives and rolling stock

To avoid too much disruption to the text, the scale drawings of typical motive power and rolling stock have been concentrated here. Most are by the author, either from maker's drawings or from field notes and photographs but a small number are "cleaned up" reproductions of maker's drawings. They are presented in the same order as the text references and the relevant pages are noted below.

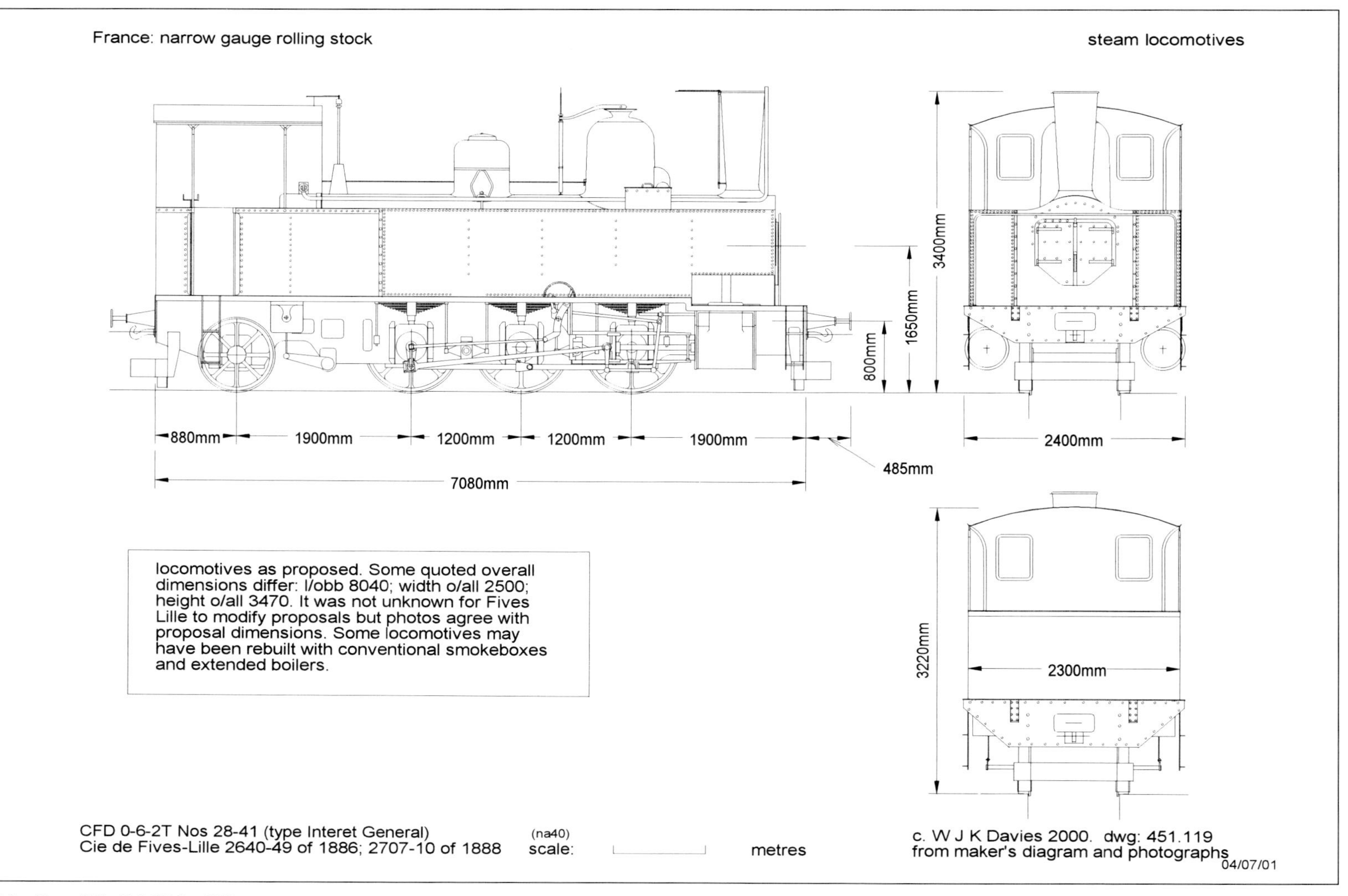
France: narrow gauge rolling stock
steam locomotives
3400mm
1650mm
800mm
880mm
1900mm
1200mm
1200mm
1900mm
485mm
7080mm
2400mm
3220mm
2300mm
locomotives as proposed. Some quoted overall dimensions differ: l/obb 8040; width o/all 2500; height o/all 3470. It was not unknown for Fives Lille to modify proposals but photos agree with proposal dimensions. Some locomotives may have been rebuilt with conventional smokeboxes and extended boilers.
CFD 0-6-2T Nos 28-41 (type Interet General)
Cie de Fives-Lille 2640-49 of 1886; 2707-10 of 1888
(na40)
scale:
metres
c. W J K Davies 2000. dwg: 451.119
from maker's diagram and photographs
04/07/01

D1 Fives Lille 0-6-2T for CFD

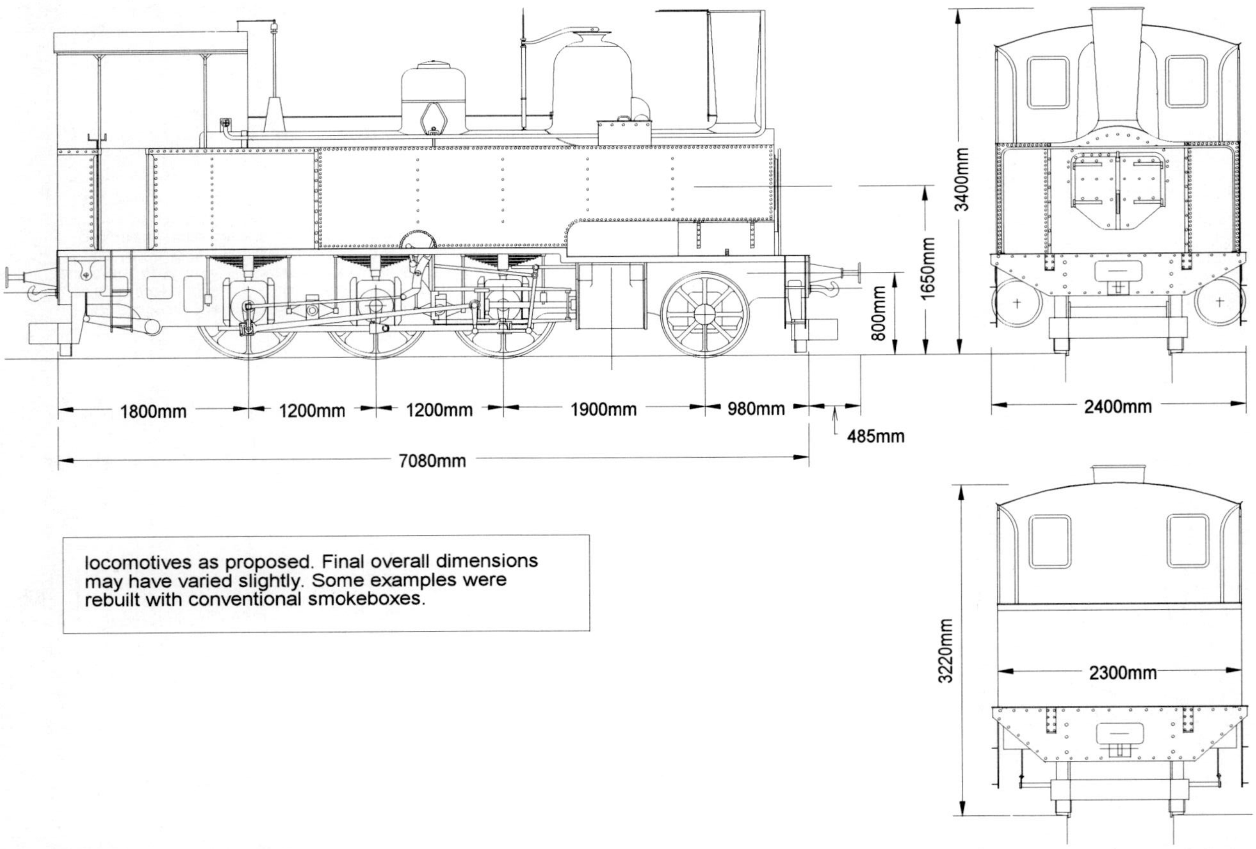

France: narrow gauge rolling stock

steam locomotives

3400mm
1650mm
800mm
2400mm
1800mm
1200mm
1200mm
1900mm
980mm
485mm
7080mm

locomotives as proposed. Final overall dimensions may have varied slightly. Some examples were rebuilt with conventional smokeboxes.

3220mm
2300mm

CFD 2-6-0T Nos 53 - 62 (type Interet General)
Cie de Fives-Lille 2727-30; 2721-26 of 1890-91

(na40)
scale: metres

c. W J K Davies 2000. dwg: 451.118
from maker's diagram and photographs
19/12/00

D2 Fives Lille 2-6-0T for CFD

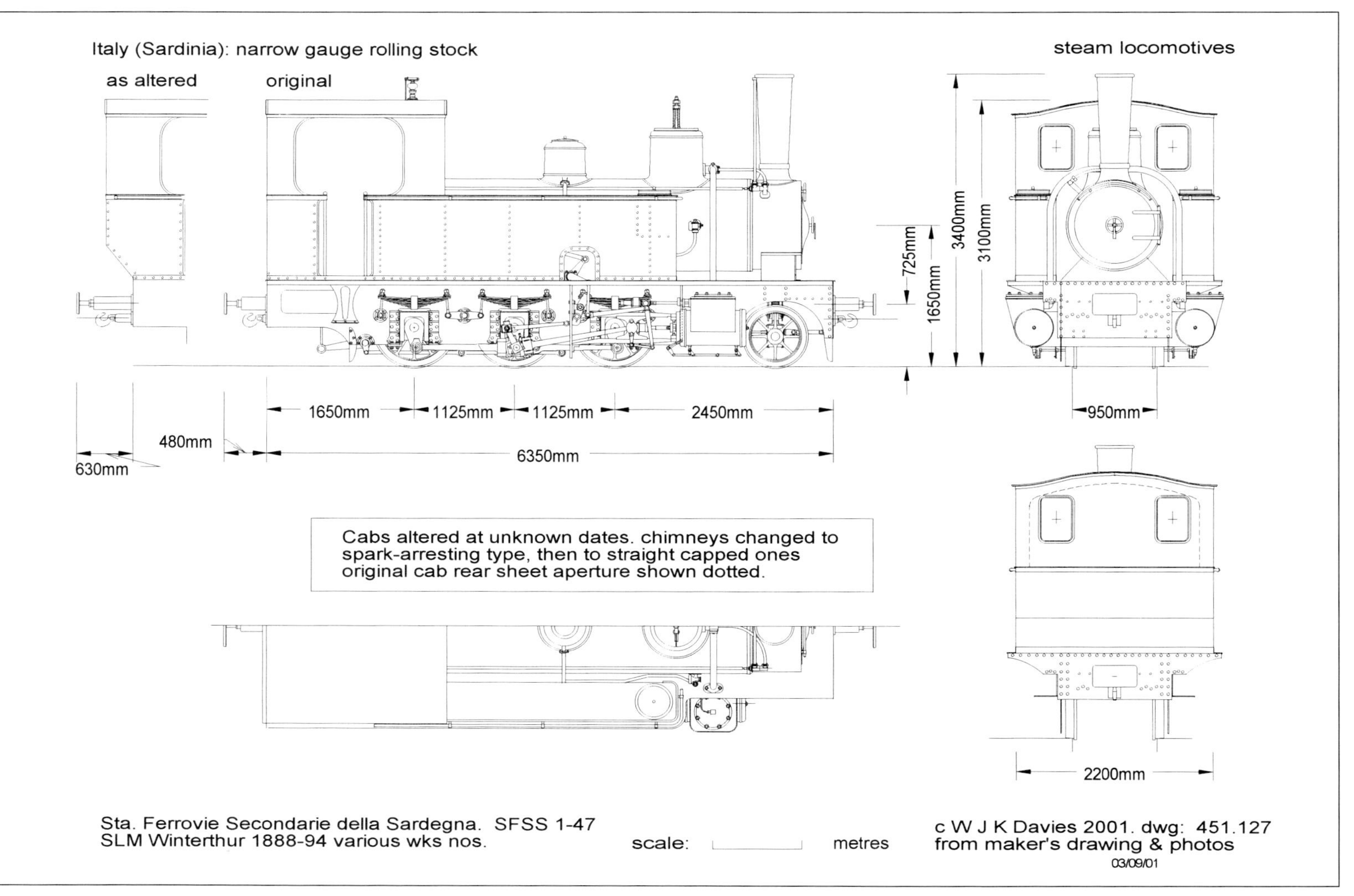
Italy (Sardinia): narrow gauge rolling stock
steam locomotives
as altered
original
3400mm
3100mm
725mm
1650mm
950mm
1650mm
1125mm
1125mm
2450mm
480mm
630mm
6350mm
Cabs altered at unknown dates. chimneys changed to spark-arresting type, then to straight capped ones original cab rear sheet aperture shown dotted.
2200mm
Sta. Ferrovie Secondarie della Sardegna. SFSS 1-47
SLM Winterthur 1888-94 various wks nos.
scale:
metres
c W J K Davies 2001. dwg: 451.127
from maker's drawing & photos
03/09/01

D3 SLM 2-6-0T for SFSS.

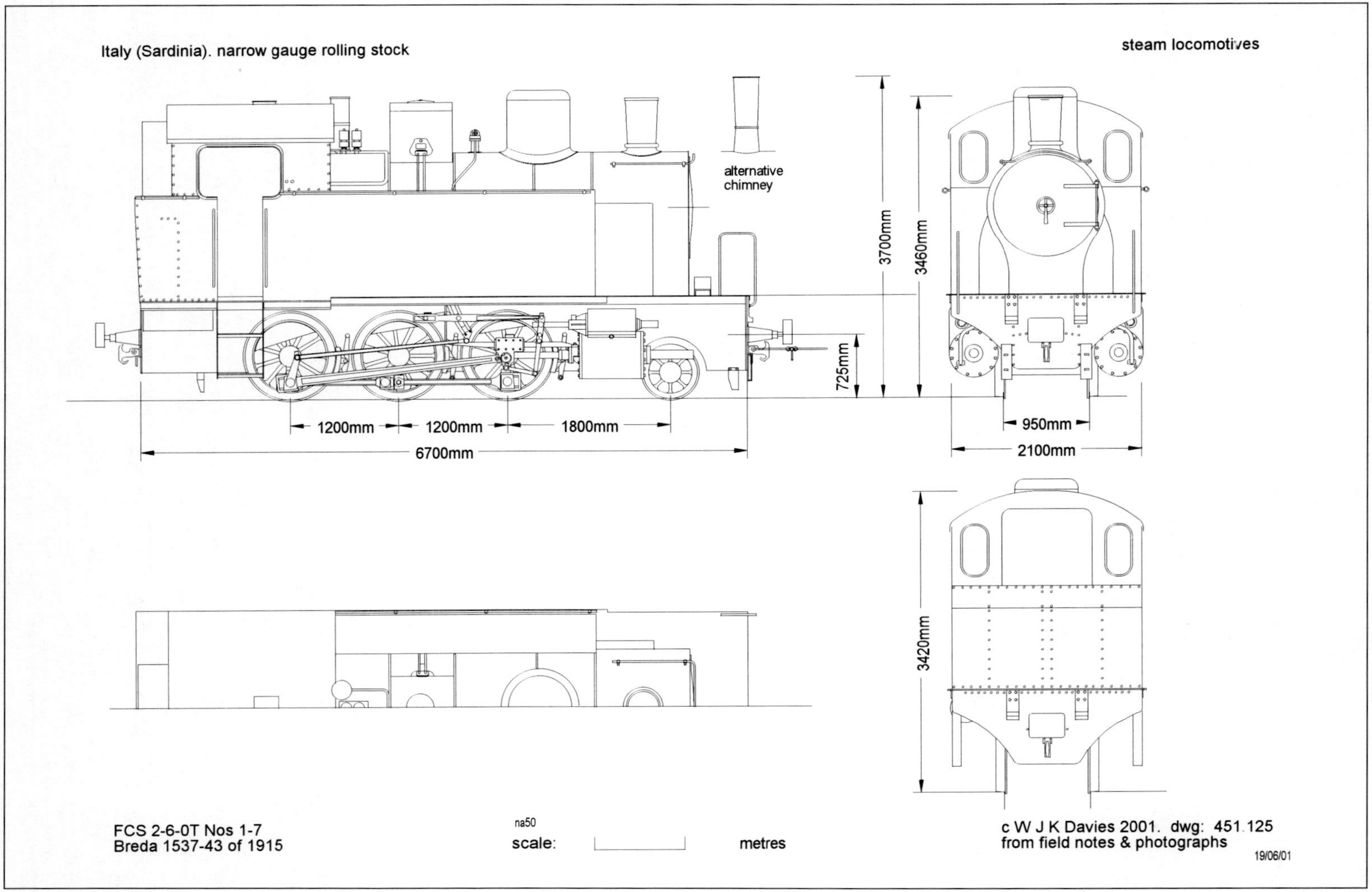

Italy (Sardinia). narrow gauge rolling stock

steam locomotives

alternative chimney

3700mm

3460mm

725mm

1200mm

1200mm

1800mm

6700mm

950mm

2100mm

3420mm

FCS 2-6-0T Nos 1-7
Breda 1537-43 of 1915

na50
scale: metres

c W J K Davies 2001. dwg: 451.125
from field notes & photographs

19/06/01

D4 Breda 2-6-0T for FCS

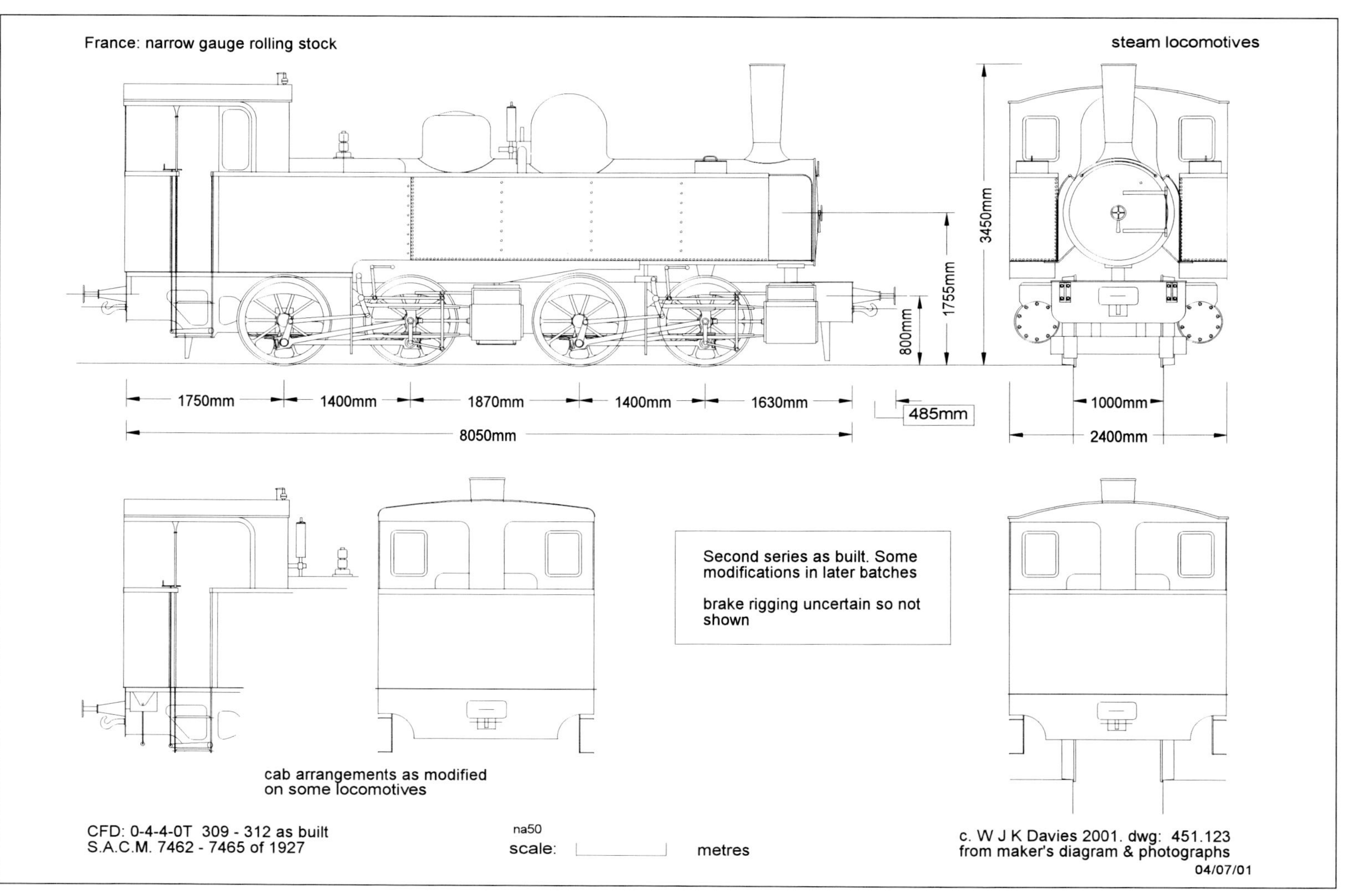
France: narrow gauge rolling stock
steam locomotives
3450mm
1755mm
800mm
1750mm
1400mm
1870mm
1400mm
1630mm
8050mm
485mm
1000mm
2400mm
Second series as built. Some modifications in later batches
brake rigging uncertain so not shown
cab arrangements as modified on some locomotives
CFD: 0-4-4-0T 309 - 312 as built
S.A.C.M. 7462 - 7465 of 1927
na50
scale:
metres
c. W J K Davies 2001. dwg: 451.123
from maker's diagram & photographs
04/07/01

D5 SACM 0-4-4-0T Mallet for CFD

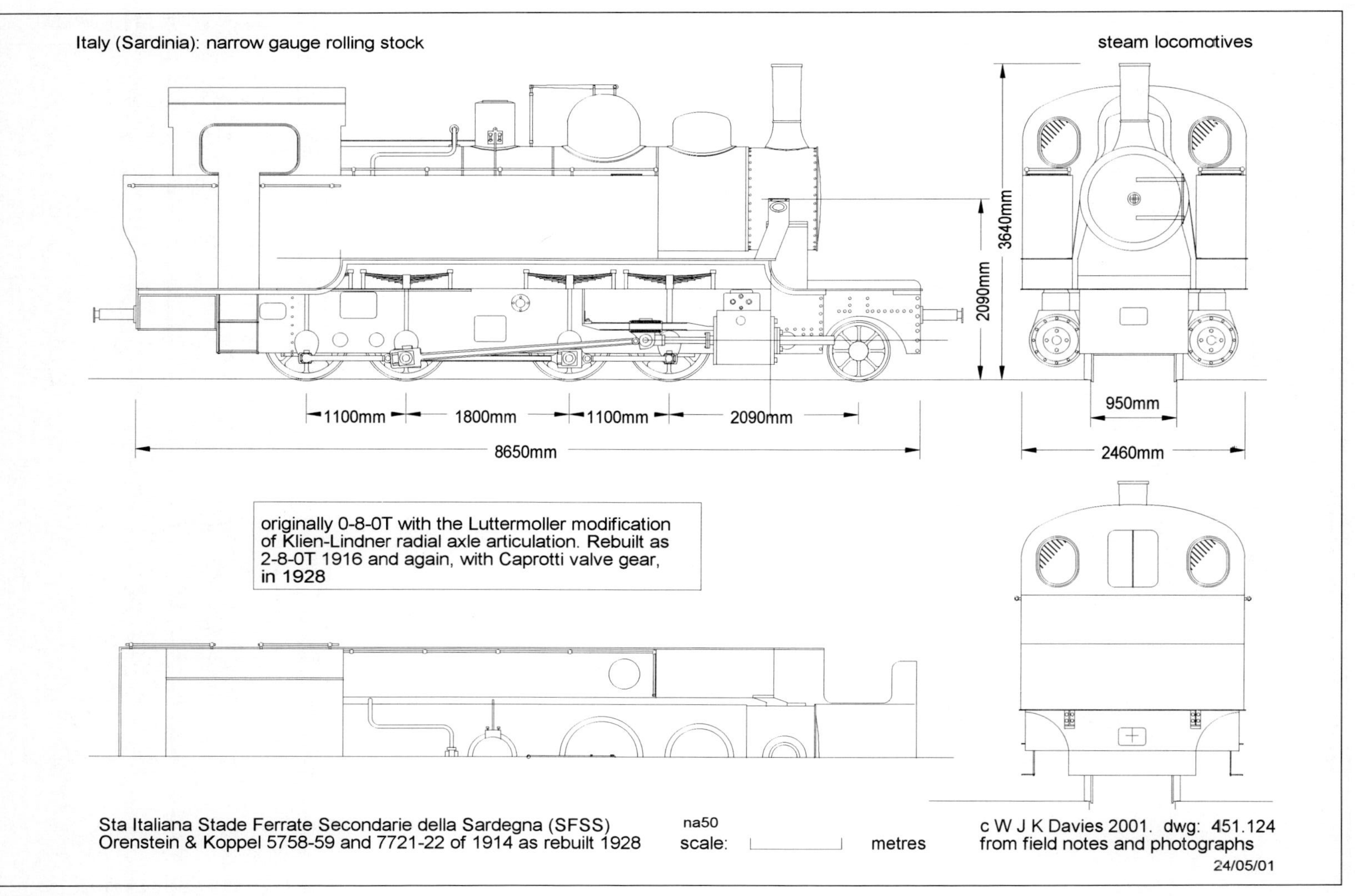

Italy (Sardinia): narrow gauge rolling stock
steam locomotives
3640mm
2090mm
950mm
2460mm
1100mm
1800mm
1100mm
2090mm
8650mm
originally 0-8-0T with the Luttermoller modification of Klien-Lindner radial axle articulation. Rebuilt as 2-8-0T 1916 and again, with Caprotti valve gear, in 1928
Sta Italiana Stade Ferrate Secondarie della Sardegna (SFSS)
Orenstein & Koppel 5758-59 and 7721-22 of 1914 as rebuilt 1928
na50
scale:
metres
c W J K Davies 2001. dwg: 451.124
from field notes and photographs
24/05/01

D6 O&K 2-8-0T for SFSS as rebuilt

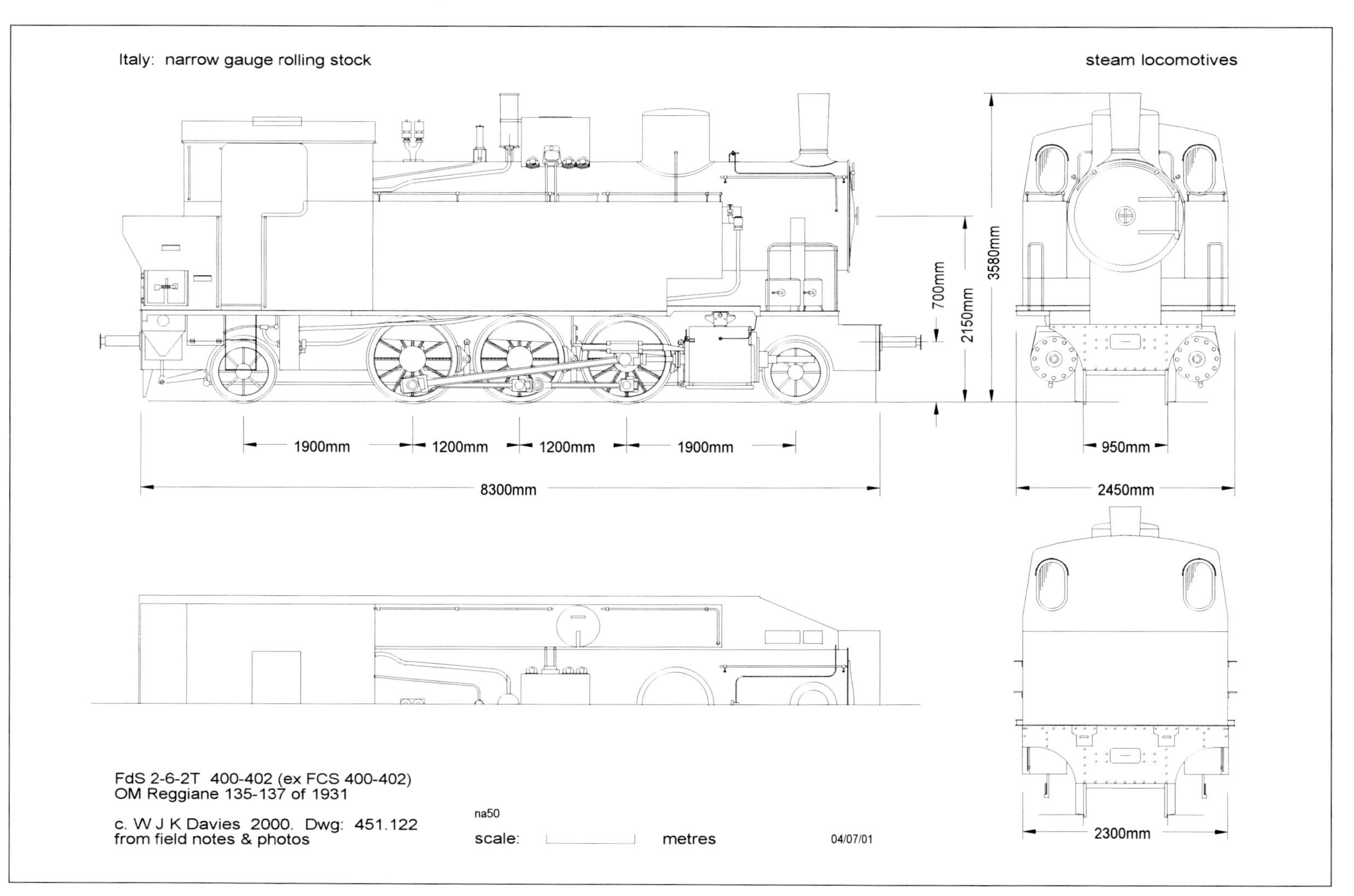
Italy: narrow gauge rolling stock
steam locomotives
700mm
2150mm
3580mm
1900mm
1200mm
1200mm
1900mm
8300mm
950mm
2450mm
2300mm
FdS 2-6-2T 400-402 (ex FCS 400-402)
OM Reggiane 135-137 of 1931
c. W J K Davies 2000. Dwg: 451.122
from field notes & photos
na50
scale:
metres
04/07/01

D7 OM Reggiane 2-6-2T for FCS

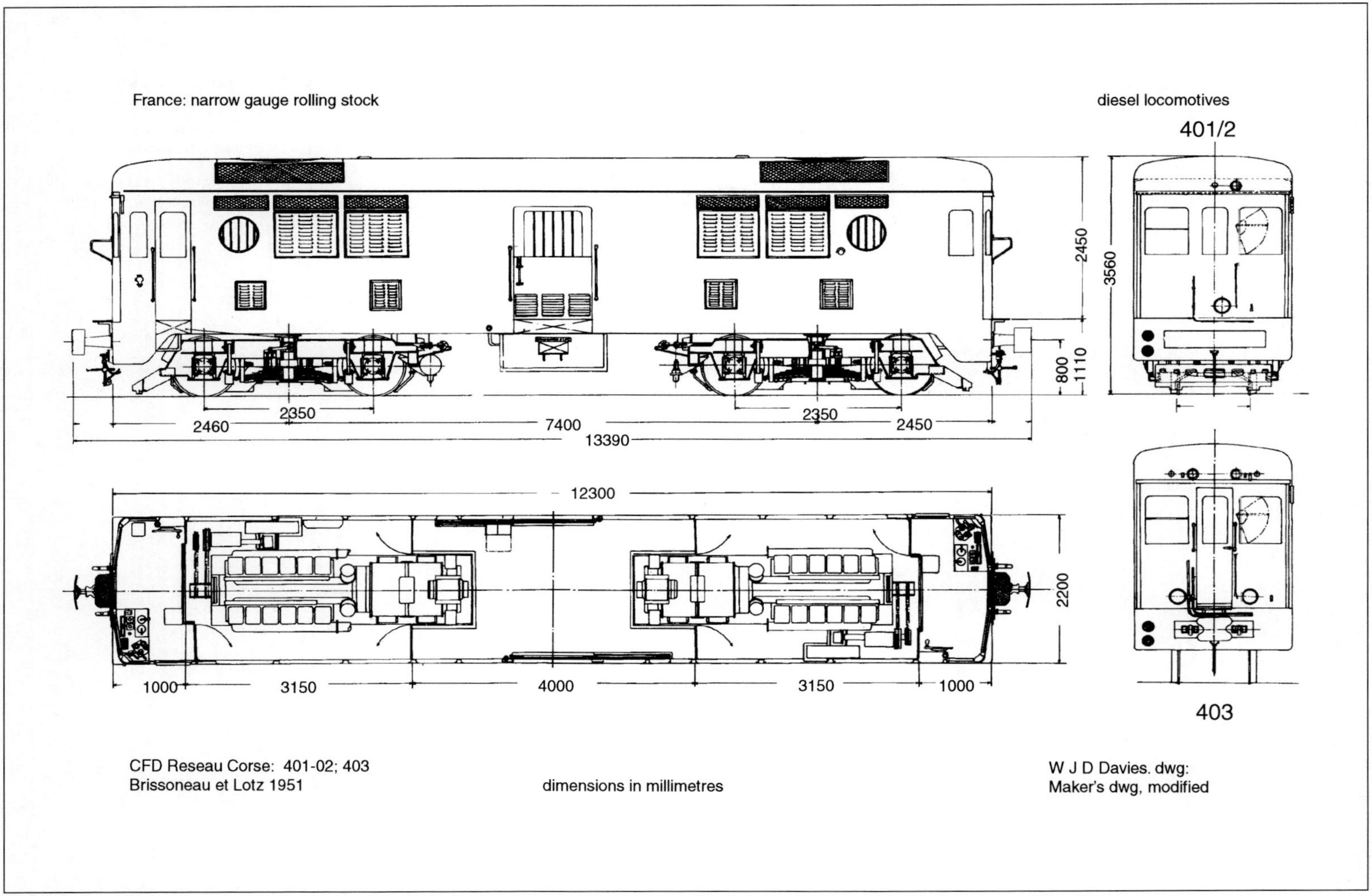

France: narrow gauge rolling stock

diesel locomotives

401/2

2450
3560
800
1110
2460
2350
7400
2350
2450
13390

12300
2200
1000
3150
4000
3150
1000

403

CFD Reseau Corse: 401-02; 403
Brissoneau et Lotz 1951

dimensions in millimetres

W J D Davies. dwg:
Maker's dwg, modified

D8 Brissoneau et Lotz BB DE loco for CFD

France: narrow gauge rolling stock

diesel locomotives

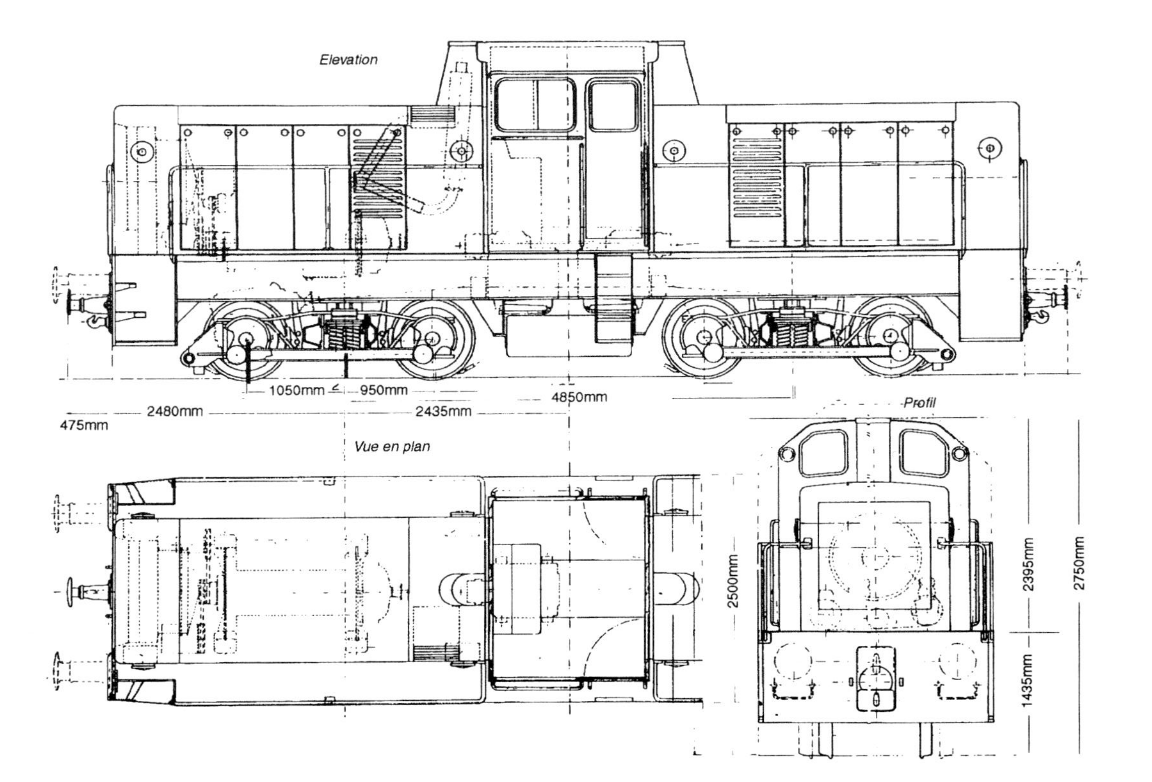

400hp BB locomotive for metre gauge
Cie des Chemins de Fer Departementaux 1962

source: Maker's photo, redimensioned

D9 CFD BB locomotive for CFD

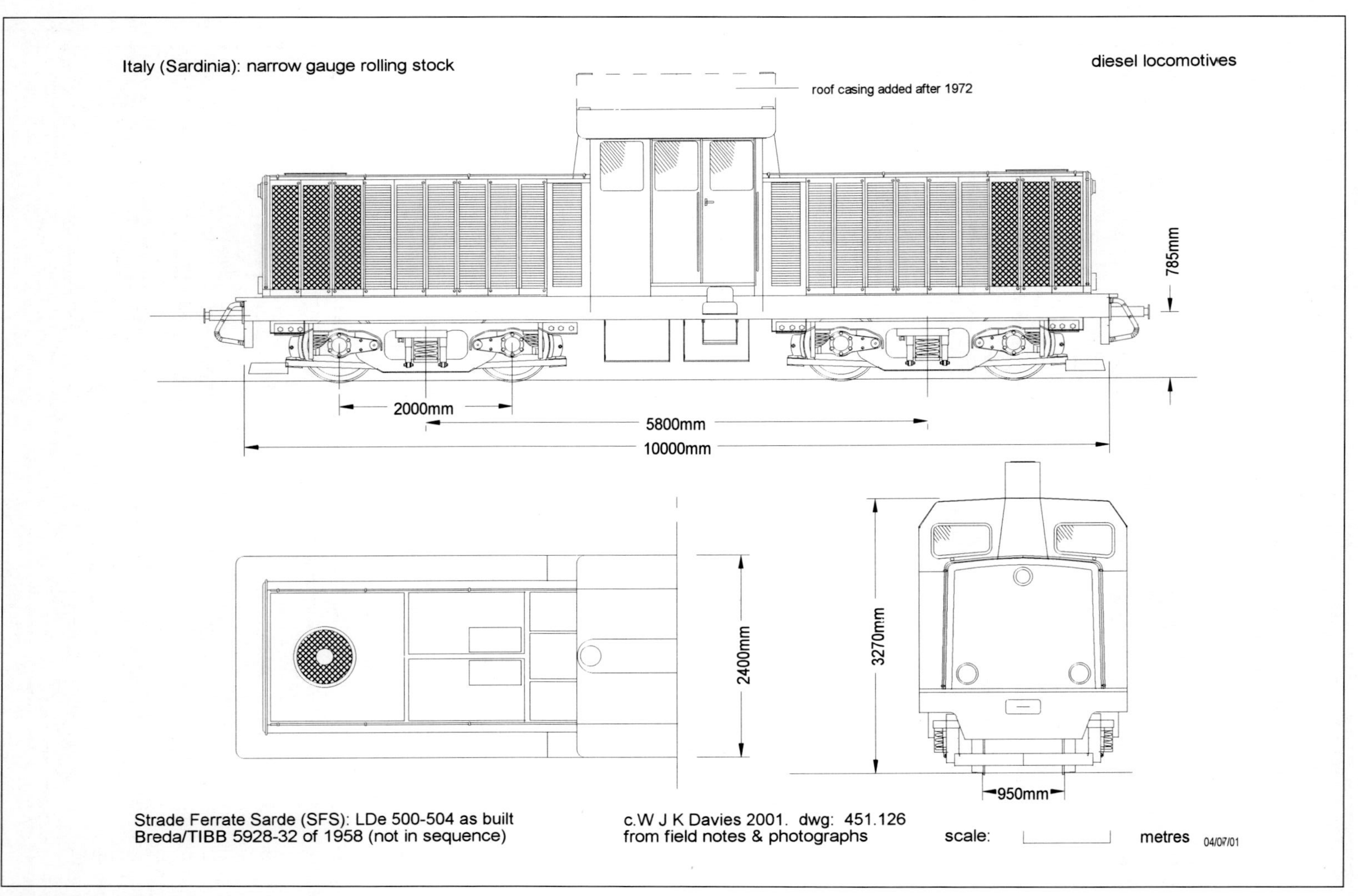

D10 Breda/TIBB BB DE locomotive for SFS

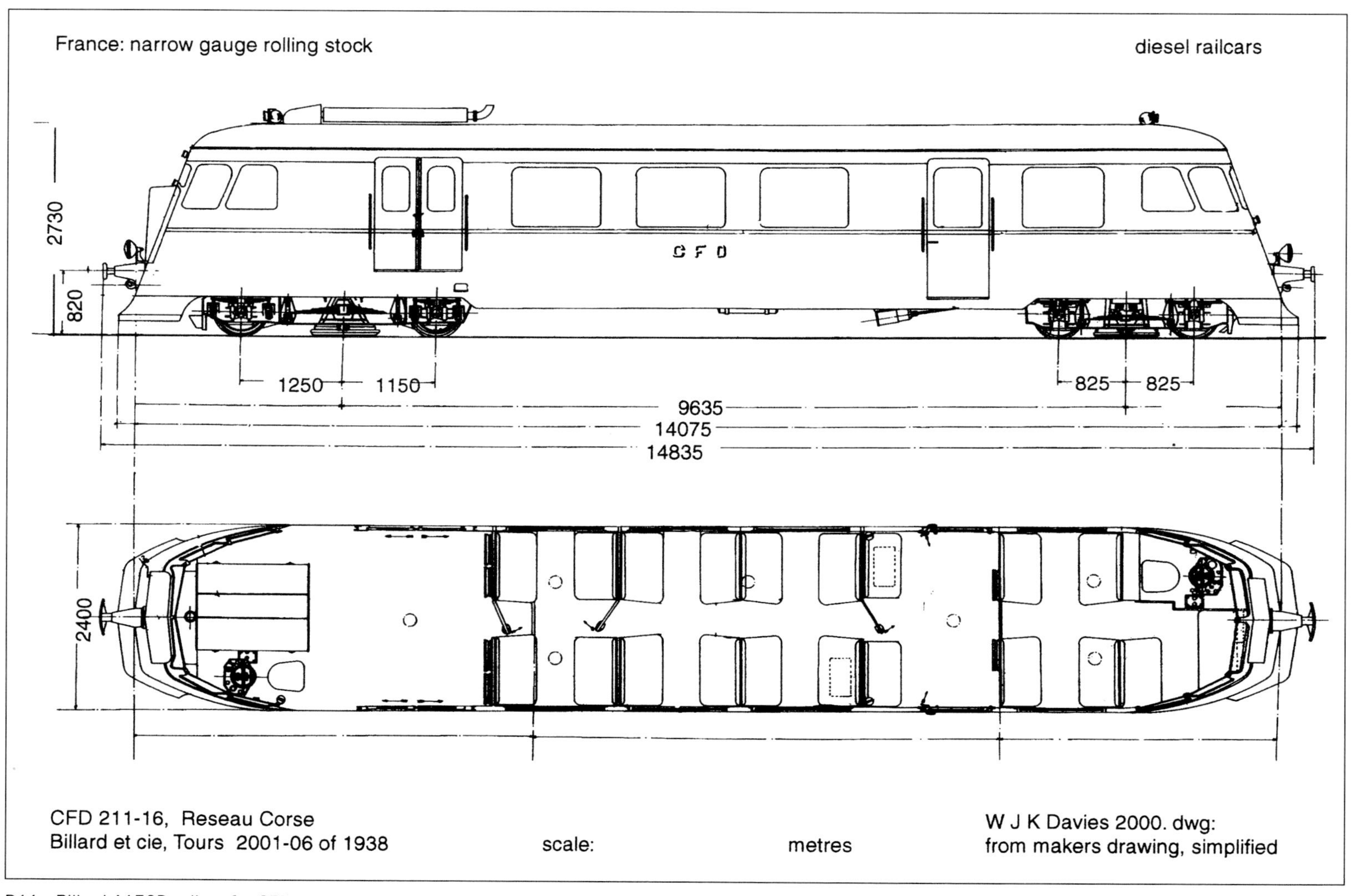

D11 Billard A150D railcar for CFD

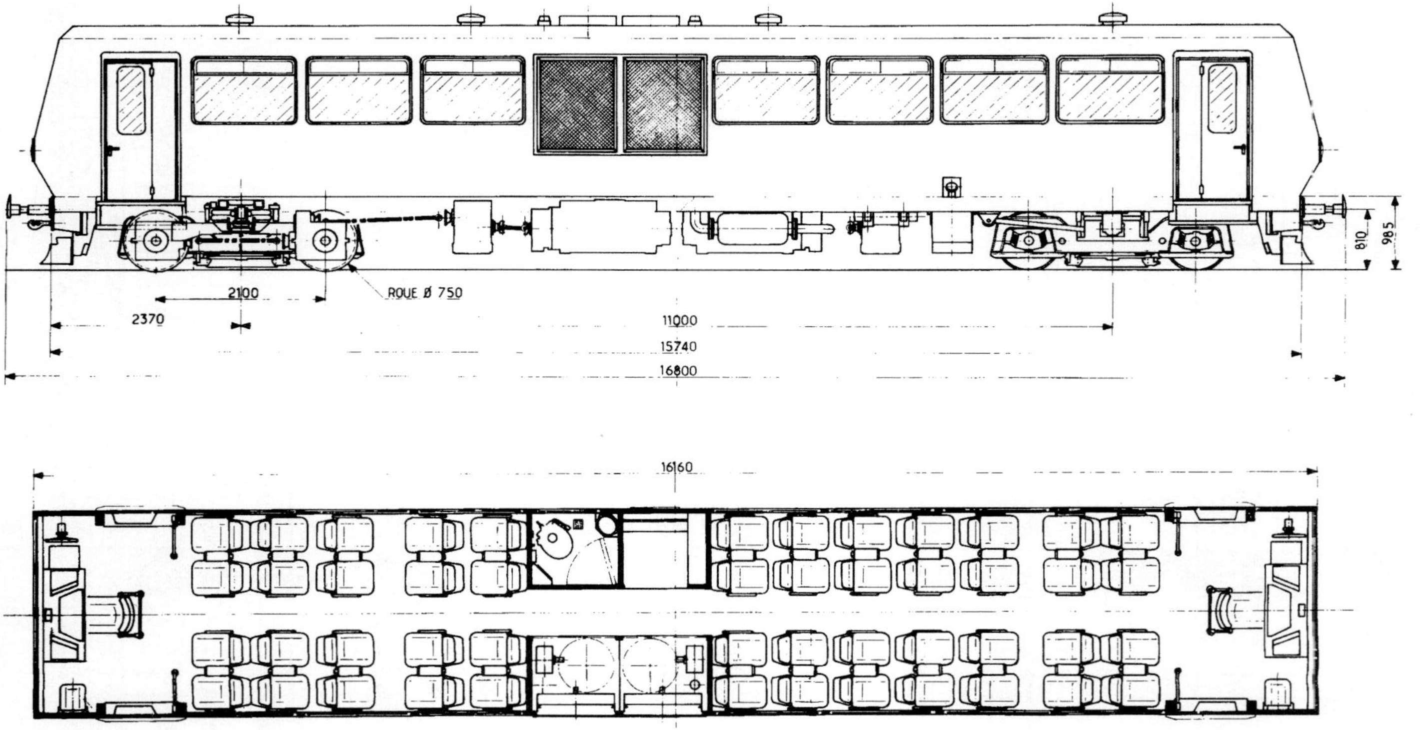

CFC Reseau Corse: X5000-01
CFD Montmirail 1981-2

dimensions in millimetres

Maker's dwg, reduced

D12 CFD 5000 series railcar for CFD

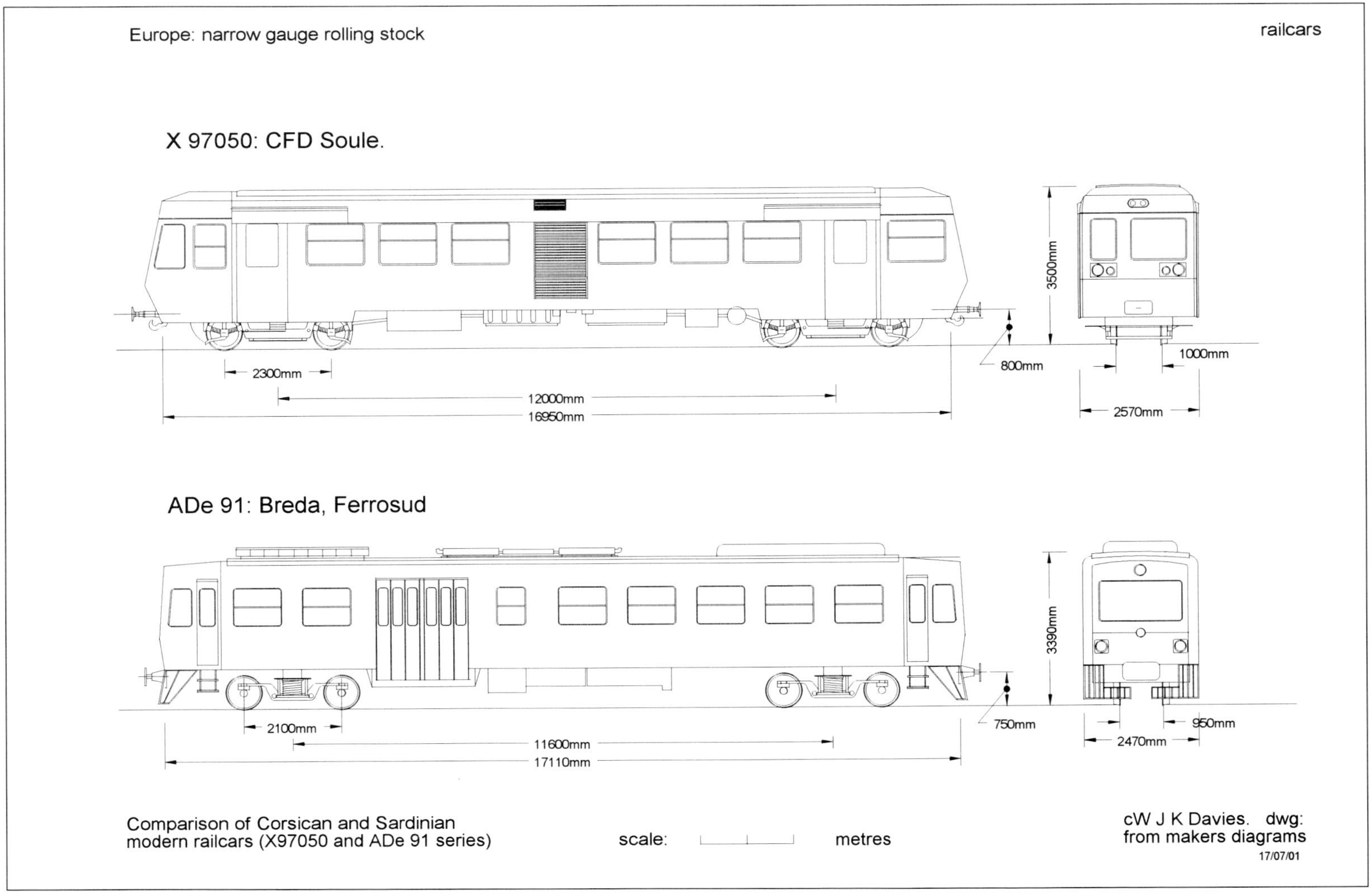

D13 Modern Soule (CFD) and Ferrosud (FdS) railcars compared

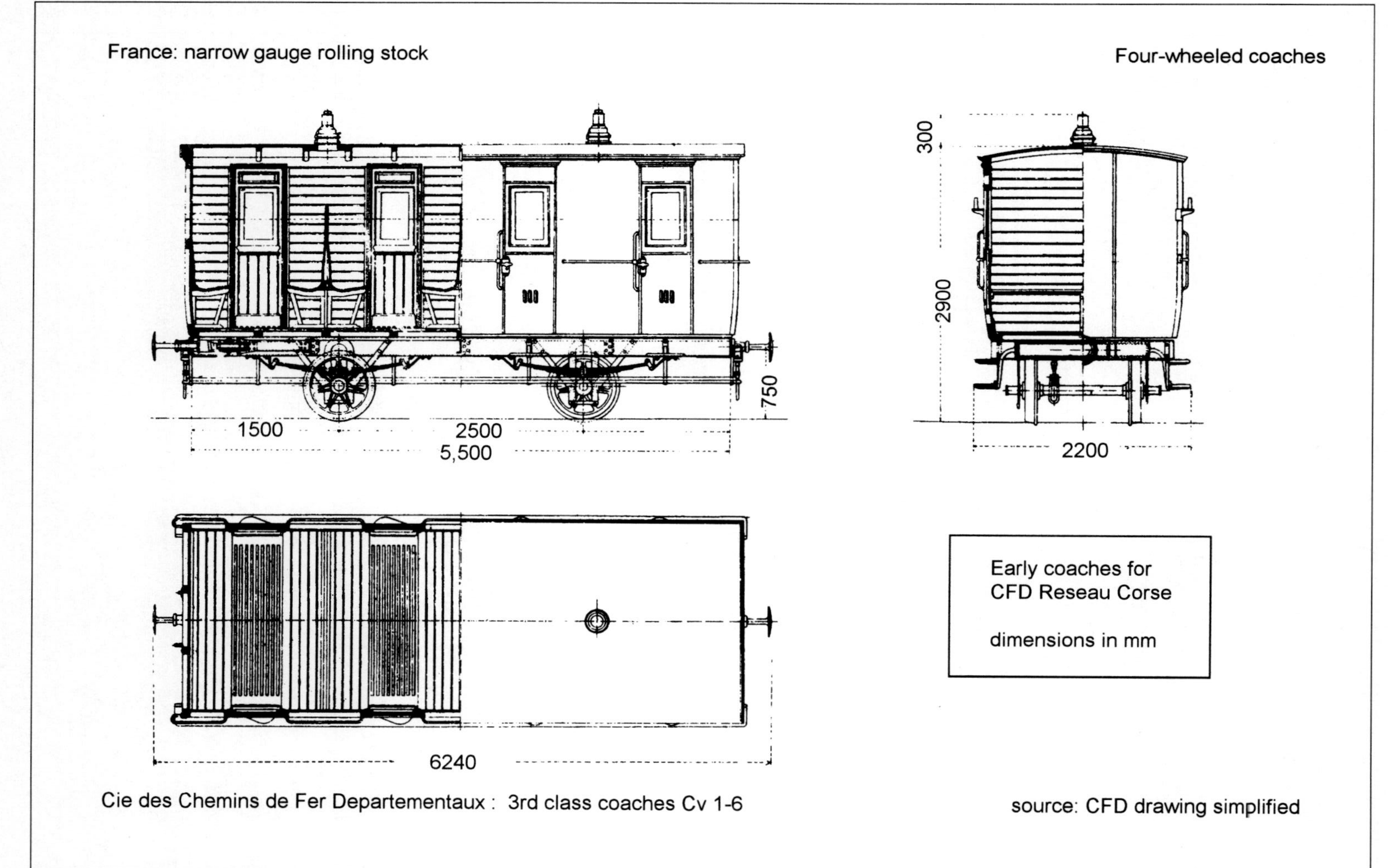

D14 CFD 4-wheel 3rd class coach

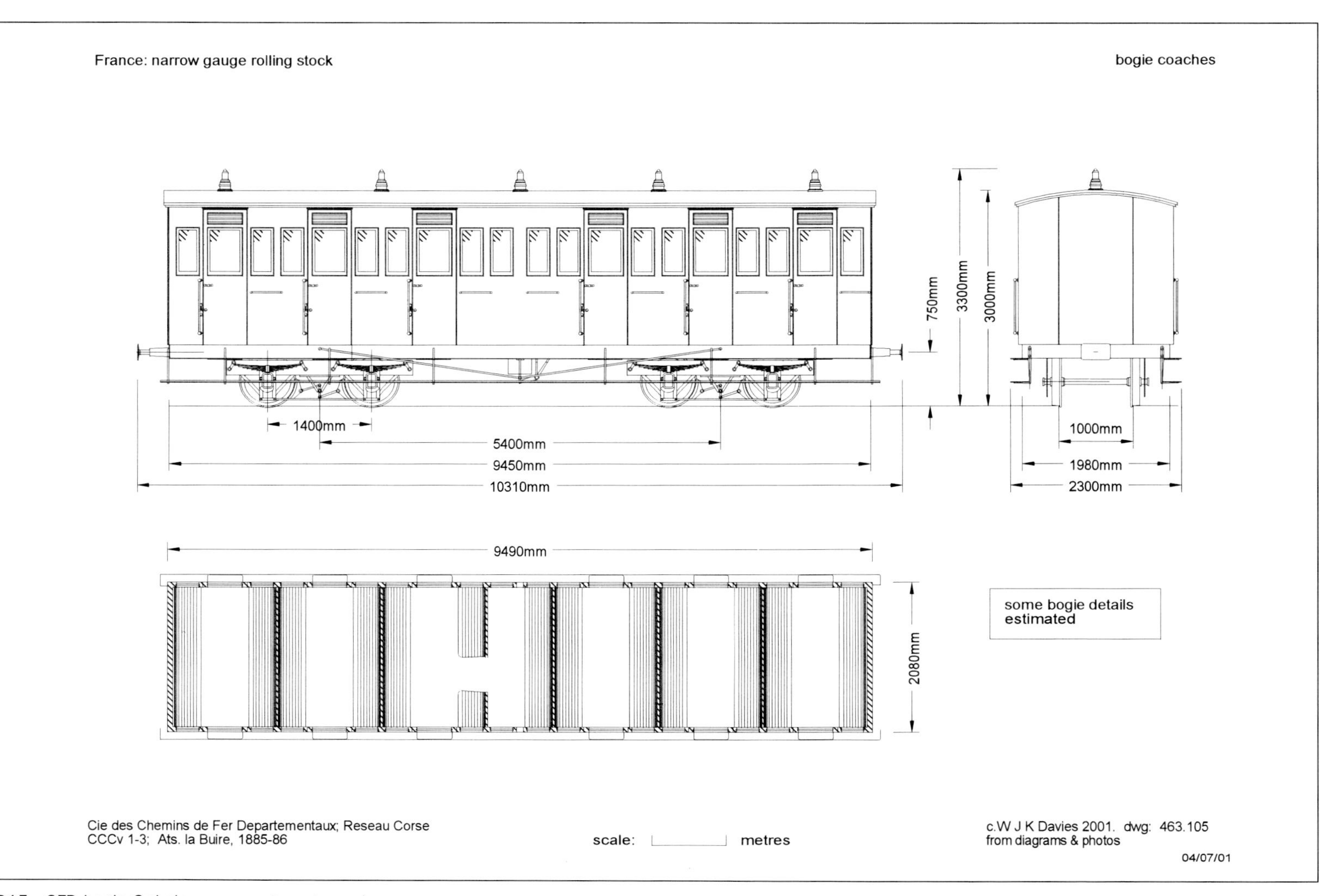

D15 CFD bogie 3rd class compartment coach

France: narrow gauge rolling stock

bogie coaches

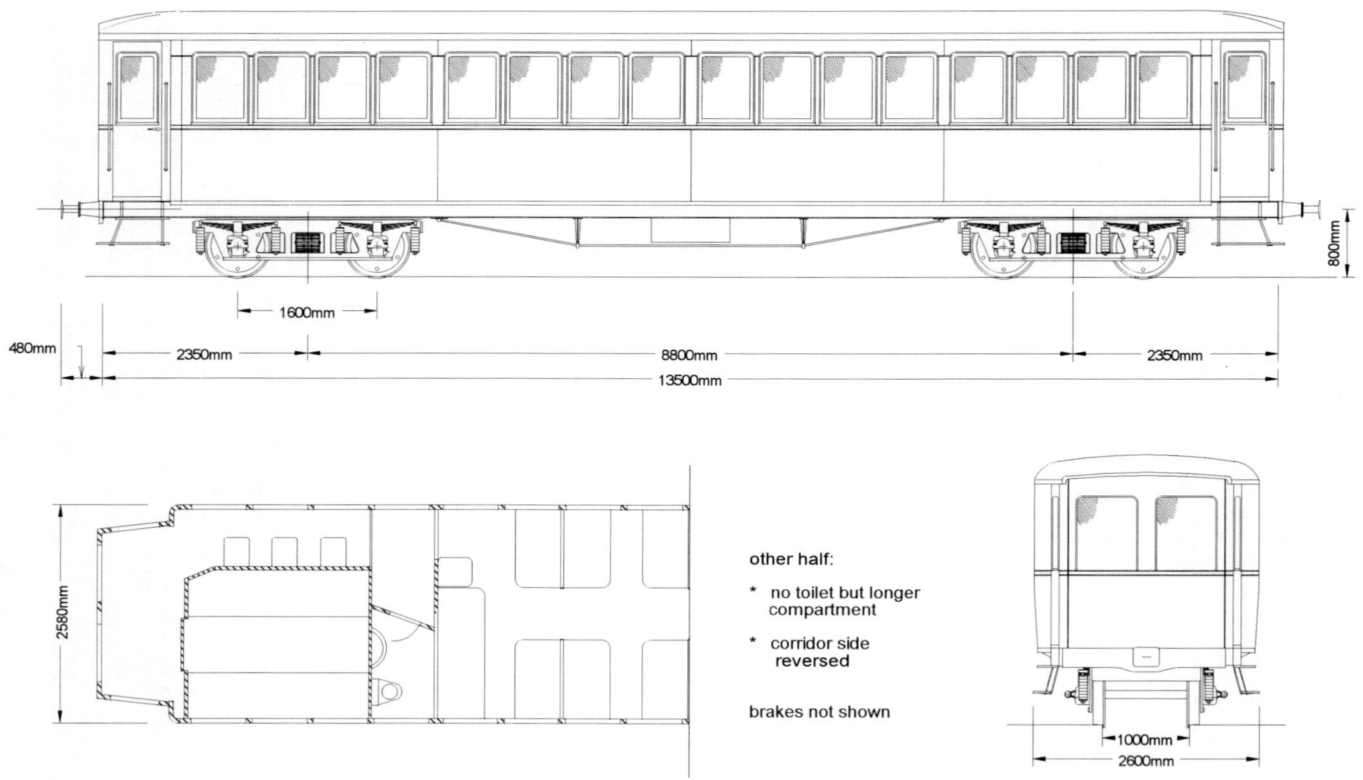
800mm
1600mm
480mm
2350mm
8800mm
2350mm
13500mm
2580mm
1000mm
2600mm

other half:

* no toilet but longer compartment
* corridor side reversed

brakes not shown

CFD Reseau Corse: CCC 1651-56
Ste Lorraine, (Anciens Ets. De Dietrich) 1920/27

na50
scale: metres

c. W J K Davies. 2001. dwg: 463.104
from diagrams and photographs

04/07/01

D16 CFD bogie saloon coach

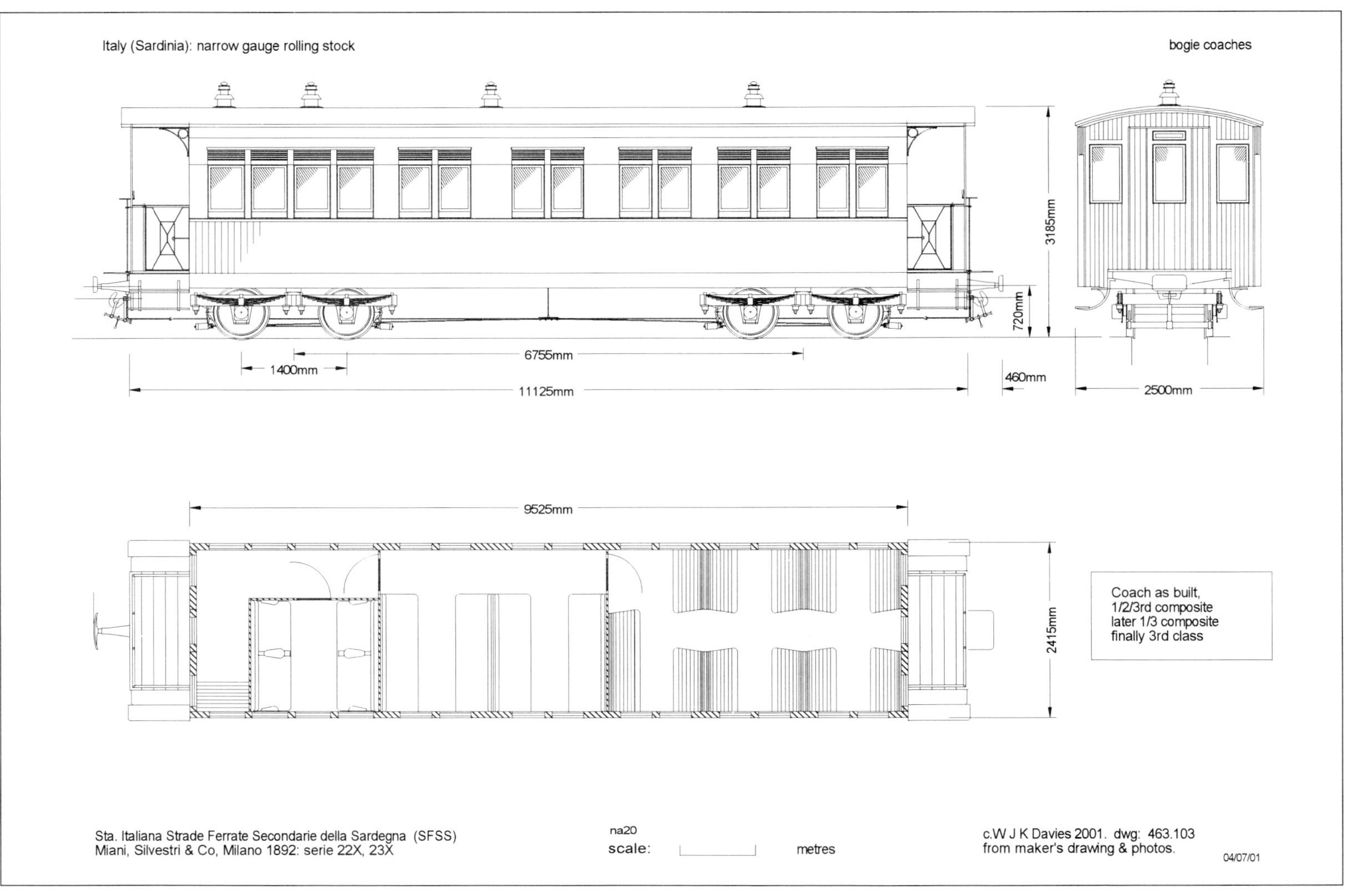

D17 Miani & Silvestri tricomposite for SFSS

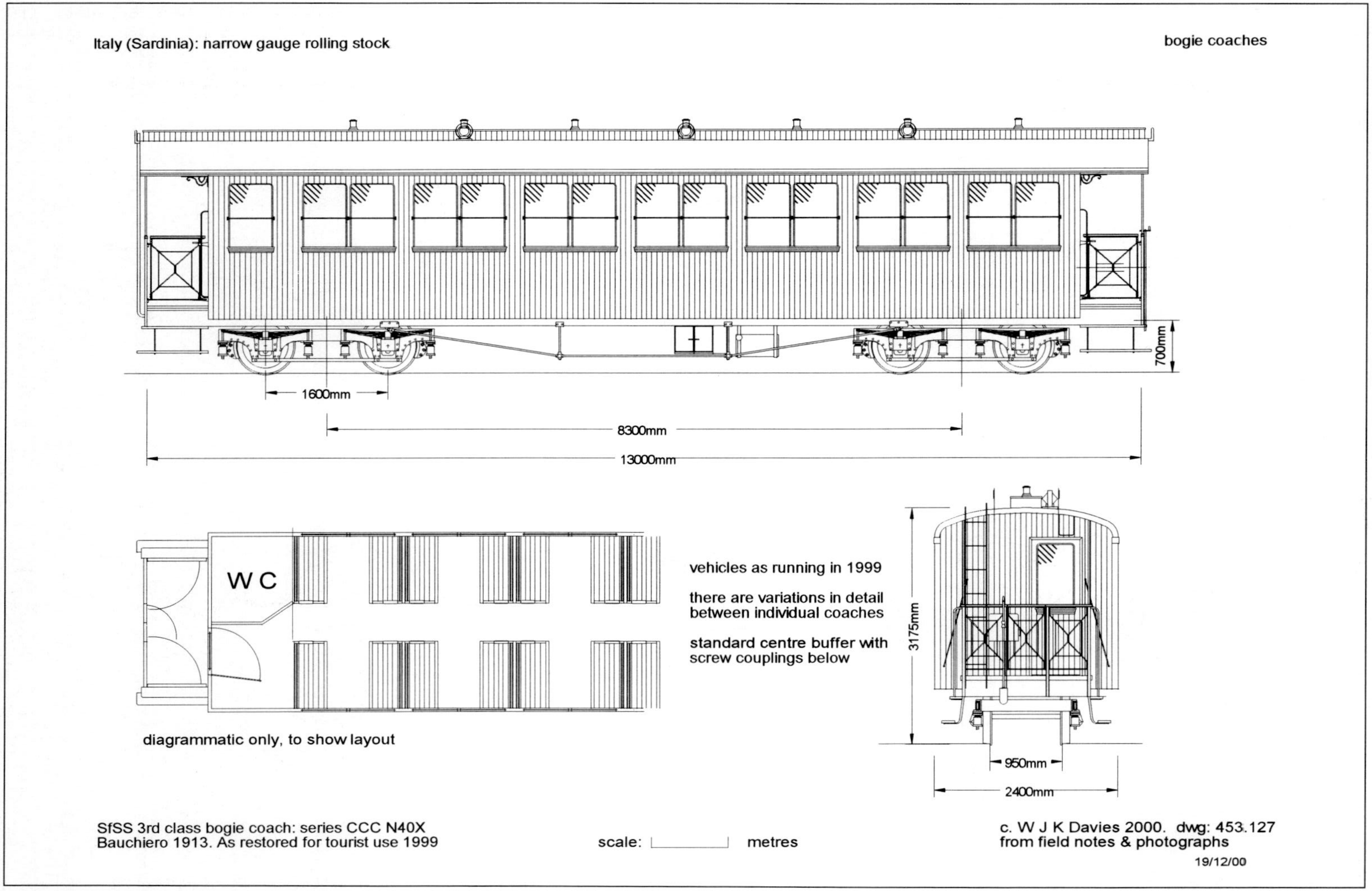

Italy (Sardinia): narrow gauge rolling stock

bogie coaches

700mm

1600mm

8300mm

13000mm

W C

diagrammatic only, to show layout

vehicles as running in 1999

there are variations in detail between individual coaches

standard centre buffer with screw couplings below

3175mm

950mm

2400mm

SfSS 3rd class bogie coach: series CCC N40X
Bauchiero 1913. As restored for tourist use 1999

scale: metres

c. W J K Davies 2000. dwg: 453.127
from field notes & photographs
19/12/00

D18 Bauchiero bogie coach for SFSS as restored

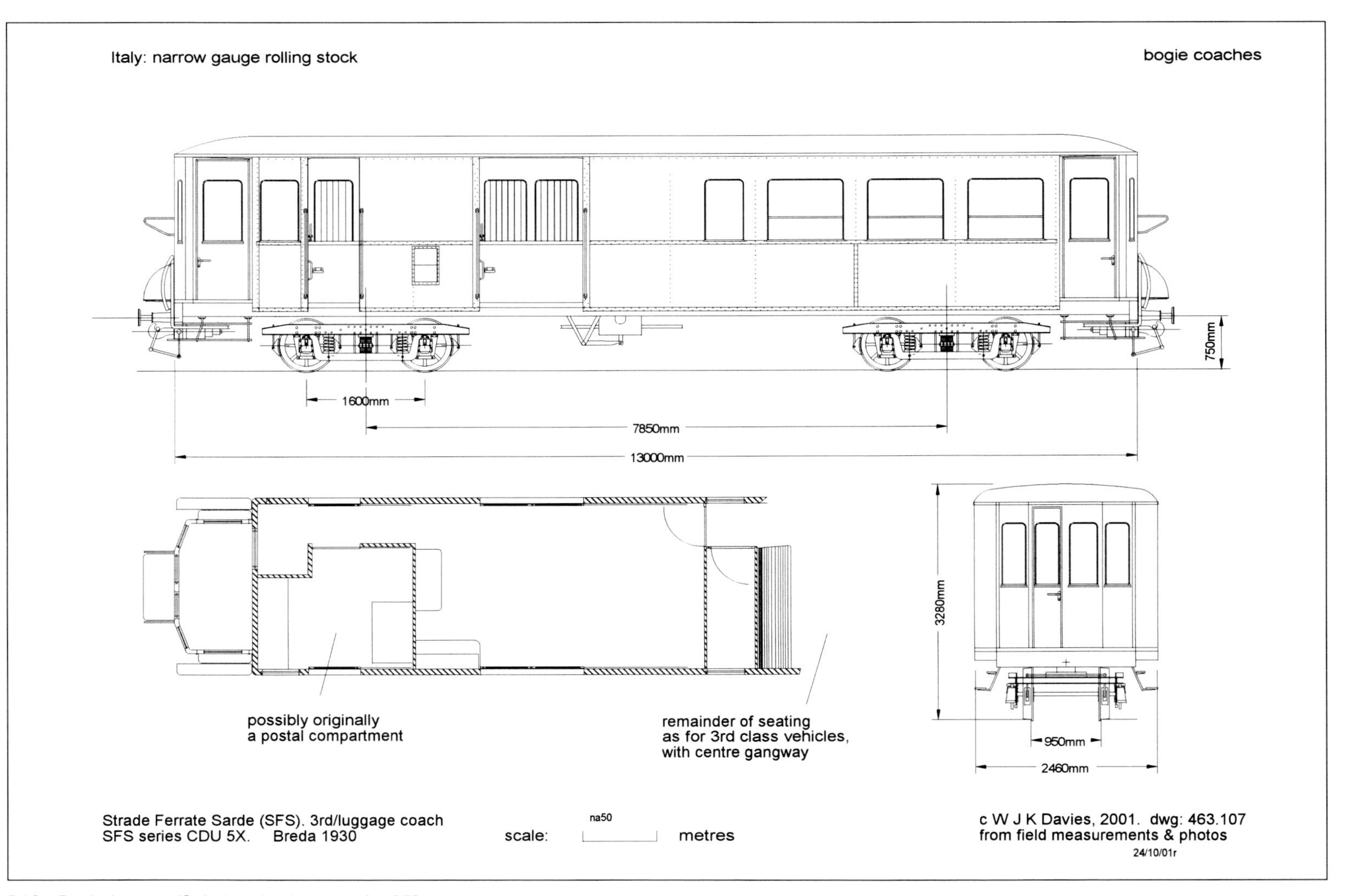

D19 Breda luggage/3rd class bogie coach for SFS

France: narrow gauge rolling stock

railcar trailers

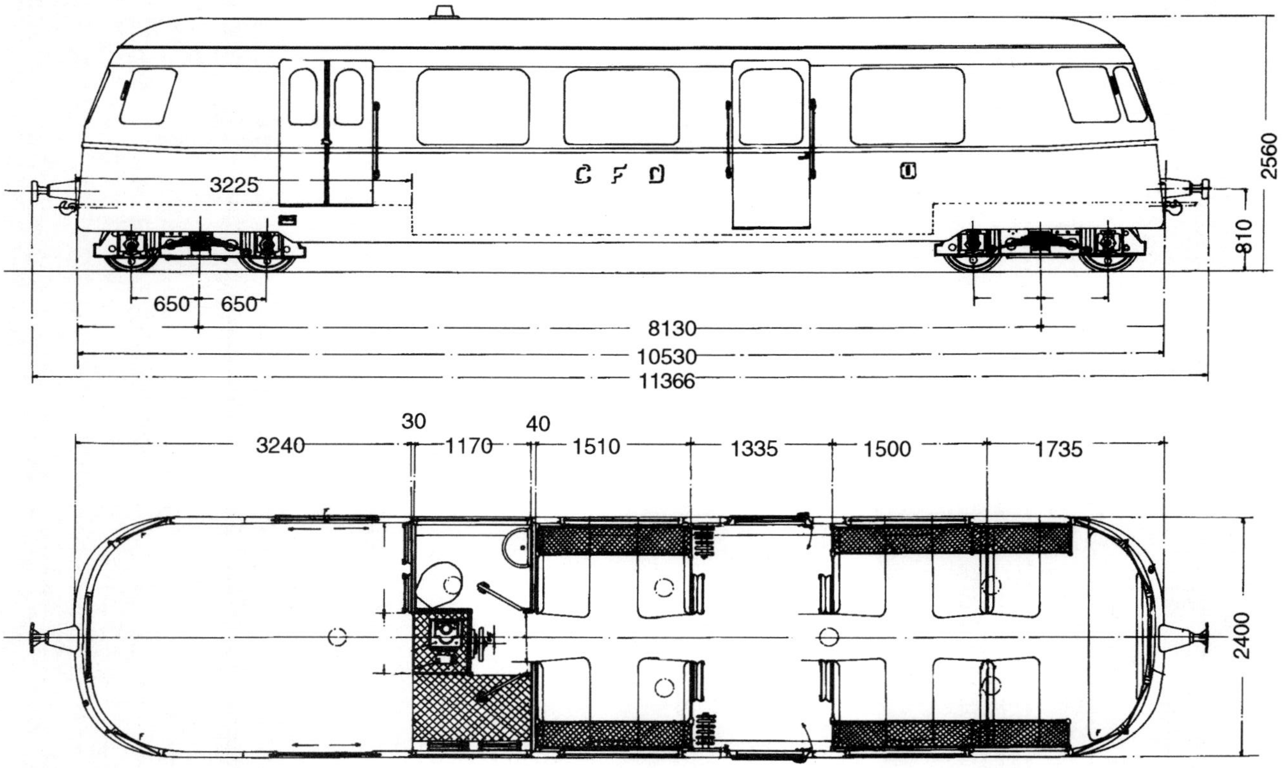

CFD Reseau Corse: railcar trailers 1 - 8
Ancien Ets Billard, Tours type R210 of 1938

scale: metres

W J K Davies. 2001.dwg:
from maker's drawing, simplified

D20 Billard R210 trailer

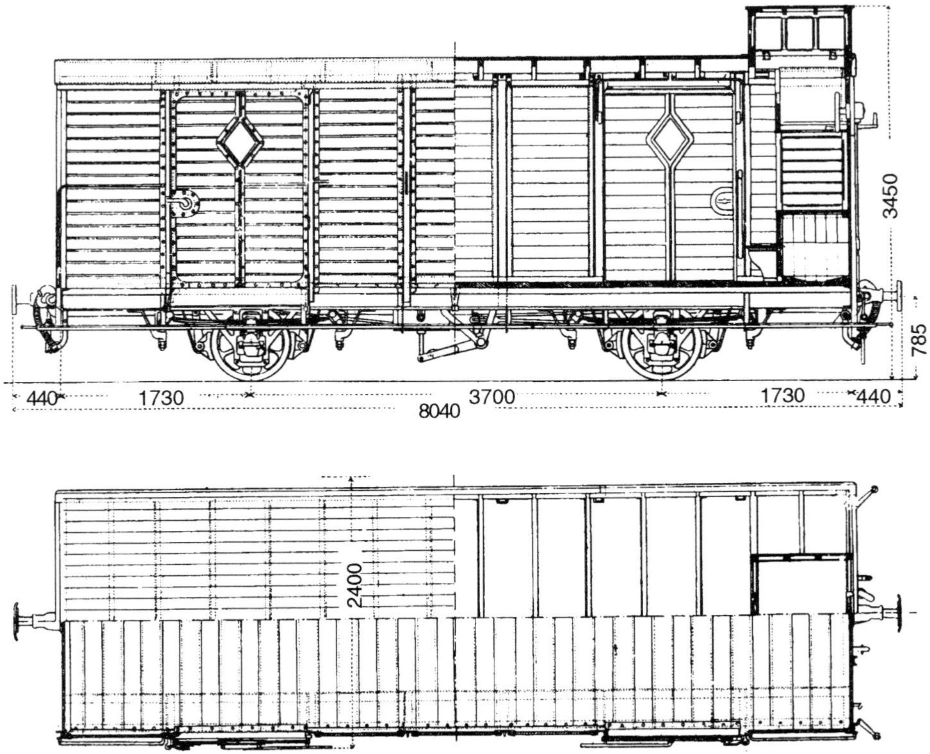

3450
785
440 1730 3700 1730 440
8040
2400

CFD Reseau Corse: DDify 2216-25
De Dietrich, Luneville 1915 & 1927 to Decauville design

dimensions in millimetres

from Decauville dwg, retitled

D21 De Dietrich large luggage van for CFD

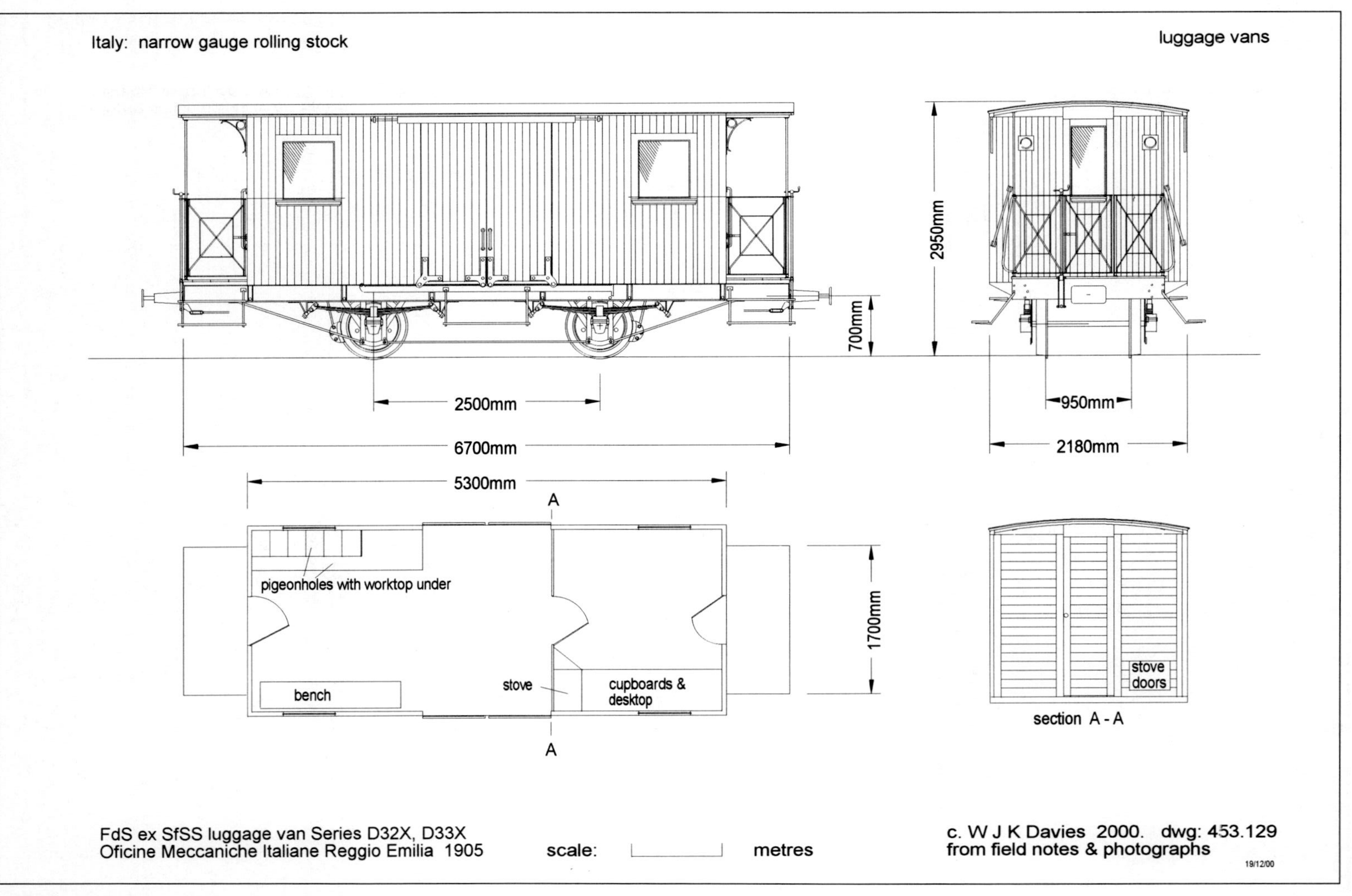

D22 Reggiane D 32X series luggage van for SFSS

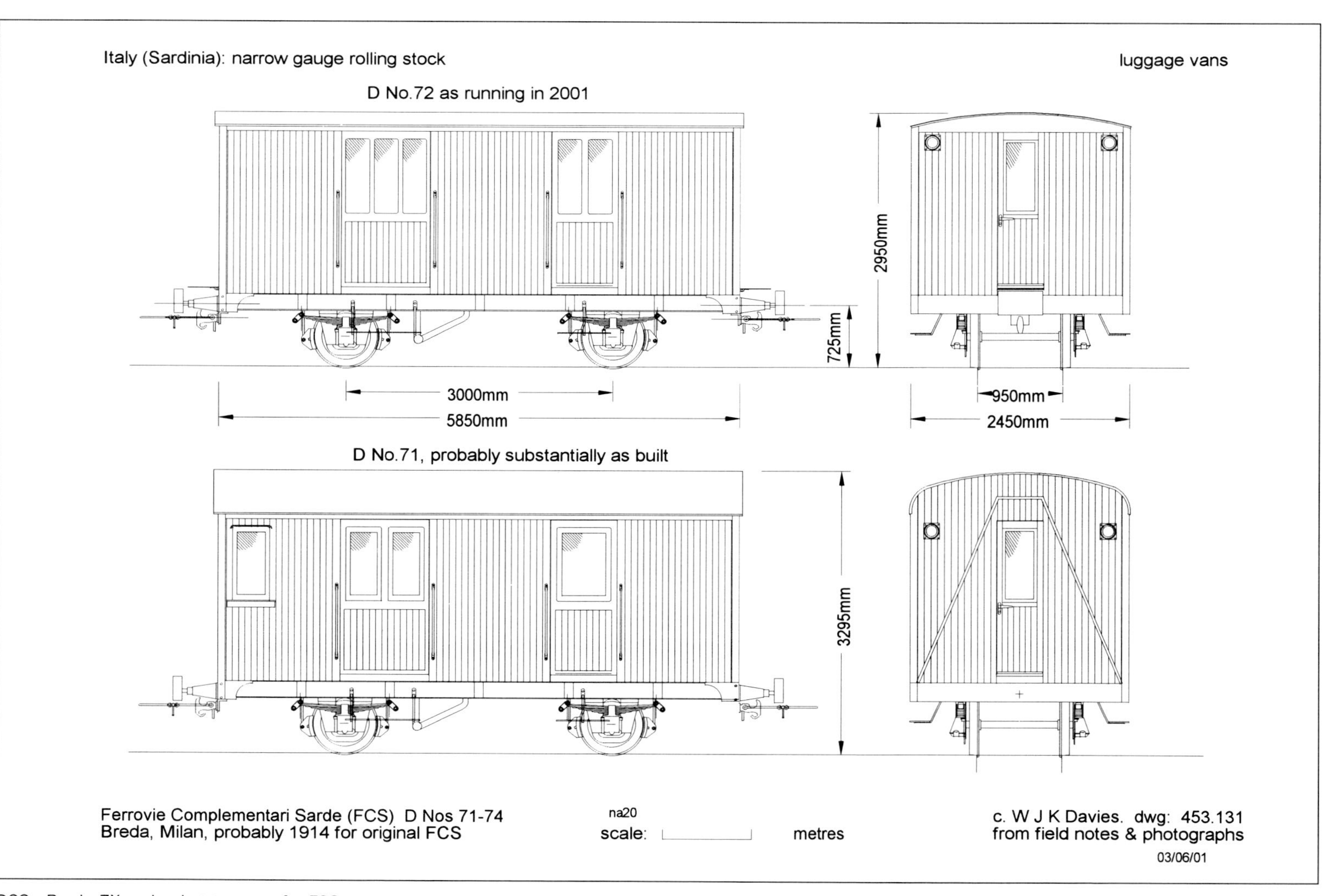

D23 Breda 7X series luggage van for FCS

France: narrow gauge rolling stock goods vehicles

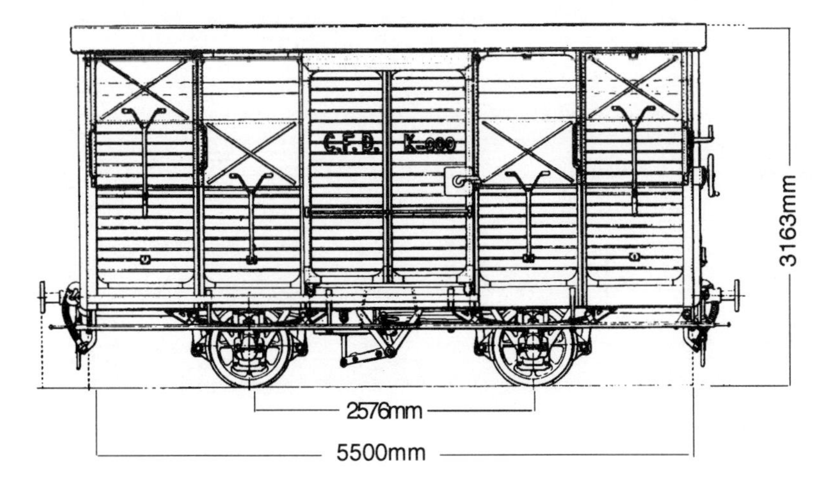

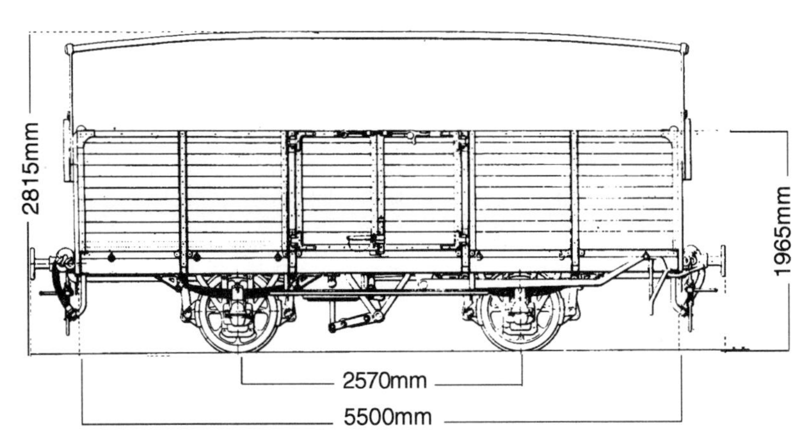

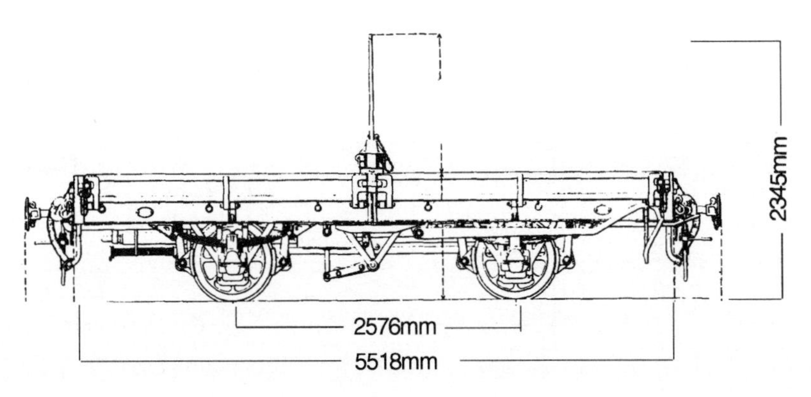

CFD : typical standard goods vehicles from: Decauville catalogue

D24 CFD standard goods vehicles

Italy (Sardinia): narrow gauge rolling stock

goods vans

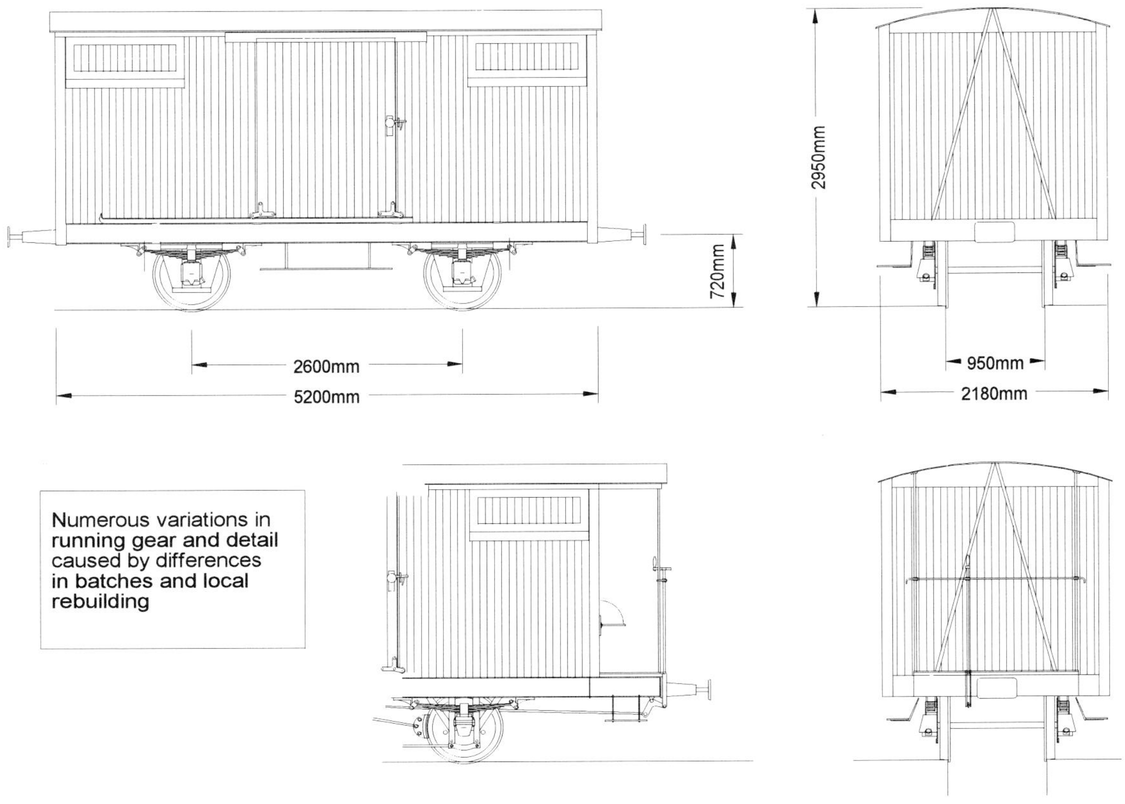

720mm

2950mm

2600mm

5200mm

950mm

2180mm

Numerous variations in running gear and detail caused by differences in batches and local rebuilding

FdS ventilated goods van ex FCS/SfSS
Series M: various makers.

scale: metres

c. W J K Davies 2000. dwg: 454.110
from field notes and photographs
19/12/00

D25 CFD standard goods vehicles

Italy: narrow gauge rolling stock

covered vans

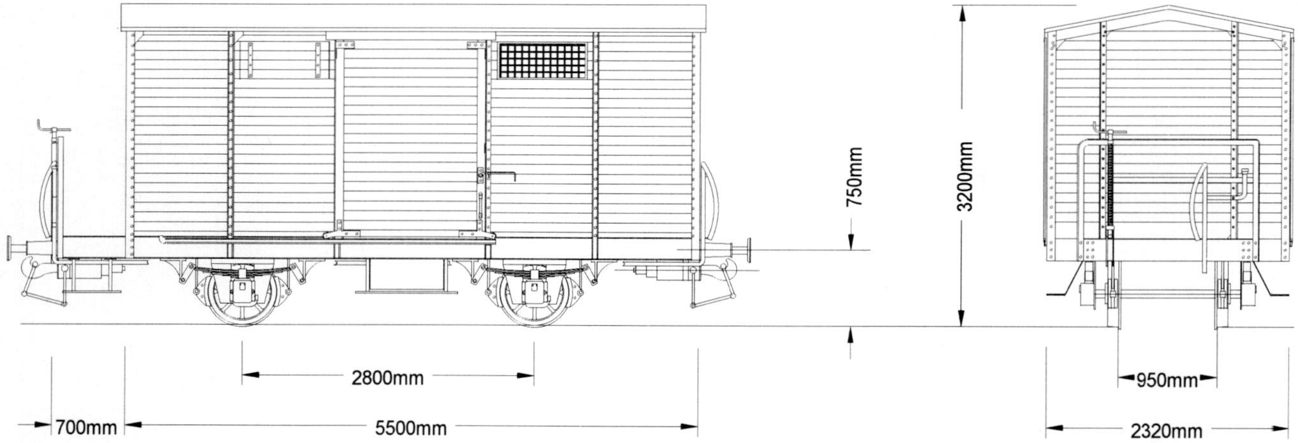

750mm

3200mm

2800mm

700mm

5500mm

950mm

2320mm

Strade Ferrate Sarde (SFS). ventilated goods van
series Fv 1XX. Breda, Milan 1930

na50
scale: metres

c. W J K Davies 2001. dwg: 454.114
from field measurements & photographs
23/10/01

D26 Breda ventilated, braked van for SFS

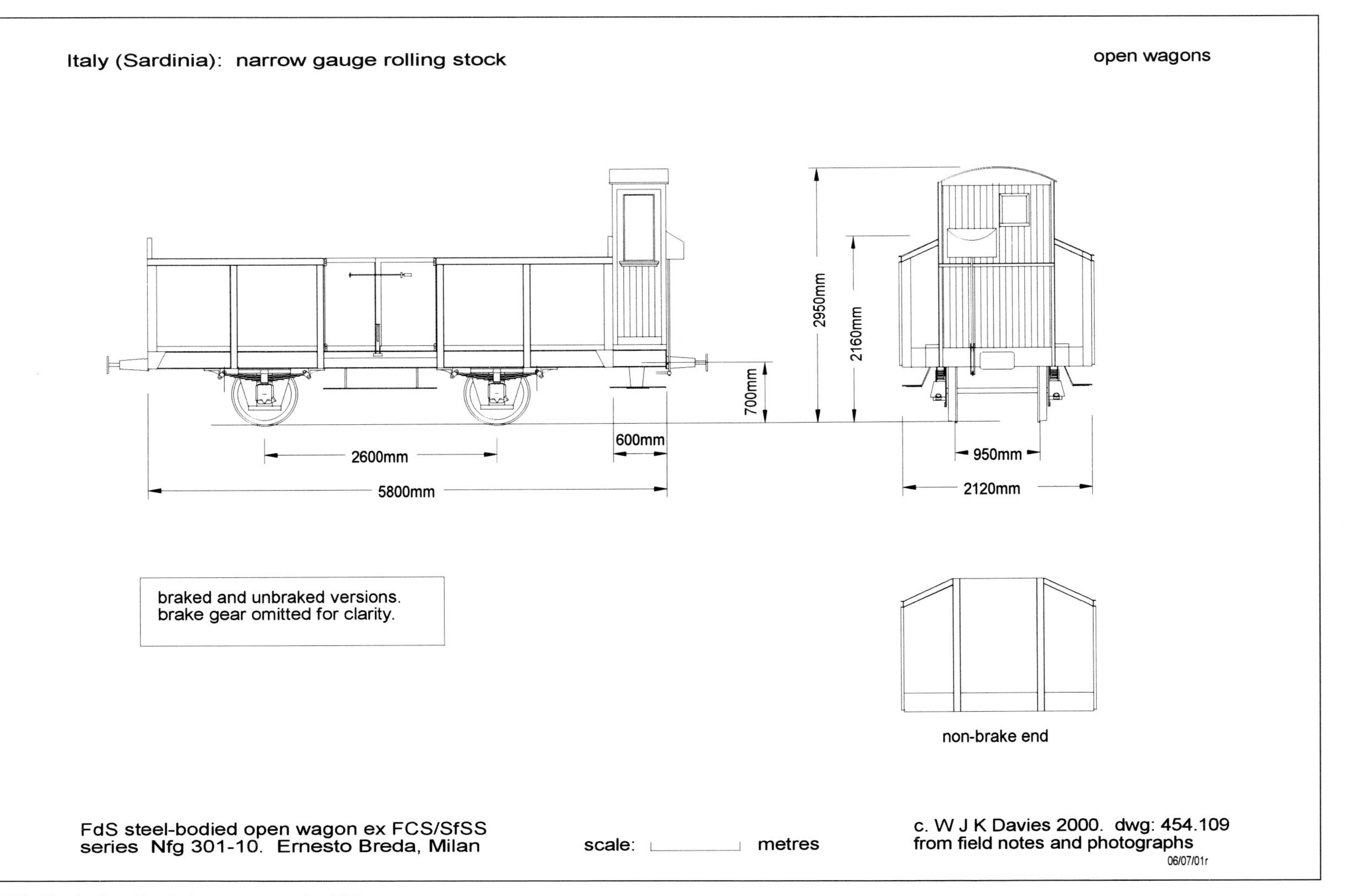

D27 Breda Steel-bodied open wagon for FCS

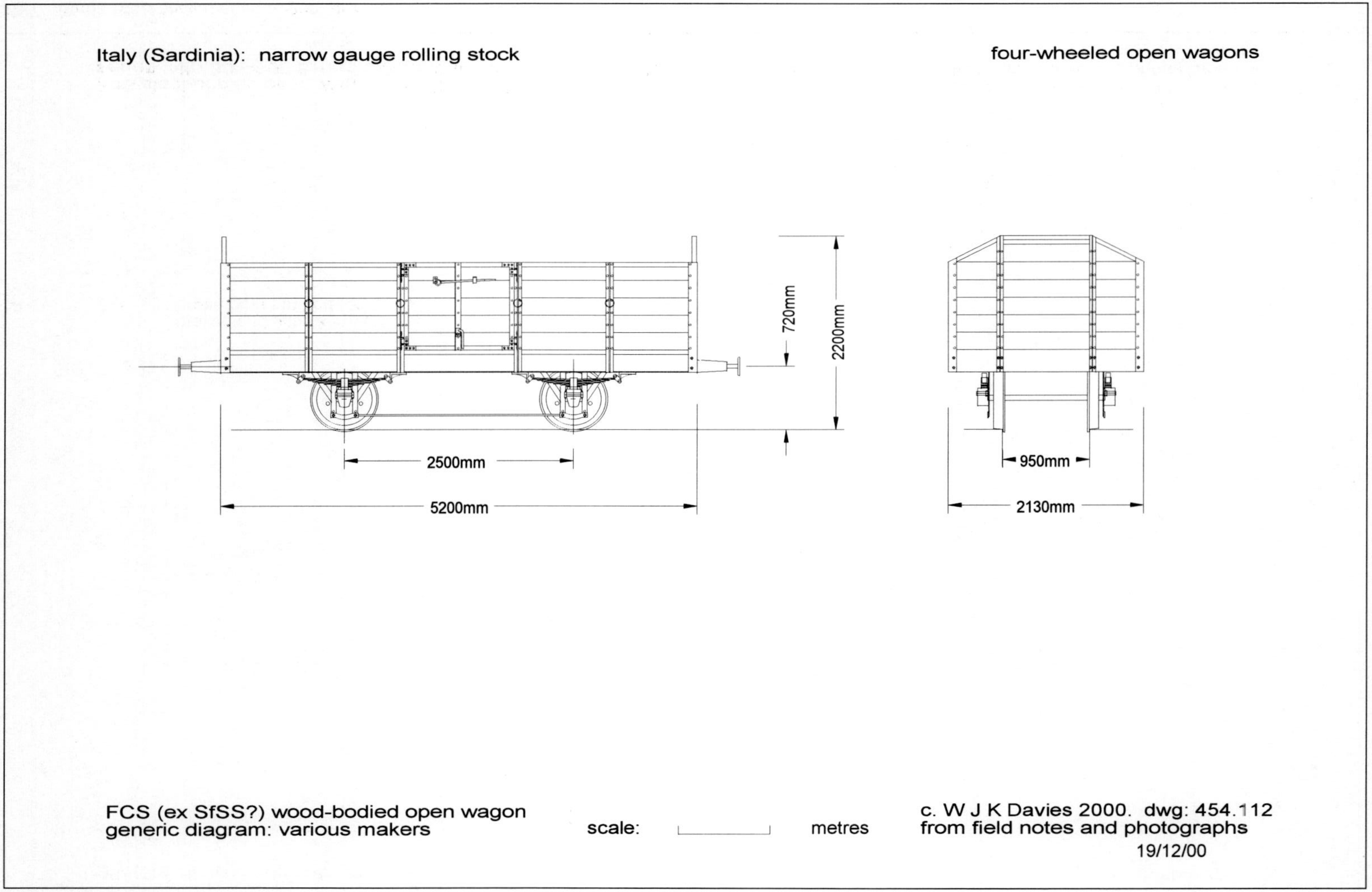

D28 Wood-bodied open wagon for SFSS

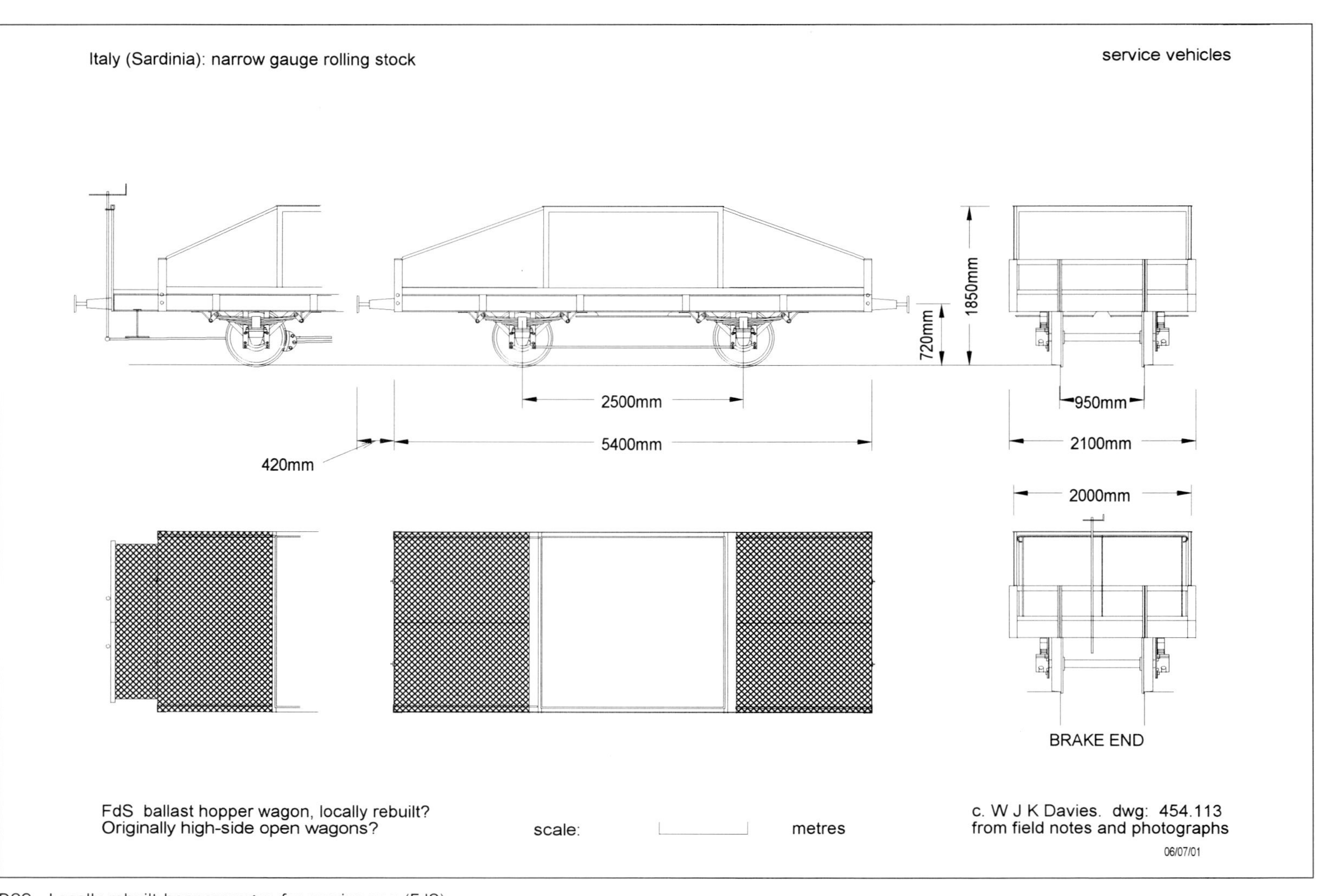

D29 Locally rebuilt hopper wagon for service use (FdS)

APPENDIX 6

A note on urban and suburban tramways in Sardinia

Cagliari

Up to the present, Cagliari has been the only town in the two islands to have had an urban tramway system. The story of Cagliari trams is surprisingly obscure, at least so far as enthusiast sources are concerned, and the following notes are offered more as a starting point for further research than as a definitive record. The story begins with the SA Tranvie del Campidano e Poetto which opened a 950mm gauge steam-worked suburban tramway from Cagliari town via the, then separate, settlements of Pirri and Monserrato to Quartu S. Elena (10km to the north east)) on 32 September 1893 with a branch eastward from Cagliari standard gauge station along the coast via the SFSS station to Poetto (7km) on 14 July 1913. It operated with a succession of standard Krauss tram locomotives towing railway-type trailers and at some period became the SA Tranvie della Sardegna with head offices at Viale Bonaria, Cagliari. For the record, the locomotive stock was noted by GA Baddeley and others as six Krauss 0-6-0 tram (see appendix 1).

The Poetto route was electrified in 1924-25, using three-phase current supplied by the Societa Elettrica Sarda and converted in a Cagliari sub-station to 750v DC with overhead collection by bow collector. Brown Boveri's Italian subsidiary supplied four bogie motor cars powered by two 49kw axle-hung motors and equipped for towing both purpose-built and ex-steam tramway trailers. The urban tramway system, consisting basically of a single route from Piazza San Michele, in the north west, down to the sea front at Via Roma and then up again into the centre of town via Piazza Amendola and the FCS railway station at Viale Bonaria, followed in 1926, being equipped with six four-wheeled cars, again by Brown Boveri. Presumably at least part of the Quartu S. Elena route was also electrified at this period, since the old depot at Santa Maria was reused. The full Quartu S. Elena route via Monserrato was electrified in 1930, a turning loop being provided at the original FCS Monserrato station to accommodate urban workings on what

Four-wheeled car 20 on route 2 in central Cagliari, 1952. (H LUFF)

Bogie car 314 ex Trieste on route 1 at San Michele, 1952 . (H LUFF)

became Route M. Final equipment comprised a mixture of new and second-hand vehicles from a variety of mainland tramways such as Padova and Trieste and included a single Bo-Bo steeple-cab locomotive for maintenance and transfer work. Basic dimensions of the original electric cars were (in millimetres):

Dimension	*4w*	*Bogie*
Length o/body	8500	13230
Width o/body	2300	2300
Wheelbase	2600	5300
Bogie centres	–	8000
Wheel dia	840	950
Weight (kg)	12000	18000
Seats	22	56
Standing	24	18

The System survived the second world war and the suburban routes were still running under the Tranvie della Sardegna label in the 1950s although the whole system was at some time taken over by a municipal company, the Azienda Communale Transporte de Cagliari. Under TdS control the urban routes were numbered (1 and 2 identified) but later (? under ACT) they became I and M. In 1966 the Quartu S. Elena route was converted to trolleybus operation and in 1969 or 1970 the urban routes I and M were closed also. Route P (FS station – Poetto), however, continued in operation certainly until the summer of 1973 and was probably closed about 1973-74; until then a stub of the former route M was kept to provide access to Santa Maria depot.

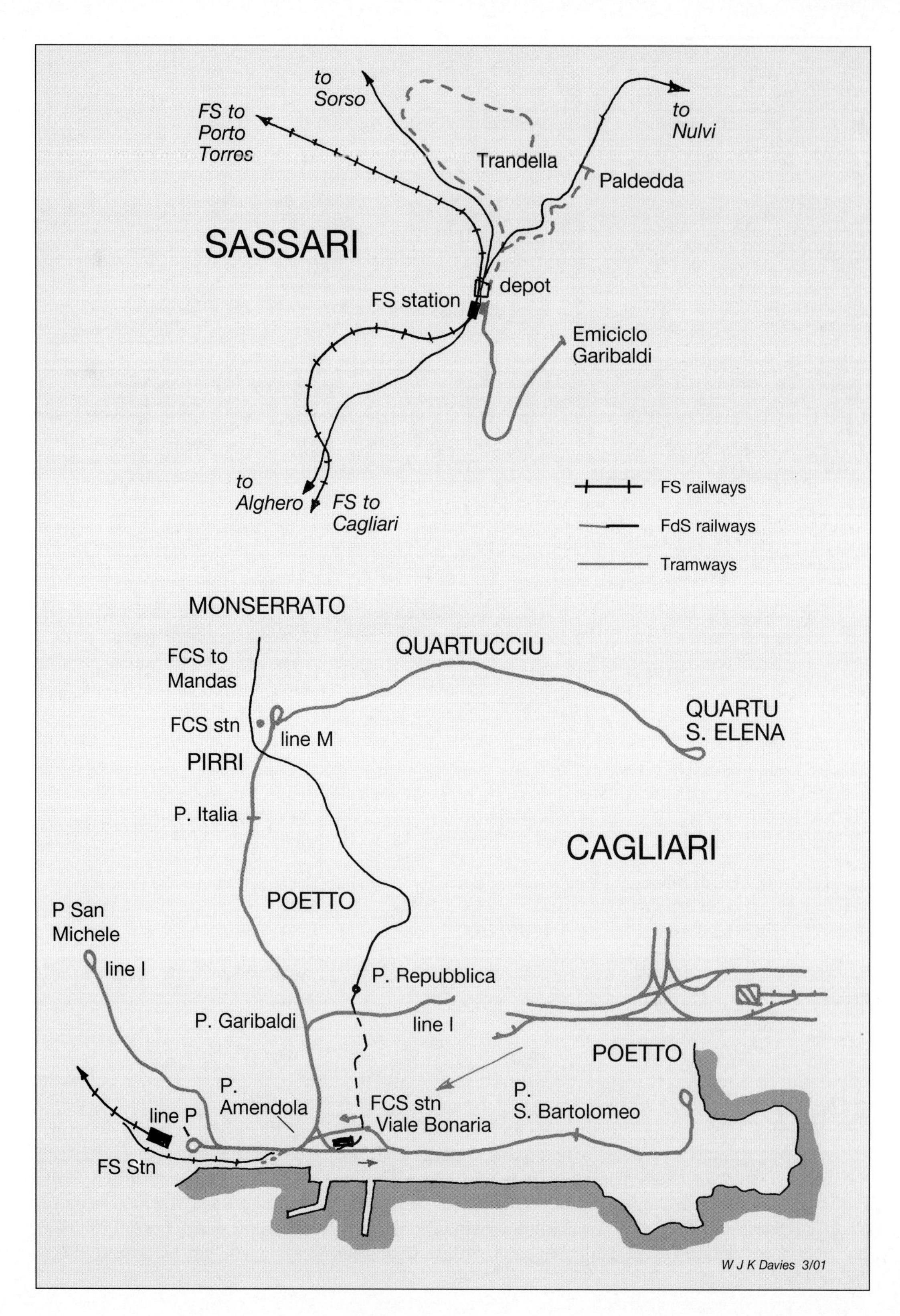

to Sorso
FS to Porto Torres
to Nulvi
Trandella
Paldedda
SASSARI
depot
FS station
Emiciclo Garibaldi
to Alghero
FS to Cagliari
FS railways
FdS railways
Tramways
MONSERRATO
FCS to Mandas
QUARTUCCIU
QUARTU S. ELENA
FCS stn
line M
PIRRI
P. Italia
CAGLIARI
POETTO
P San Michele
line I
P. Repubblica
P. Garibaldi
line I
POETTO
P. Amendola
line P
FCS stn Viale Bonaria
P. S. Bartolomeo
FS Stn
W J K Davies 3/01

The TIBB Bo-Bo steeple cab electric locomotive at Santa Maria depot in 1952. (H LUFF)

Sassari

In the past few years another tramway system has been initiated at the opposite end of Sardinia, to serve its second city Sassari and its hinterland. Planning for this, officially a light surface metro, started in 1996 and construction work started in March 1999. It is to be electrified on the "normal" tramway voltage of 750v DC and will be the first modern tramway in Italy to be built on the 950mm gauge. This is specifically so that it can interwork with – and later possibly subsume – some of the existing narrow gauge railways and operation is to be entrusted to FdS. As planned, the system will be built in stages. The first 3.240km of a planned 7.633km Line 1 is currently under construction for completion by July 2002. It will run from Emiciclo Garibaldi, in the town centre, south, west and then north in a big 'U' shape to a planned "intermodal interchange" at the FS railway station. Future extensions will run partly on or alongside the existing FdS branches to Sorso and Nulvi, to serve Sassari's northern suburbs and the depot will be on FdS property contiguous with the existing rail depot; from observation much of the initial work on these sections has at least been started under the railway modernisation programme. At the same time a feasibility study is being started to see if the modernised Alghero branch can later be incorporated in the system, possibly with a branch to Alghero airport and a relaying of the old line back along Alghero seafront to the harbour area. Much of the trackbed for this latter still exists and it should be quite feasible. It will not be surprising if all or part of the Sorso branch is also incorporated at a later date.

Initial equipment is being provided by Ansaldo Breda to a narrow gauge variant of their "Sirio" type currently being built for several standard gauge systems on the mainland. In essence it is a five-section, articulated set on three bogies, bi-directional and with a low floor for easy loading and unloading. Current diagrams give dimensions as 27000mm length, 2400mm maximum width and 3300mm height to roof. Four sets are currently on order but more will certainly be required as the system extends.

Bibliography of published items

Books

Description Raisonnée de Quelques Chemins de Fer à Voie Etroite, C. Ledoux, Dunod, Paris, 1874
Articulated Locomotives, L. Wiener, 1930, republished Kalmbach Publishing 1970
Mediterranean Island Railways, P. M. Kalla-Bishop, David & Charles, 1970
Railways of North Africa, E. D. Brant, David & Charles, 1971
The Continental Steam Tram, G. E. Baddeley, LRTA, 1982
Les Petits Trains de Jadis Vol 6: Sud-est de la France, H Domengie, Edns du Cabri, 1983
Les Chemins de Fer Corses, P. Bejui, Edns du Cabri, 1987
Le Ferrovie Calabro-Lucane, S. Rongone, author, Bari, 1987
Die Dolomiten Schmalspurbahnen, P Muscolino, Calosci, Cortina, 1988
Railways of Sardinia, W. Simms, author 1999
Renault, Le Material Ferroviaire, M Grannec, ETAI Boulogne, 1999
Minor Railways of France, W. J. K. Davies, Plateway Press, 2000

Brochures

Sardegna, Il Trenino Verde. series of guides produced by Sardinian Tourist Office, 1990s

Major articles treating directly of Corsica and Sardinia

Brown Boveri Review 10/27
- The Cagliari Municipal Tramway and Cagliari-Poetto Railway

CFS/CFRU
- CFS 79 (1967) Corsica
- CFR 119 (1973) Corsica
- CFR 270 (1998) Corsica

I Treni
- 3/01 (224) A Sassari arriva il tram

La Vie du Rail:
- 19.05.68 "Les nouveaux Chemins de Fer Corses"
- 27.10.83 "Ou en est le Chemin de Fer de la Corse"
- 31.10.65 "Chemins de Fer en Sardaigne"

MTVS

1982-4 (24) Les Auomotrices Billard
1984/4 (32) Les Chemins de Fer de la Corse
1986-2 (38) Numero Special Locotracteurs

Narrow Gauge World,
- Issue 6. Narrow Gauge in Sardinia

Tutto Treno

– Tema 14: Lo Scartamento Ridotto in Italia

Voie Etroite

– 1/80 (56) Chemins de Fer Corses
– 1/86 (92) Chemins de Fer Corses pt 1
– 2/86 (93) Chemins de Fer Corses pt 2

Videos

Trains de Corse, Edns La Regordane
Speciale Treno Vapore – la Ferrovie Cagliari–Mandas–Arbatax. Museo Ferrovie, Cagliari

General notes and news

Binari (Journal of the Italian Railways Society)
Chemins de Fer Regionaux et Urbains
Chemins de Fer Secondaires
Continental Railway Journal
I Treni
La Vie du Rail
Magazine des Tramways à Vapeur et des Secondaires
The Narrow Gauge
Voie Etroite

Island finder index

Treating the two islands of Corsica and Sardinia as a comparison has, hopefully, made the history of their railways more interesting to read. Those who simply want quick reference, however, may find it frustrating, hence this specialised index. numbers in **bold** indicate plans or diagrams; *italics* indicate photograph.

Corsica

Sardinia

Journey's end: SFS 3 and train pull in to the dead-end spur at Palau Marina. (AUTHOR)